LIFE LESSONS

ESSAYS ON PARENTHOOD, AMERICA, 9/11 AND DETROIT

ROCHELLE RILEY

Detroit Free Press

600 W. Fort St.
Detroit, MI 48226
www.freep.com

Other recent books by the Free Press:

Portraits of War
Razor Sharp:
   Drew Sharp
Hang 10
Time Frames
The Detroit Almanac
HeartSmart Kids
   Cookbook
State of Glory
The Corner
PC@Home

Fishing Michigan
Hockey Gods
Motoons:
   Mike Thompson
Ernie Harwell:
   Stories From
   My Life in Baseball
Corner to Copa
Century of Champions
Believe!
Stanleytown

➤ To order any of these titles, please call
   800-245-5082 or visit **www.freep.com/bookstore**

➤ To subscribe to the Free Press, call 800-395-3300.

Life Lessons
ISBN 0-937247-43-X
$14.95

FOR MY DAUGHTER

MY THANKS ...

... to the colleagues whose nurturing sustains me: deputy managing editor Julie Topping, features writer Cassandra Spratling, assistant features editor Nicole Avery Nichols, library director Shelley Lavey and deputy managing editor Dale Parry; to my editors: assistant managing editor Sharon Wilmore, features editor Tina Croley and former assistant features editor Sally Mahan; to every copy editor who has handled my columns, especially Helene Lorber and Susan Hall-Balduf; to my "secret" editors and confidantes, Oneita Jackson, Shauné Jackson Hayes, Kelley L. Carter and Chastity Pratt; to my fellow columnists, Desiree Cooper and Susan Ager; to our office managers, Thelma Oakes and Robin Payne; to the men who know everything Detroit and don't mind sharing, deputy metro editor Bill McGraw and deputy nation/world editor Peter Gavrilovich; to our computer systems staff, who never treat me like "Chicken Little" when I say my computer is exploding; and to a dynamic library research team that helps me find anything, anytime, no matter how obscure: Shelley Lavey, Patrice Williams and Chris Kucharski. My greatest debt of gratitude is to Robert McGruder, the late executive editor of the Free Press who convinced me to move to Detroit, whose work to make newsrooms reflect America should be a road map for all newspapers and whose standards still guide my work.

THE LIFE LESSONS TEAM

Shauné Jackson Hayes, editor
Mauricio Gutierrez, designer
Rosa E. Castellanos, designer
Helene Lorber, copy editor
Dave Robinson, project coordinator

SPECIAL THANKS

Heath J Meriwether, publisher
Carole Leigh Hutton, executive editor
Thom Fladung, managing editor
Eric Seals, photographer
Steve Dorsey, design and graphics director

INTRODUCTION

Why do I write?

I write because the words tumble from my fingers unbidden. And I write because there's a song in my head. I hear the singing and want to share the song. It is a song about life and the things I've learned about the past, about the present and about how I see the future. Having been a writer since I was 3, I can tell you that writing is easier for me than speaking. Having written a column for seven years, I can tell you that writing it down makes it real. Written conversations can be more powerful than the cantankerous bluster that sometimes passes for dialogue these days. It is so important for all of us, particularly Americans, to voice a chorus of thoughts so that, years from now, people will know that the America of patriots, full of disagreement and compromise, existed.

For me writing is still a noble, honorable, dutiful task. I am helping to create a history that our children will remember us by. Every news story, every debate, every turn of phrase will be stacked somewhere for someone to look at in 20, 50, 100 years and wonder: "What the heck were they thinking?" I want American newspapers to reflect the variety of opinions that make up America. One of those belongs to me — a divided loyalist to North and South who grew up in North Carolina with a fondness for New York, who loves the Southwest but also has cleaved to Michigan. I want that background and the psyche it has produced to be a part of the harmony of voices in American newspapers.

That is why I write.

ROCHELLE RILEY

FOREWORD

When the world feels like it's spinning out of control, Rochelle Riley offers "life lessons" that bring us right back down to earth. You have to admire her willingness to confront the tough subjects and events that affect us as individuals and as a community.

But what lures us in and keeps us coming back are her personal stories, which she shares so unselfishly, like the time she made her daughter pay respect to the Queen of Soul. Boy, did that bring back memories of my own children, Jessica and Joey, and the first time they saw Aretha Franklin live in concert. Her columns speak to the universal experiences that we all share. When she talks about her daughter, we remember the same experience with our own children.

There is one other thing about reading Rochelle's essays. An essential element in any successful relationship is trust. Ask any Rochelle Riley fan and they'll tell you they trust her. She brings a sense of truth and balance to her work that makes you believe.

With "Life Lessons," whether you're a new fan or an old fan, you can revisit her essays over and over again. Like a good painting or good music, they are meant to be enjoyed, to be savored, to be appreciated. The lessons and stories and analyses of news and her sweet chats about raising a daughter touch us in such a way as to make us laugh, make us cry and help us to celebrate our similarities and embrace our differences.

Rochelle, you go, girl!

CARMEN HARLAN

CONTENTS

CHAPTER ONE
LIFE LESSONS

Some kids just want to be different

It happens with kids. They have a bad day and want to go into the witness protection program. They have a school dance coming up and would rather fake a stomachache than dance in front of kids of the opposite sex.

And sometimes, they just want to be different.

They wake up and dye their hair or ask for a tattoo or beg to pierce some place that hurts.

Thank goodness my daughter hasn't asked for a tattoo, and she's too young to get into the hair color of the week thing.

But she did bring up something last week that she does want to change: her name.

It's not that she hates the name that I gave her. It has suited her and served her well for a while.

But her preparations for high school have meant more than figuring out which designer's clothes will become her signature style.

It means more than deciding whether she's an actress first or singer first, or veterinarian instead of artist.

It means taking on a moniker that is hip, exciting and something that I wouldn't have chosen. That's a requirement. If I like it, it doesn't work.

In her case, she wants to be Nikki. Not Nicole. Not Nicoletta. Just Nikki. I held out hope that at some time I'd mentioned Nikki Giovanni, the Knoxville, Tenn., native who edited the literary magazine at Fisk University, organized Cincinnati's Black Arts Festival and offered reflections on African-American identity that were unique in the '60s and '70s.

Her poetry sustained me in college, and her "Ego Tripping" remains my favorite poem, and reads, in part:

> *I was born in the congo*
> *I walked to the fertile crescent and built the sphinx*
> *I designed a pyramid so tough that a star*

That only glows every one hundred years falls
Into the center giving divine perfect light
I am bad

I sat on the throne drinking nectar with allah
I got hot and sent an ice age to europe
To cool my thirst
My oldest daughter is nefertiti
The tears from my birth pains
Created the nile
I am a beautiful woman.

I gazed on the forest and burned
Out the sahara desert
With a packet of goat's meat
And a change of clothes
I crossed it in two hours
I am a gazelle so swift
So swift you can't catch me

For a birthday present when he was three
I gave my son hannibal an elephant
He gave me rome for mother's day
My strength flows ever on...

But there was nothing profound or literary about my daughter's choice of Nikki. She just liked the sound of it.

So I treated this flight of fancy like any other. I put the onus on her and explained that she'd have to earn $250 to change her name. She, of course, was apoplectic!

"Why!?" she queried in the plaintive wail of teenage angst.

I explained: She'd need $125 for legal fees, $90 for a new passport, $10 for the doctor's visit.

"What doctor's visit?" she asked.

"The one where you get all your school shots over again under your new name?" I told her. "Your co-pay is $10."

I haven't heard anything about the name change since. And I didn't even get the chance to tell her that Nikki Giovanni's real name was - Yolanda Cornelia.

March 23, 2003

A girl who likes going out with Mom

It began during vacation when my friend Karol and I took our daughters to the movies.

The girls immediately found seats for themselves away from us, the first time my daughter didn't sit with me in a theater. I thought it was darling.

But then, I missed her.

I missed catching her silent question at the end of a preview as we either give a coming attraction two nods or two grimaces, our version of the thumbs up-thumbs down game. I missed watching her laugh at the funny parts and sharing snacks.

It happened again when I took her and another friend to the movies in Southfield. They paired up the way girlfriends do, and I took my place walking 10 paces behind, close enough to pay for the tickets and buy snacks, but not to hear comments about the cute boy in the next line.

That used to be me she chatted with, speculating on how long the Nerds Ropes had been in the display case and whether to get nachos or elephant ears. But this time, she wondered aloud: "Mom, when are you going to let me do that?"

"What?" I asked her.

"Go to the movies with my friends like those high school kids," she said, nodding to the obviously popular group of kids nearby. "You answered your own question," I told her. "When you're in high school."

But it happened again — last Wednesday as we watched the Pistons spank the Los Angeles Lakers, a game I attended as much to cheer Chauncey as to stand in awe of Shaq.

From the moment we sat down, she was antsy to be somewhere else. And she began cheering for the Lakers. "Are you doing that because I'm cheering for the Pistons or because you really like the Lakers?" I asked.

"I love the Lakers. I love Shaq and that other guy — what's his name?" she said, laughing as she pretended to recognize anybody else.

Oh yeah, "Contrary" becomes the middle name of every child who turns 13. And they become either bored with you or embarrassed by you.

She was stunned that I would eat a creamy, drippy Popsicle. She hated that I talked to fellow fans — strangers! And she was horrified when I cheered, even though I cheer at everything — football, basketball, baseball, concerts. And I was pretty tame. I wasn't throwing out the random, shrill shouts that cause people to look more at you than at the game, but just participating in the synchronized "BEAT L-A!" prompted by the announcer.

Still, she rolled her eyes, wishing for a buddy and seats six rows away.

But something happened.

By the time the Pistons were up by double digits, she was holding onto my arm and screaming for the home team. By the time it was apparent that the guys who go to work didn't fall for the hype, and I'd screamed "Make it happen, Chauncey!" for the sixth time, we were in sync.

She didn't say she'd wished that someone else had been there. She didn't wish to be somebody else who seemed to be having more fun.

Nope, for a minute, she was the girl who liked going places with her mom. It was another reprieve from that milestone of high school that we're preparing for. It let me know that we have a few adventures left before her life gets rated NP for No Parents.

She even let me hold her hand as we walked to the car. And that was a bittersweet moment I filed away for the future.

March 16, 2003

Britney style puts Mom in a tight-fitting bind

Oh, if my grandmother could have seen me. She would have just laughed that hearty but ladylike snicker of hers and let only the twinkle in her eyes say, "I told you so."

I was standing in the kitchen checking to see whether the bottom of my daughter's shirt met the waistband of her jeans. And behind her, a nearly naked man was dancing on TV.

You've seen the guy advertising Joe Boxer underwear. He's hopping around excitedly, hands clenched in little marimba-like fists, and nothing's coming between him and his briefs. My daughter didn't even notice. She was waiting for word from on high, my lofty perch at the top of the Oh-Mom-you-are-so-ancient mountain, saying she could go to school in what she liked.

So I'm watching Dancin' Joe and watching her and wondering what the point is of vetoing the spaghetti-strap tops, too-short shorts and shirts that aren't really shirts but elaborate sports bras when there's a man dancing in underwear on TV.

As you watch your children grow up and you wonder whether you're being the parent you swore at 11 that you would one day be, the answer can be found in the juniors department of every store. They've been designed by and for Britney Spears, for girls who do rock concerts between their middle school classes.

There is no more universal connection between most parents or gap between parents and teens than style.

And, honey, I apparently don't have it.

At least not in the eyes of 13-year-olds who roll their eyes when they have to tell you, yet again, that everyone wears the item of clothing in question, which, when you get to school every day, you actually see everyone wearing.

What's worse, my continuing effort to inject feminist activism into clothes shopping is met with either stony silence or loud laughter, as if

I've just told the best joke.

For instance, you've heard me complain before about how girls' clothes keep getting tighter and tighter while boys' clothes just keep getting bigger and bigger.

For the life of me, I can't see why I'm looking at pants two sizes too small for a 13-year-old girl when her 13-year-old male friends are wearing pants big enough for my father, and my father's a big man.

The boys' pants not only drag the ground so that what was once a hem is now just a memory, but the pants are nowhere near their waists, as if they're in a perpetual state of readiness to go to the bathroom.

Meanwhile, the girls can only wear their pants in the morning. They have to pack a different pair for after lunch when the tiniest expansion in their waists means the zipper's not going anywhere.

I wasn't always like this. I was a teen once. And no, it wasn't that long ago. And my favorite outfit was a pair of light-blue hip-hugger jeans (I can hear my daughter laughing now) and a yellow shirt. But to get my grandmother to let me wear the outfit, that shirt had to cover everything. So it was a yellow-popcorn bodysuit that fastened and stayed put. No glimpses of bare skin, but it was hip.

Now I'm the old person, the one whose daughter laughs at the idea that I used to wear mini-skirts. She wants no part of back-to school shopping. No matter how I cajole, plead, nag, she says she'd just rather wear her old clothes.

As a matter of fact, she's going into boxes of clothes that she wore to school last year and the year before. Why, they must be at least two sizes too small.

Duh.

August 30, 2002

For anything else, there's a mom's love

Canceling a trip to New Orleans to hang out at the Essence Music Festival: $296. That was the cost of four unused tickets to hear the Isley Brothers and India.Arie, Luther Vandross and Frankie Beverly and Maze.

It would have been the first concert I'd attended since Jill Scott and Sting sang at the Palace last year.

It would have been the first time I'd seen one of my best friends, Janet, since she came for Thanksgiving dinner last November. We get to see each other only two or three times a year, which is about 50 times less than I'd like, but a blessing whenever it happens.

It would have been my first time in New Orleans in more than a decade, having missed every Mardi Gras I'd ever hoped to make because of work or school commitments.

And it would have been my first trip with a new Detroit friend who has made living here a greater joy than it otherwise might be.

Visiting Target to find just the right standing fan for a lakeside cabin with 12 girls in it: $94.19.

The fan cost only $39.99. But I've never shopped at Target without buying more than I went in for.

I can walk into Target for a $2.99 toothbrush but still wind up buying a shirt, a book, some snacks and at least one of something that's on sale.

On this trip, my bill included $2.69 for a National Enquirer (yes, I sometimes read it, and yes, I paid $2 more than I should have), insect repellant, two bags of smoothie mix (you blend it with ice and water, and, as the new It drink, it's supposed to replace fresh fruit), two pillows and, of course, that 4-foot fan, which was all I had wanted in the first place.

Driving to northern Michigan to take that fan because the heat spell that hit the country last week didn't skip Grand Traverse Bay and its surrounding communities...

Driving to northern Michigan because I got a phone call, and a small voice on the other end said, "I don't want to stay at camp. It's hot and I can't sleep, and I'm so tired. Can I please come home?..."

Driving to northern Michigan and being greeted in the woods by a hot, tired 12-year-old who hugged me so tight I gasped, and who, for the first time, didn't let go first: Priceless. And it didn't even matter that the temperature had already dropped nearly 20 degrees, because she was as glad to see me as the fan.

Sometimes when I think that I'm missing out on my life because my life became my daughter's life from the moment she arrived, I have only to remember that the life I chose with her is the only one I really want.

It is her smile that brightens my day. It is her A on a test that I celebrate as much any column I write.

It is her art that I buy special frames for and hang on the walls of our home right along with Romare Bearden and Ellis Wilson.

And when I think of 3-year-old Adonnis and 10-month-old Acacia Maynor, whose mother left them in a hot car in Southfield, where they slowly and painfully died, and little Amari Ware who died after a bullet burned its way into her stomach, when I think of those children, I cry.

I cry for those parents who are parents too young and too soon and who don't understand the magnitude of the lives in their hands.

I cry for neighbors and relatives who watch those too-soon, failing parents but do nothing.

I cry for myself as I pledge to be a better parent, which makes it so simple to cancel a concert for the joy of driving five hours to take a fan to camp.

In fact, it was the easiest decision in the world.

July 10, 2002

It's OK to break rules, sometimes

I knew that I'd blow it. As soon as we climbed into the truck for the five-hour journey to take my daughter to summer camp, I knew that, at some point, I wouldn't follow any of the rules I'd set for myself:

No crying.

No sharing with the counselors a list of things that make her happy.

No telling of sappy stories to her new cabin-mates.

And there was one last rule, one I made the night before. After I'd dropped her off, helped her unpack and said good-bye, I'd go home.

Straight home.

And I had fully intended to do that.

But then I experienced the nightmare. If you're a parent, you know the one. It's that moment just after you've dropped your child off somewhere. If it's the movies, you circle the block to make sure no one kidnapped her from the sidewalk. If it's a slumber party, you go back to make sure the parents didn't leave right after you did. (You of course use the pretense that your child left something in the car, which is why you're standing there holding an ice scraper in June.)

As I drove away, I thought of a dozen things I should have said. Did she remember the rubber bands for her braces? Did she need more money? She wouldn't mind my coming back to ask her that, would she?

But deep down, what I really wanted was to watch her million-watt smile introduce and endear her to people. So I went to the movies, right in Traverse City. I sat watching "The Bourne Identity," killing two hours (sorry, Matt) until I could drive back to camp just to make sure.

To make sure she was safe ...

To make sure she was happy ...

To make sure she was there.

As I parked near the cabin, I saw no movement. No one was there. Oh, God. I just bet there was some major catastrophe and they were all at the hospital! Maybe she fell down the steps on her way to lunch!

I climbed back into the truck, deciding whether to sit or drive around, when suddenly, there they were, a group of beautiful girls and their counselor, stopping by the cabin on their way to somewhere else.

I walked up slowly, tentatively, and stood until she looked my way.

I got a grin, and then a "What are you doing here?"

She didn't run over to hug me. After all, she'd just seen me leave. She just smiled.

"I was just making sure that you didn't need anything else."

"Nope. All fine."

And there, I'd done it. Broken the rule, disobeyed my pledge to leave. I would have been in Pontiac by then.

But instead, I was standing there, having broken one rule and deciding whether to break another, to get mushy in front of the girls.

I decided against it. I casually blew her a kiss and turned to the truck, acting as if I was headed down the street, not 250 miles away.

And I rejoiced that the nightmare wasn't real.

Nothing else happened.

Except that, after driving for five hours, arriving home and feeding her hamster and jumping into bed to watch "Trading Spaces" reruns, the phone rang.

"Hi, Mom. I'm having such a good time. Camp is awesome. I'm glad you got home safely. It was so sweet that you came back."

Sometimes rules are made to be broken.

June 23, 2002

8-year-old learns a royal lesson

I remember it like it was last night.

My daughter was 8 years old and decided that she was going to run away. It seems I wouldn't let her have dessert without eating her vegetables or watch TV without doing her homework, or something sinister like that.

She grabbed a few things, put on her coat, walked out the door and stomped across the front lawn to the edge of the street in our cul de sac.

She didn't step out of the yard because 1) it was dark and 2) it was dark. So she just stood there.

It was a defining moment for me as a parent. I could let this tantrum go — again — and await the next one, or I could do something to nip them in the bud. So I put on my coat and told her to come on.

Then I called my friend Barbara, director of a homeless shelter in Indiana, about 10 miles away from our Louisville, Ky., home, and told her I had a person who needed her shelter.

As we drove to Barbara's house, my daughter asked where we were going. I told her, "Since you've decided not to live with me anymore, I'm going to take you to a homeless shelter. You can stay there until you're able to afford a place of your own."

I thought of when I read that Prince Charles had sent his youngest son Harry to a drug clinic to see what his life might be like if he kept drinking and smoking marijuana.

The punishment occurred in August after the queen's son discovered that Harry had been smoking at the vacation castle and had been drinking at a pub when he was 16.

At the clinic, Harry "met some people in recovery — heroin and cocaine addicts mostly — and heard their life stories, complete with harrowing details," Bill Puddicombe said in news reports of the visit to Phoenix House Treatment Service for Drug Dependency, which Puddicombe runs.

"He was relaxed and friendly with the residents, and they responded warmly. Most people here thought this was responsible parenting."

It's not the least embarrassing way to learn a valuable lesson about the risks and detriments of drinking and drugging. But when you're a public figure, the son of a prince, the grandson of a queen, well, your punishments tend to be a little public.

Prince Charles set a tone for parenting that gained stellar reviews not only from the nosy British press, but from this parent who's glad not to have heard, "Oh, boys will be boys."

Children will be children. Or they'll be worse if we let them. Sometimes nipping something in the bud early will keep them away from a path to destruction. It will keep them out of harm's way.

It will give them something to tell their grandchildren about someday.

Like my daughter, who I hope will someday tell her daughter about the time she decided to run away from home. She'll remember that running away creates more problems than it solves, and how she almost wound up in a shelter.

Actually, at my friend's house, she was offered a bite to eat and a lap to sit on. And since they were watching one of her favorite Drew Barrymore movies, her mom's friend said she might as well wait until that was over.

So my daughter, in the arms of my friend, talked things over. And when they were done, she decided that she didn't want to run away after all.

And she hasn't since.

January 20, 2002

Quiet vacation to nowhere allows time for pondering

Vacations can make or break you. I know because I've had both kinds.

You know how some vacations are: You spend months saving to pack 1,724 activities into six days and then come home tired and poor and not ready for work. You've done it before, gone and visited some place where you felt you had to see everything to get your money's worth and had to eat everything so you could recite your culinary adventures.

I've done all that, and more. Then I'd come home and need two weeks to recover.

This year was different.

About a month after Sept. 11, after I was no longer numb to what happened and could actually measure the impact on my life, I realized there was no immediate or physical impact on my life. I suffered no injuries, save a broken heart. I didn't know anyone who died or lost a job.

But the spiritual and emotional impact was easy to document. Sept. 11 taught me to pay more attention. Thousands of people got a phone call that someone they loved was gone in an instant. If there was something a wife had planned to tell her husband that night, she couldn't. If there was a party where a husband planned to dance with his wife, the music had ended.

So when my annual holiday vacation came, I remembered Sept. 11 and remembered that tomorrow isn't promised and that phone call could come for any of us at anytime.

For my vacation, my daughter and I did — nothing.

We spent the holidays in pajamas, playing endless Uno and watching scary movies. We ate breakfast at noon and vegetables when we felt like it. My daughter created a collection of artwork, colorful faces, worth hanging in the Detroit Institute of Arts. We rearranged furniture and played in snow and baked biscuits and ate them with honey and real butter.

We visited university libraries to learn about growing tomatoes without soil. But the trips were via the Internet, so we didn't need shoes. We also

talked, really talked about things, my 12-year-old and I, that were personal
and sometimes go unsaid, about what we like about our lives and what we
could and should change. We talked about our jobs — mine is writing and
hers is school — and how we could get better.

And, as much as we tried to flee the news, we talked a little about
Afghanistan and a misguided boy's heartbreaking attempt to show support
for a stranger by flying a plane into a building.

She wondered how the husband of a woman who had attempted suicide
and was obviously depressed could leave her at home alone with five kids
every day. I wondered how she got so smart.

I recalled the debate over a basketball superstar's return to the court,
whether he would mar the perfect sports legacy he had left. No one argued
about the broken promise to a wife and kids, who finally, after years of
NBA travel and celebrity, had a husband and father home. So another
marriage ends. And more children grow up with a visiting daddy.

That made me think of how important family is, which is what vacations
should be about, not time away from those you love, but time really spent
with them, even if it means sipping Starbucks coffee in your pj's and
watching "Jaws" for the 20th time.

It's not the destination that makes a vacation. It's the journey. Our
holiday journey was from the kitchen to my room, from the dining room to
the "closet," our name for the den.

It's the best trip we never took.

January 11, 2002

Daughter's 12th birthday represents a last chance

My daughter is 12 years old today. It would be any other birthday except for the way we carve our lives into sections: childhood, teendom, Generation X, Generation Confused, the Pepsi Generation and Baby Doomed, uh, Boomed and the Golden Years.

So after this final year of childhood, she'll become a person whose age ends in "teen." But what rings greater for me is the farewell to pony rides and Barbie cars, ice cream parties and poofy dresses with yards of taffeta designed solely to itch your legs.

Now, the job becomes simpler yet more complex as she moves into another phase. It is a phase where I'll get graded by society and grade myself on what I've taught her.

The biggest lesson I hope she'll take into teendom is that she's loved.

When I was around her age, birthdays were celebrated as a part of daily living. We were thrilled with birthday cards hiding $5 bills and mouth-watering cakes my grandmother made from scratch. I remember one birthday my grandparents forgot. I moped around, dragging my feet, my eyes downcast until my grandfather finally asked "What's the matter with you?"

"It's my birthday," I told him. "And everybody forgot."

The look in his eyes made up for every bad thought I'd had that morning. My paw-paw leaned forward in the La-Z-Boy recliner that he lived in on the weekends, reached into his front pocket, the change pocket, the one we used to stare at on Friday evenings because we'd just die for a nickel to run around the corner to the store where you could buy 25 cookies for that single coin.

He reached in and handed me a dime. It was a new one, pretty and full of a bigger story than 10 pennies can really tell.

I kept that dime for a long time — at least two days, before heading around the corner to the store. But I kept that memory for a long, long time. That dime healed what might have been a bigger wound and reminded me that I was loved.

Teendom requires simpler, but more important gifts. This will be my last year to help her review the materials I've given her for life. Next year, when she actually becomes a teen, it will be too late.

Oh, I can remind her. I can try to be a role model for lessons learned. But more often than not, I won't be there for the tests. She'll be hanging out with friends. She'll be riding in cars with boys.

As I mourn with strangers in Grosse Pointe Woods whose teenage children's lives ended last week in a night shattered by a loud crash and a louder heartbreak, I know that, beginning in a few years, there but for the grace of God go I.

I know my daughter will, on some nights, face situations I can't talk her through, and I won't know until later whether she followed the rules.

She'll have to decide not to drink or smoke or be tempted by a sweet smile and a great come-on. She'll have to decide whether to call home when the choice is between waking me or climbing in with a drunk driver. She'll know I don't sleep when she's out.

For this birthday, besides useless but fun gifts, I plan to give her a dime. It won't pay for a phone call anymore. But I hope it will represent for her what my paw-paw's dime meant to me — a lifetime of love and a reminder of the things that cannot be bought, the things that, as our children grow older, they must remember without us.

I hope it will help her remember the greatest two lessons — tomorrow isn't promised, but it can be given away, quickly, with one bad choice. And, no mistake is too great to take to a parent.

August 8, 2001

Mom's TV ratings system is error-proof

It's one of my daughter's biggest pet peeves. We'll be watching something on TV, and suddenly I'll change the channel or turn it off.

Sometimes, she gets it: We will have heard more than one bad word, or someone is about to act on amorous feelings before 9 p.m. Or it seems that more than one or two people are going to be killed. (It's a shame that CBS canceled one of our favorite shows, "Diagnosis: Murder." There usually was only one victim and the typical single death, most times, was off camera or so badly acted that it wasn't horrific.)

But the problem points to something that a Michigan State University study found to be true, something that parents have known for years.

TV ratings, which flash in the upper left-hand corner of the TV screen at the start of a program, are confusing and, many times, inaccurate.

Bradley Greenberg, an MSU distinguished professor of communication and telecommunication who has edited a book about it ("The Alphabet Soup of Television Rating Programs," Hampton Press. $65 hardbound, $26.50 paperback), found that ratings for violent shows have been inaccurate about two-thirds of the time and inaccurate for shows with high sexual content about four-fifths of the time.

If four out of five are wrong, what's the point?

Spurred by Congress, family advocacy groups and concerned parents, the TV industry began using ratings four years ago to give us at least a heads-up on content. But like movie ratings, TV ratings are subjective. TV networks and individual production companies rate their own shows. It's the old fox-watching-the-hen house syndrome. And the ratings system is voluntary.

"I was surprised by the lack of comprehensiveness in telling parents what kind of content there is," Greenberg says. "There are a lot of programs with sex and violence, and no content ratings appeared.

"But," he says, "I think the thing that bothers me the most is the lack of standards by the television industry. Each independent production company creates its own definition of what sex is, what violence is and what age appropriateness is. That is the largest contributor to the lack of believability by parents. They know the rating on one show doesn't mean the same thing as the rating on another show because the two shows don't share the same standards and the different networks don't talk to each other."

What Greenberg concluded was not only that the ratings are mostly inaccurate, but also that parents are confused by the labels. The study also found that:

* Networks failed to provide ratings for about one of every four shows in time to be included in TV Guide.

* Parents least likely to need the system are most likely to use it, while parents most likely to need the system are least likely to use it.

* Young people misuse them (like the X-rated labels on CDs that warn kids right into buying them).

Until Hollywood does it, we'll have to just rate programs ourselves.

So here's a thought. Instead of TV-Y (for all children) and TV-14 (requiring parental guidance), we could use the W and DW system. If I could have watched it with my mom, then it's W, for watch. If I couldn't have, then it's DW, for don't watch.

June 24, 2001

A belated message to mentor: Thank you

How do you thank someone for teaching you how to write? For showing you how important it is to care about the little guy and getting his story right?

This is my thank-you to Ginny Carroll, one of my first editors when I was an intern at the News & Observer in Raleigh, N.C. I was a sponge. She helped supply the water.

She taught me the difference between an obituary and a story about someone dying and leaving behind memories, baggage, loved ones and some dirty laundry. She taught me how to deal with those who cared and some who didn't.

She taught me the difference between a police story and a story about an event — whether it was a traffic accident, fatal shooting or knife fight - that forever changed the lives of those involved.

She taught me that any story, no matter how mundane, could make it to Page One with effective writing.

She taught me that details are everything. They make the difference between telling someone that Sadie Jones' goat died and telling someone that Sadie Marie Jones' father gave her a goat for her 13th birthday because she'd gotten an A on her report card and she loved that goat so much she kept it in her room. So it didn't seem unusual — when the goat met his untimely end - that Sadie Marie would want to give her goat a funeral.

And Ginny taught me to laugh on deadline — not at deadlines; that would be sacrilege — but to laugh to relieve tension.

When the phone rang last week and a woman said she was calling from the prestigious Medill School of Journalism at Northwestern University, I knew she was calling about Ginny.

Apparently, Ginny's students were worried when she didn't show up for class, so they checked her condo. Police officers found her at home, where she'd died.

Her death, at 53, was of "natural causes." But there's something unnatural about losing a person who took in stray people as quickly as she would stray cats. She was a workaholic whose best friends were those she'd just made and nearly everyone she'd ever met. You couldn't help but love her.

She loved her job, whether it was working at the News and Observer and the State newspapers in Columbia, S.C., or for Newsweek, where she'd been its Detroit and Houston bureau chiefs.

She returned to college four years ago to complete her bachelor's, master's and doctoral studies, all so she could teach. This was her first and last school year as a professor. But the impact she made on her students at Northwestern was as powerful as the effect she had on me as a young University of North Carolina intern learning to walk the walk in that first job.

Through the years, we've been there for each other's highlights and nearly always met on the road. We toasted her coverage of presidential campaigns and the arrival of my daughter. She taught me to cook and to like cats (even though I'm allergic to them).

I'm trying not to think about the visit we were supposed to have this summer. She would have seen the mother I've become; I would have seen the professor she'd become. But I didn't need to go there to know she was the best.

I won't see her again on this side, but one day, I'll stop by her peaceful place in South Carolina near her daddy and sing a gospel song, tell a joke and talk about the first time I saw my byline in the paper — and how she helped me get it.

May 16, 2001

Time doesn't fly; we fly through it

As my daughter stood between the bathroom mirror and me so I could brush her hair, I realized that it was harder than usual.

Suddenly, it dawned on me why that was. I couldn't see the top of her head.

I had seen the top of her head the week before. And the week before that. And though I had accepted the fact that I could no longer rest my chin on it, at least I could see it.

But that morning, I was brushing blind. And it filled me with such a rush of emotions that I almost wanted to sit down. Instead, I cheerily commented on how quickly she was growing up, and how fast time was passing.

But only one of those was true.

Time doesn't really pass. We do. Time is our constant companion until we leave it and our children take its hand to walk through their lives.

Time watches us when no one else does and marks the monuments of our lives: high school graduation; first jobs; first loves; the birth of our children; the deaths of our parents. It is there through all of it, for the ones who came before and the ones still to come.

It hasn't changed, not in the 11 years of my daughter's life and not in the hour since I began this column to reflect on how much happens to us as we move through life, and how time just is.

We've counted 30 years since the Beatles broke up, but it is an artificial measure that is meant to reflect what has happened since: the death of Paul McCartney's bandmate John Lennon, his own rebirth as a frontman for Wings and then again as a poet.

We've counted 4 1/2 years since JonBenet Ramsey was found beaten and strangled in her family's Boulder, Colo., home, but what we've measured is the frustrating number of days a killer is free.

We've counted four months since America watched the swearing-in of a president who has been the greatest gift the writing staff of "Saturday

Night Live" has had since, well, the previous president. And the country has not become a province of Canada or become one Baldwin brother less in population.

Sometimes we forget what we have forgotten. The most heinous crimes fade. The most vicious attacks yield the spotlight to worse ones.

And sometimes we insulate ourselves because we don't want the memories. Like the six years we've counted since a truck bomb toppled half of the Alfred P. Murrah Federal Building in Oklahoma City, Okla., and killed 149 grown-ups and 19 children.

Except for the families of those lost to the actions of a madman, I don't believe we've dwelled on it. We've relegated it to that corner where we store historic events we'll never forget. And there they sit until we're reminded by something, such as the over-the-top coverage of the bomber's pending execution. I wish we'd just let the killer sit alone in a cell for the rest of his life, a much harsher punishment than to die a martyr.

At a ceremony in February to dedicate a museum devoted to the bombing, President George W. Bush encouraged America to step up to its most important task: "to confront evil wherever and whenever it manifests itself."

Time has seen the best and worst of us. Occasionally, we pay homage to its constancy. And we notice that time forgives us for being confused by who's moving. We are passing, not it. It will be here long after we're gone.

And time looks the other way the day a mother cries because her daughter has grown so tall.

May 9, 2001

First car still rolling down memory lane

One of the great things, among many, about the North American International Auto Show is we can do two things at once: see the future and see ourselves.

We define ourselves and each other, in part, by what we drive. We have loved in Thunderbirds, caroused in Corvettes and hauled revolutions in Volkswagen minibuses.

We have watched political observers declare soccer moms a voting entity driving minivans. (Sometimes, I miss my van. I'd remove the middle seat and my daughter would sit in the back seat and pretend she was in a limousine.)

But no matter how many identities we grab with accompanying sets of car keys, we never forget the beginning.

We always remember our first car.

For me, it was a 1974 Ford Maverick, blue with a white top. Its striped seats were like lightning, and I felt empowered.

It became my biggest responsibility, a sign that I truly was an adult. It also was evidence that my grandparents were finally letting me take my life in my own hands.

It came without the typical anticipation and mouth-watering wait. After four years of high school and three years of college without owning a car, I never thought I'd have one. Then I was offered an internship at a newspaper 40 miles from the college where I was studying journalism.

That 40 miles may as well have been 400.

I headed home for the weekend, back to the growing-up house where my grandparents solved all problems. Defeated and dejected, I fell asleep.

Bright and early the next morning, my grandfather woke me. Fully dressed and ready for breakfast as he had been at 7 every morning that I'd been aware of time, he asked me go see who had parked in front of our house. My grandfather was not to be questioned, so I went.

Parked at the curb, near our unpaved driveway, was a blue and white car, with no papers and no keys.

"I can't tell whose car this is," I shouted back up to the man who had been my father for most of my life.

"Now you can get to work," he said.

I hated to leave the car, but needed to hug his neck. So I made quick work of a dozen or so kisses, grabbed some clothes, then sat in my car.

Before me lay a dozen paths made available because my grandparents had paved my destiny. My car became my buddy, my leg-up on car-less friends. She took me to that first internship and to my first job at a second North Carolina newspaper.

Four months later, I sat at a red light reading a phone bill so enormous I missed the light turning green. The driver behind me honked. I looked up, hit the gas and drove into blackness. I woke up in a hospital with a broken jaw and cracked sternum. I never saw the drunk driver and don't remember being knocked out the passenger door, the only time I wasn't wearing a seat belt.

It would be days before I could visit the salvage yard where she'd been towed. There was no saving her. The impact had crushed her.

I've had five cars since then. And I may find a sixth among the more than 700 beauties at the Auto Show.

But none will be as special as the Maverick, who as much as the minivan was suburban mom, was a young, sassy woman starting out in life.

January 10, 2001

Holocaust hits home through child's eyes

There came a moment when my daughter was reading aloud from "The Diary of Anne Frank" that time stopped and I felt what I should have when I read the book years ago: the emotions of a frightened 13-year-old caught up in war:

"When we walked across our little square together a few days ago, Daddy began to talk of us going into hiding. I asked him why on earth he was beginning to talk of that already. 'Yes, Anne,' he said, 'you know that we have been taking food, clothes, furniture to other people for more than a year now. We don't want our belongings to be seized by the Germans, but we certainly don't want to fall into their clutches ourselves. So we shall disappear of our own accord and not wait until they come and fetch us.' "

Hearing Anne through my daughter made what happened to her even more real. I could feel the suffocating fear of hiding from government-sanctioned terrorists, spending two years and one month in near silence in the walls of her father's office building.

I could sense the claustrophobic loneliness of having only seven other people become your world. It hurt more than it had when I first read the diary. Back then, I tried to feel connected, tried to imagine someone my age being forced to cower like a rat in a warehouse or die, tried to imagine not knowing fresh air or the heat of sunshine on my face for months and months.

But I couldn't. I felt sympathy, but not empathy.

But oh, as a parent, hearing my daughter read of eating rotten potatoes and being so tired of grown-up complaints; of being forced to share quarters so tight that others' odors become your air, their daily quarrels your mournful symphony — that was easy to do.

We were reading Anne's diary before heading to Stratford, Ontario, with a mother-daughter book club to see "The Diary of Anne Frank" at the Avon Theatre.

We packed lightly, carrying only what was essential for the 150-mile trip. We're new to Detroit and to being this close to the Canadian border, so we had no idea where we were. Our group drove past farms and countryside to reach the town with three theaters and many of its original buildings.

After the show, we had dinner, then headed to the hotel. We slept, eight of us, in one room, a mirror image (for a night) of what life was like for young Anne. There were eight in her secret annex: the Franks and their two daughters, Margot and Anne; the Van Daans and their son, Peter; and a dentist named Dussel.

It was impossible not to be aware of every sound, every sniffle, every scent. It was impossible to imagine what that must have been like for eight people for so long, people whose greatest fear was bootsteps on the stairs.

"First, I hear a sound like a fish gasping for breath; this is repeated nine or ten times, then with much ado and interchanged with little smacking sounds, the lips are moistened, followed by a lengthy twisting and turning in bed and rearranging of pillows..."

Hearing Anne's words through my daughter's voice made me feel the horror and makes it easy to join the fight to make sure historic tragedies such as slavery, the Holocaust, ethnic murders in Bosnia and tribal murders in Rwanda never happen again.

It is not enough to condemn in words the tragedies that befall those we don't know. We must do more. Anytime we forget the horrors of history or don't think they belong to us, we should just imagine our own children there, and then the fight becomes ours.

October 18, 2000

Tears of loss well up
a year after a flood

A year has passed since terrible floods, urged on by Hurricane Floyd, ravaged my hometown, displacing my grandmother and her neighbors.

We didn't know its true destruction, however, until a few months later, when first my grandfather, then 50 days later, my grandmother, died.

The floods killed them.

I've recounted many times the story of going home after the floods and finding 70 years of bad luck in the yard — 10 slivers of broken mirror from my grandmother's bedroom, amid photos and knickknacks that once resided in the living room.

My friends cried with me as I relived how the waters took the house and my grandparents' sense of peace. They took the floods as God's message that it was time to move on.

And they did, he in January and she in March.

They taught me many lessons in their lives, some I didn't get until months after they'd said good-bye.

The greatest? Two people loving each other their whole lives isn't hard. If you remember that's what you're supposed to be doing after the fights, after the bills, after the children get on your nerves, after you forget to take care of each other's errands.

After everything, if you remember that you're still supposed to love, loving for a lifetime is easy.

They would have celebrated 68 years in November. And they nearly always went to bed mad.

The idea of pretending that you weren't was silly when you'd been with the same person all your life.

If they argued and went right to bed, you could hear the sniping into the night. Yet every morning, she got up, gently kissed his head and made his breakfast, for 66 years.

And every morning, he walked into the kitchen and ate her breakfast because it was the best in the world.

I try not to blame the floods, try not to question God's work because His is not to question, but to accept.

That's like not going to bed mad at each other. It's fake. It doesn't work.

Still, I keep my questions simple: God? Are they happy? Are they together? Are they watching me? Do they think I'm doing a good job with my daughter? Do they know I love them so much more now than ever?

But I never ask why.

She taught me that. I never heard her ask why, not when tragedy struck, or when her baby daughter, my mommy, was diagnosed with multiple sclerosis, not when she herself was diagnosed with cancer. Never.

She would have been 87 week before last, and she would have worn that age as well as she did her favorite suit, a sky blue linen affair.

Today, she'd be on her way to Sunday service to sit in the same pew — second row, right side — that she'd sat in every Sunday for 80 years.

That is, when she wasn't in the choir stand, on the front row, her clear soprano soaring into the rafters and rippling up and down the stained glass windows like angels in flight.

She would have been so proud of my moving to a new city and trying to make a difference. She would have reminded me to wrap my head because it is the only part of your body that you can never let get cold.

As I celebrate her birthday, I know she would have liked where I am. She would have liked my confidence in a new place, where I have a new mission among new people.

That's how she raised me.

October 15, 2000

Daughter pays respect to the Queen of Soul

The lights dimmed. The music swelled. Three ladies in red — and one sassy guy in the same color — sashayed onto the stage and over to microphones at stage left. They began the chorus of "Uptight" — six songs away from "Ain't No Way."

The crowd roared, a subdued, still-can't-believe-we're-here roar. Then, before we could take a breath, before the anticipation could rise again, she strolled out into dual spotlights and just started singing — just started, before we could curtsy. The voice was the one I'd expected, the one I'd heard nearly all my life, the one that told my boyfriend the things I would do "Until You Come Back to Me," the one that demanded "Respect."

The night was a Valentine's Day field trip for my daughter and me. Most of the audience was couples: the nice lady (and her husband, who didn't mind that she and I clapped through nearly every song); the brunette with the great haircut who quietly, but persistently, maneuvered to sit with her husband, even though their tickets were in separate spots.

All were there to see the Queen of Soul, something that everybody should do once if they truly want to experience what real music is and has been.

My lifelong adoration for Aretha Franklin began long before I moved to her hometown. It was a simple respect for her God-given abilities that led me to appreciate every song she's ever sung. But it was a healthy respect. I abandoned my initial plan to drive up to her suburban home and camp out until I could shake her hand. And I had never seen her in person.

My daughter's fascination with the Queen began two years ago when we moved into a new house, and the Queen was constantly on the CD player while we unpacked. I played the same songs over and over. (That's the good thing about CD players. You can program them to play "Ain't No Way" until your daughter says there ain't no way she's listening to that song again.) As my daughter endured, she finally asked: "Who is Aretha Franklin?"

I was stunned.

"Who's Aretha Franklin?!" What had I taught her about black history, about rock history, about the world's greatest singers, if she didn't know the Queen of Soul?

"We're listening to her!" And we stopped everything to dissect her music and talk about a royal life: her church beginnings, the early anthems, the ballads, the ability to jump on sophisticated hip-hop with "A Rose Is Still a Rose."

Then we returned to "Respect," which along with "Chain of Fools," started it all for me. For weeks, I played "Respect" every day.

Soon my daughter hated nothing more than being a little snippy with me and getting two choruses of "Respect" in return. After a while, she began apologizing profusely to cut me off.

"Mom, I'm sorry I talked back. Please, please don't sing that song!"

Not long after we moved to Detroit, I read a newspaper ad about the Queen's appearance at Music Hall. My daughter became my best date.

This summer, she'll see the Grand Canyon. One year, she'll see the Matterhorn in Switzerland and Victoria Falls in southern Africa.

But this year, this Valentine's Day, she got to see the Eighth Natural Wonder of the World. She knew the importance of the moment. And she gave the Queen her propers — singing and clapping along, and sharing a mother's love.

February 21, 2001

Parenting is a good detour in mother's career path

When I first learned of Sylvia Ann Hewlett's book outlining the woes of older women who reached professional success but forgot to have children along the way, I was offended as a woman and mother.

But a closer look at "Creating a Life: Professional Women and the Quest for Children" (Talk Miramax, $22), reveals that Hewlett just focused on the wrong numbers.

Hewlett interviewed highly successful women — at the top of their game in a league that didn't used to let us play — and discovered that many of them didn't have children. She focused on that and found, she says, that "none of these women had chosen to be childless."

I thought, "How absurd."

In a national study to be released next week, she surveyed 1,186 female high achievers, ages 28 to 55, who earn at least $55,000 a year.

She found that 33 percent of these high achievers were childless at age 40; 49 percent of ultra achievers, those women who earn more than $100,000 a year, were childless. Nearly a third of those ultra achievers, the highest money earners, still want children, despite their age.

What Hewlett's book didn't say is that for those 33 percent of successful women who didn't have children, 67 percent did! Or they didn't want to have children. And those 49 percent of ultra achievers who didn't have children? Well, 51 percent did have children or didn't want them. I called Hewlett, and she confirmed that the numbers were right even though the figures she didn't use are more positive.

In a country where professional women once could not work once they got married or pregnant, it's progress that women not only are breaking through the glass ceiling, but many are taking their children with them.

The women I'd like to meet are those who made lives that included careers and motherhood.

But I'm not dismissing Hewlett's research. What she did uncover was the amazing level of regret among some of our best and brightest.

They didn't lose the option to have children. They just chose a rise to the top over motherhood.

Hewlett writes poignantly about her own struggle later in life to have children and how she felt forced to leave her corner office in midtown Manhattan when she did.

I know that feeling.

My daughter was 5 when, as a rising newspaper executive, I spent a great deal of time traveling on business. I remember checking in one night, as I did every night I was away.

Her nanny said, "Before I put her on the phone, I have to tell you something. I wanted to make her a surprise. So I cooked a burger and fries for dinner. When I put it on the table, her eyes got wide and she looked at me and said, 'I didn't know you could get this at home!'"

That moment lived past that day, and within a year I climbed off the executive ladder and returned to writing, my first love. More importantly, I haven't missed a theater performance or major field trip since.

I have no regrets about changing my priorities, but I do have regrets about waiting so long. My daughter is my first career. The goals I set for her life are as important as those at my other job.

So ultimately, "Creating a Life" is a book about the regrets that come with success and how some women learned that making a life can be as important as building a career and that a child's laughter can bring so much more joy than the view from a corner office.

April 12, 2002

Family church, 1872-2002

We spent Thanksgiving evening visiting my mother at the nursing home that has been her home for years. After she'd fallen asleep, we headed back to my aunt's house, the family gathering place since the floods that accompanied Hurricane Floyd drowned my growing-up house three years ago.

On the way, my cousin took us by the place where our church, St. Paul AME Zion, once stood.

The church was razed in February, three years after becoming a water-soaked ghost in the floods. By the time it finally dried out, it was apparent that the 130-year-old building couldn't be saved.

Unlike other sites, where the hole left by a razed building is filled to be level, the site of my childhood church rises up like a giant grave. My aunt and other members of the church's historical committee raised the funds so the grave could be adorned with headstones, three monuments to remind the new of the old.

The first headstone is a tall granite obelisk bearing the history of the church — a history I knew almost by heart. It used to hang on the wall at the front of the church, a paragraph containing names of people I never knew.

The second headstone commemorates the history of the Tarboro Colored Institute, the first school for children of color in my hometown of Tarboro, N.C.

Since my family is a family of teachers, I was stunned to learn about it. But the remaining teachers in my family had never known of it either.

Such is the way with the history of so many black communities across the South. If there is no one to write it, that history gets lost.

When you're a child in church, most of the things you are taught come from the Bible and from the hearts of men and women trying to guide your walk through life. City and church histories are things you learn later on, from other sources, if you spend your life in the town where you grew up like so many people do.

I was proud to learn that the first school for black people in my hometown was one that my ancestors attached to our little church.

The final monument on that little hill above the Tar River is a granite encasement shaped like an L. It holds the bell from the old church, the only thing that survived the waters. I used to hear that bell every Sunday. It is as much a part of my memories as Jackson Five hits, the rumble of our old washing machine and the sound of the horn on my first car.

Touching that bell made me miss Paul Everett, the Sunday school superintendent who used to ring it early every week to announce faith time.

A jovial man with Emmett Kelly eyes and a laugh that was always larger than he was, Mr. Paul, as we called him, sometimes let us ring the bell, because he knew that when you were teaching faith to children, you had to add a little fun.

The bell was rung last at Mr. Paul's funeral in the 1980s, and not touched again until it rang at the church's funeral two Sundays ago.

I never knew how much I missed that bell until I stood looking at the grave of a building where good people helped mold the lives of children for 130 years. I missed that bell and what it stood for, the place where I learned about faith.

Sometimes, Thanksgiving is just for giving thanks. And sometimes, it's a time to go home and learn the things you never knew when you thought you knew it all.

December 4, 2002

Professor pushed students in the right direction

Every now and then, I go back in time.

I don't go far. Just back to the campus where I became a grownup.

Everyone I know remembers college with fondness and regret. It was a time of first loves and broken spirits, of pizza dates and lost virginity (a great myth since I don't know anyone who doesn't remember exactly where they left it).

It was a bridge from youth to the great beyond. And for me, that bridge still swings in the southern part of heaven, the campus of the University of North Carolina at Chapel Hill, where my life changed with a single question:

What are you going to do?

It was asked by a man for whom "simple" will never be a description, my mentor and former journalism professor, Harry Amana.

Harry was then and will ever be a demanding teacher, a patient adviser and a jokester for whom life is one great stand-up act. He's one of those professors you always tell people about, the one you call every time you change jobs, when you need a shoulder.

When I think, with fondness, of the people who have made my life the life that it is, Harry is among those who made a difference. He taught me that no question is stupid (unless it's stupid), and no detail is too small to get right. He showed me how to listen to people in a way that makes them want to tell you secrets. He told me I had talent.

I only half-listened. I was torn between wanting to make great grades and losing my ambitions in a swirl of dating, dancing and finding my soul mate instead of my path.

But in my sophomore year, it was Harry who grabbed me by the shoulders, looked me in the eye and asked: What are you going to do?

He wasn't asking what classes I planned to take. He was asking me to choose my mission. He had watched me chase myself all over campus, dabbling in drama, French literature and political science, even though I'd known for 16 years that I wanted to be a writer.

Harry saw much in me and reminded me that to whom much is given, much is required. He told me I didn't have years to decide because those years that I'd be deciding were years I could be working, accomplishing and being a role model for others with decisions to make.

He made me get off the pot and start growing up. He did that for a lot of people, and 50 of them gathered in Durham, N.C. last month to thank him. It was supposed to be a surprise 60th birthday party. But it wound up being a news story about Harry written by people like the online editor who recalled riding to journalism job fairs in Harry's old white station wagon. And the Atlanta news executive who watched Harry warn a hotel clerk who had lost his kids' room reservations not to make him jump across the desk and act like a "park ape." That former student waited 30 hours and the entire trip back home before asking Harry a single question: "What's a park ape?" And the Cleveland columnist who sent a letter reminding his fellow students that he helped hire Harry, but lamenting that he never had the pleasure of Harry's tutelage.

Harry cried when we gave him a commissioned portrait of John Coltrane, but later was himself again, telling jokes and stories we wished he'd forgotten.

The trouble with Harry is that he doesn't like public sentiment. He was stunned that we came back. But the pride in his eyes said more, as he looked over a room full of former students doing what he taught us.

His mouth said, "You guys." But his eyes said "Thank you" — and "You're welcome."

November 9, 2001

A blessing in birth and burial

Last year on my birthday, I was in a convoy of grief riding behind a white hearse. As we slushed in sleet and rain, cars pulled to the side of the road, their headlights dim beacons on a gray day.

The line stretched more than 30 cars long, a good showing in a small town.

We arrived at a tiny church, whose pews were unfamiliar. This wasn't our church, the one where I'd memorized Bible verses. This was the church around the corner that stood up to the '99 floods and lived to tell about it. Our old church wasn't so lucky. It drowned, taking with it memories of Sunday school lessons learned on tummies full of salmon croquettes, biscuits and molasses — and grits, always grits.

In the days before the funeral, I kept saying, "We shouldn't do this on my birthday. I won't ever be able to celebrate again." But that was selfish. That Saturday was the only time relatives could fly in and out before work.

It made sense. And in the small towns of America, where tradition is greater than grief, making sense is everything.

Grief, for us growing up, was something you tied a knot around. You could loosen the knot at funerals but had to tie it back tight afterward and return to work, to life.

So on my birthday last year, I loosened the knot a little. I watched a preacher who grew out of a boy I once knew say kind things about the man who had been a father to me all his life. I cried. I hugged strangers. Then I drove along icy roads back to the airport, taking off minutes before a storm stranded others.

Since that day, I've revisited my grandfather's life through old photographs, seeing again the gruff giant who had slowly shrunk into a man I no longer feared, a man who laughed more easily and was able to express love and pride.

This year, I expected to wake on my birthday with a heavy heart. I expected to see only endings. Instead I saw beginnings, something Kentucky writer Neil Chethik explained about men and the deaths of their fathers: "Michael Jordan quit his basketball career after the death of his dad. H.L. Mencken launched his legendary newspaper career. And the poet Dylan Thomas, witnessing his father's losing bout with cancer, composed one of the most oft-quoted couplets of the past century: 'Do not go gentle into that good night. Rage, rage against the dying of the light.' "

Men may experience grief differently than women, but there are similarities. Grief can make you do things. Having cataclysmic events occur on signature dates can make you do more. Some turn to drink. Others throw off entire lives and begin new ones. Some just stop.

For me, burying my grandfather on my birthday was a blessing. It has changed the way I view every day. It reminds that life is shorter than we think and full of more joy than we ever truly appreciate. If there's something we haven't done, it isn't too late. Not today. Not while the snow falls softly and those who love you still watch from a different perch.

It's never too late to remember and use the memories to push you higher and farther than you ever dared.

From now on, I will let my birthday welcome me to new ideas and new challenges. And each time, even as I recall his final sunset, my grandfather will join me in new dawns.

January 31, 2001

Election has lessons for us all

We had planned to take in a movie. But a funny thing happened on the way to the presidential election outcome.

My daughter and I watched the unfolding Florida vote recount instead. And we learned something vital: America can still make history every day. This year's election is Neil Armstrong walking on the moon. It's Dr. Martin Luther King Jr. preaching at the Lincoln Memorial.

Like space shuttle launches, presidential elections are exciting, confusing, cerebral events that had lost luster. The shuttles launch. Some watch. Most don't. Every four years, some vote. Some don't. Pundits guess. Networks broadcast (too early). Winners celebrate. Losers concede. Only the politically obsessed live the details.

But like the tragic Challenger launch, when something goes terribly wrong, we are captured. We are watching rescuers pull survivors from a bombed Oklahoma City building. We are seeing Nixon resign the White House.

Nothing else matters.

The past week has taught us again that American elections are not black and white, but gray. We cannot be saved by easy answers that force us to look for absolutes. Gray dares our daily suppositions, fuels how we think, hurts us because it isn't clear. It's the reason problems with race persist in America. We refuse to deal with gray, looking for easy.

This one has teachers running for history books and children watching the news. It has grandmas watching other grandmas fight over betrayal by ballot. And somewhere in all this, I hope there's a young Floridian asking: Why didn't I vote?

This election makes us stop working for a minute. We forget to fuss about the traffic or fret about homework. We forget to watch "Friends." This is the greatest civics lesson of all.

Our children need to see that dirty politics exist. They need to see Americans fight over our most basic right: the right to choose. They must learn the sadness of watching vote fraud charges sprout across the nation, dragging this election like quicksand into our national memory.

Our children must know that every vote counts and that every vote should be counted. They should hear Republicans calling Democrats whiny spoilers and Democrats calling Republicans cheaters. Why? Because this is how our country was founded, hateful rhetoric and all.

We must teach the context behind the most serious issue in Florida: allegations that some black voters were turned away from polls. That used to happen decades ago, we must tell them. It must never happen again.

But we should explain why that issue takes a back seat to upset seniors. The elderly have more clout.

Still, every allegation must be resolved.

In the end, what is most frightening and disheartening (besides the number of votes "found" during the recount) is the number of people asking: Why should I vote?

Their answer came this past week from a U.S. soldier abroad who said: To think that my vote could be the one that could elect a president, that's something.

To think that your vote could elect a president should be enough to participate. That's the best lesson we get as we consider one pundit's advice: Parents, bring your kids to the TV. This is history in the making.

November 12, 2000

Being mom turns into hands-off role

It was a typical weeknight with the typical chore of trying to squeeze five hours of activity into two hours of time — dinner, catching up, reviewing the activity planner and homework.

But we didn't have the typical assignment. I always say "we." It's a mom thing. "We" have algebra. "We" have choir rehearsal. "We" have to find a new binder for a play script. "We" have to find a pair of jeans that aren't flooding. You know — high-waters. OK, jeans that don't announce your socks a block before you arrive.

Oh, never mind.

Anyway, it was a night of more-than-usual homework, because my daughter had to create a way to present and discuss the ancient Chinese dynasties.

Her usual array of books and papers covered the kitchen table, which sits directly across from the computer desk. And she was working on top of all of that stuff.

She had decided to do a Chinese scroll that would feature a different dynasty on each of several pages. She would tape all the pages together and then draw a long green dragon along the entire scroll.

I stepped out for only a minute, or what we moms think is only a minute until we get back to find the grilled cheese sandwich the color of charcoal or the dishwasher oozing suds.

When I got back, her scroll was about 20 feet long, the entire length of the kitchen, and she was trying to figure out how to maneuver it to work on each sheet.

"Honey, it might be too long to work on that way. What if you —"

"I can do it myself."

I stopped for a minute, hearing words I'd heard nearly every day from the time she was 2 until about a year or so before teendom, where we live now.

But I hadn't heard them in a while. For a minute, I thought it was a flashback.

"I was just going to suggest —"

"I can do it myself," she said, more emphatically the second time.

So for the next half hour, I let her, watching her slowly move those connected sheets of paper along until she got tired. As I watched, I saw her reaching up for her bowl of cereal from the counter to take it to the table herself. I saw her tying her shoes. I saw her struggling to get her favorite white sweater on, putting her head in the sleeve. I saw her using a pair of scissors for the first time.

It wasn't that I wanted to push my way into her project. I'm not one of those parents who does her child's work because the first time you're not there, the teacher will know.

I think all I was feeling as I kept checking on her progress was the helplessness of a parent no longer needed.

Oh, I'll be needed for other things. But I wasn't needed for this one. And I knew there would be others.

"Mom, I can do my own hair. Mom, I can drive myself. Mom, I can pick out a prom dress myself. Mom, I ought to know who I want to marry."

The true signs of a child growing up aren't just in the lengthening of their legs or size of their clothes.

The best signs are those moments of maturity that you've been waiting for all their lives. They are signals that your job, at some point, will be coming to an end — or at the very least changing. You will no longer be a manager, but a consultant.

One who stands at the door and starts to touch something, only to hear:

"Mom, I can do it myself!"

November 27, 2002

Reflection on a job well done

When I was a young girl, back in my growing-up town, my grandfather used to clean a lawyer's office downtown. When he'd finished all his runs in his cab, he used to have the dinner that my grandmother had ready for him every evening, drink a big glass of water, then head out to empty trash cans and mop floors.

That office was spotless every morning when that attorney showed up, not because he paid top dollar, but because my grandfather took pride in his work.

That pride is missing in many people and many jobs these days. People work to make a buck, make ends meet, get through the day. But some have forgotten or don't care that the job reflects who they are.

Just stop by any drive-through, where mean hands shove over a sack of food while a scowled-up face dares you to ask for ketchup.

It sometimes makes me wish for days I've seen only in old TV commercials where gas stations provided service (with free window washes and a smile), where store floors were kept clean because someone was actually responsible for them and not just told to do them, and where people took pride in whatever work resulted in a paycheck at the end of the week.

I'd thought most of those folks were gone, until I met Jay Huckabay.

I'll get back to writing about impending war and the Michigan governor's race and why the Detroit City Council is violating its charter. But for just a day, let's celebrate someone who represents the true American work ethic, one of pride and responsibility and the belief that the customer is always right.

Jay works for the phone company. He's 42 and lives with his wife and two kids in Lee's Summit, Mo. In seven years, he has worked in customer service, billing and sales. He's in sales now, and Tuesday morning was his first day back after a week's vacation celebrating his 20th wedding anniversary.

I met him through the seven other people I talked to, after various transfers and call-backs, trying to get a customer service representative to handle my complaint. It took 37 minutes of dealing with people armed with attitude, a manual on how-to-transfer calls, and no sense that how they sounded reflected on their company.

But after that 37 minutes, I got Jay, a courteous, well-spoken guy. If he didn't like his job, I'd never have known it. Since he works in sales, I wasn't his job. But because he takes pride in who he is and how he works, I became his job. He understood my problem: I had been billed for two months after I canceled my service with his company.

By 9:50 a.m., Jay had a billing manager on the phone, one he'd gotten on his second try. They found the problem and promised it would be corrected by week's end.

Sometimes, at the dawn of a hectic day, you just want someone to work with you, to help you find a solution and not make you feel dumb for trying.

When it's their job, you want them to do it with professional respect and a sense of pride. They're representing a company you're doing business with. If they stink, you might just decide the company does, too.

Jay Huckabay did that for me Tuesday morning. He reminded me of my paw-paw.

That lawyer's office back in Tarboro, N.C., reflected well on that attorney. Every time a client sat down, she saw gleaming floors and spotless trash cans.

But that office reflected well on my paw-paw, too. His name on those floors was as important as the name on the door.

What he taught me and Jay reminded me is that, sometimes, all people will know of us is how we do our jobs. Maybe remembering that will change our whole attitude about how we work, how we treat people and how we want to be remembered.

October 9, 2002

Death teaches a lesson in family love

One of the most wonderful things about American families is that they are fabulously messy. Another is they require unconditional love.

I learned this from my father, a stranger who became one of my best friends.

I am my father's oldest daughter. But I didn't know him for years. When he married my mom, his college sweetheart, I was already on the way. My parents separated when I was 3, and he became a ghost, a wonderful memory who sometimes returned with gifts and kisses and who disappeared altogether by the time I was 11.

For 13 years, the greatest emotion I felt about him was anger. But then I met his sister when I became a reporter in Dallas, where she lived. And my Aunt Nell re-introduced us.

For the first time, my father became my father. And I got to know a man who was a genius, an intellect, a giant with a musician's heart and a scientist's acumen, who loved — truly loved — jazz, and who cared deeply about the thousands of students to whom he taught chemistry at New York's Bronx Community College.

Anger stands no chance against unconditional love. My anger for my father began to fade in my 20s when I began visiting his Harlem home and learned how much we were alike, fellow conspiracy theorists who believe the American people will never know what's truly in the federal budget, and know that Oswald didn't act alone. For my 16th birthday, he had given me a copy of the Warren Commission Report on the assassination of President John F. Kennedy.

But only as adults did we ever talk about it.

As much as we enjoyed each other, it was his relationship with my daughter that truly moved me. She met her grandfather for the first time seven years ago, when we trekked to his Peekskill home to watch golf, walk around the duck pond and take in the occasional Broadway show.

Two years ago, she visited alone and called me in tears.

"I'm so bored," she said. "Yesterday, we memorized the periodic table and tomorrow, we're doing an experiment."

When we weren't together, she'd regale him by phone with stories about her pet hamster, or he'd quiz me about my column. I heard the pride in his voice. It felt good. And I realized that, even in absentia, we had always been family.

My dad was supposed to come to visit for the Ford Detroit International Jazz Festival. But I got an e-mail from him on July 17.

Dear Rochelle,

Your voice is like an orchestra to me. In reading your columns of June and July, I can feel changes in rhythms as I go from one to another. I can hear passion like trumpets coming out of you. Your caring about the success of schools and the delivery of medical care reminds me of the left hands of Ahmad Jamal and Duke Ellington. Your analysis of politics is like a double bass chorus roaring through any political weather exposing political truth so that I can feel it in my heart.

I love your job and I love you!

We'll talk soon, but I'm going to have to postpone my Labor Day trip.

Gil

When a heart attack felled him three weeks ago, I mourned like I'd known him all my life. Because in a way, I had. I knew him during the best part of his life, and he knew me in mine.

My dad would have liked that I found lessons in his death, even prouder that I would write about them:

Anger is no match for unconditional love, and you should love your parents all your life, no matter when your life together begins.

August 27, 2003

49

CHAPTER TWO

LIFE IN AMERICA

Looking away led to deaths of Yates kids

We helped Andrea Yates kill her five children in a Houston suburb. Yes, all of us in America who treat mental illness like Aunt Martha's alcoholism (something we never speak of in public) helped pave the way for an atrocity.

Stay with me now, and think: What would you do if you were sitting at home with your five children and a psychotic person came to the door? Would you let her in? Would you call 911? Would you leave her alone with your children while you went to work?

Not in a New York minute.

Yet Yates was left alone every day with her five children, Noah, 7, John, 5, Paul, 3, Luke, 2, and Mary, 7 months. The children were left for two reasons: The psychotic person was their mother, and America doesn't like to talk about mental illness.

But people knew.

They knew there was a problem in February 1999 when, according to news reports, Yates became so withdrawn that her husband, Rusty Yates, had to move his family from the converted bus they were living in to his mother's house. She was found unconscious the next day with more than 40 anti-depressants in her system.

People knew in July 1999 when she scratched bald spots onto her scalp, and her husband found her in the bathroom holding a steak knife to her throat.

People knew, according to People magazine, when doctors, upon learning that she and her husband planned to have more children, predicted that having more babies "will surely guarantee future psychotic depression."

People knew in November 2000, when she wound up in a psychiatric hospital after having her fifth child and living through her father's death.

People knew when she was discharged but was later found at home in a full bathtub with no idea what she was doing. People knew when she was re-admitted but discharged "with suicidal impulses," according to medical records. She returned home to be a good mother. Yet all the while, police later learned, she was thinking about killing her children.

So two years after her husband found her in the bathroom with the knife, a month after her second stay in a psychiatric hospital, Yates led her children to a full tub of water and drowned them. The last one she had to chase.

Doctors testified this week that Yates told a psychiatric team she had planned to kill her children and was going to use a knife but changed her mind because it would be too bloody. Only after she killed her children on June 20, psychiatrist Melissa Ferguson recalled, was the 37-year-old homemaker medicated, stripped and placed in a suicide-watch cell.

Meanwhile, Yates sits in a courtroom, either silent or babbling, while others debate how far into hell she descended and whether she was there when she drowned her children. She has pleaded not guilty by reason of insanity. Prosecutors say she was sane and should die.

We didn't see it coming. For most of us, it was a shocking bulletin on CNN. But there were neighbors and doctors and family members who saw and either didn't ask questions or didn't demand answers or didn't slap Rusty Yates' face to wake him up and say, "Your wife isn't in a good place right now and shouldn't be caring for the kids."

But we all played a part, because, in America, we don't take mental illness seriously. We avoid psychiatrists like the plague for fear we'll be branded crazy or unfit for work, marriage, parenthood, the military.

If a friend were about to get hit by a truck, we'd shout "Watch out! Move!" But when we see a friend about to fall into an abyss we don't understand, we stand by, whispering hopes that they'll be all right.

We do that, even though lives are at stake.

Dr. Melvin Bornstein, a Birmingham, Michigan psychoanalyst, says we ignore mental illness out of our own fear of it. "When we see individuals who are mentally ill, this becomes a frightening experience for people. It's much easier to say that there is something really wrong with them that has nothing to do with me. There's no common humanity," he said.

That is why there has been such a minimization of the importance of mental illness and its effect on people's behavior, Bornstein said.

"We have a history which dates back to the 16th and 17th centuries where treatment of mental illness was inhumane — putting people in asylums, isolating them, performing horrendous procedures on them like cutting their brain, making them suffer. People see them as a part of the devil's work."

Andrea Yates, Bornstein said, might have wanted to save her children.

"She heard voices and if the voices were saying that was the way to do it — that is a display of how complex the problem is and how helpless this human being is in dealing with her pain. We don't feel OK talking about it, so people turn their back on them."

So many people saw what was happening in Clear Lake, Texas, but because mental illness is such a taboo subject, people waited. Doctors drugged Andrea Yates, yet let her leave a psychiatric hospital while suicidal.

She was used once by a husband who didn't realize his dreams of having a big family would lead to losing them all.

She's being used again as a pseudo-celebrity commercial for the unenviable toll that childbirth and early motherhood take on women.

As we search for someone to blame, we must look at those who left children at home with a psychotic woman whom they hoped would get well.

We must look at medical professionals who didn't consider the fate of the innocents they were sending her back to each time she left the psychiatric hospital.

We must look at Rusty Yates, who is his wife's biggest champion and who will forever share this burden. He left his children with a psychotic woman who couldn't keep up with life and didn't want her children to suffer. The children are gone and his wife soon will be, to jail to hear the voices or to a psychiatric hospital where she can learn to live with the pain.

And we must look at the rest of us, who'd rather misunderstand mental illness than learn that it can exist right in our own homes.

It seems that mental illness has become the leprosy of the 20th and 21st centuries, and we'd rather look away, not touch, not get involved, than understand the power of the mind and what it can cause the body to do.

It should be a crime to ignore it to the point that lives are endangered. If we had paid attention to the fact that mental illness can kill, we might have saved five innocents who happened to be at the scene of our crime.

February 27, 2002

2001: A nation and new baby discover themselves

Ladies and gentlemen, meet Brody Blackwell, son of Beth and Ryan Blackwell of Warren, just northeast of Detroit.

Yes, every baby is cute, but Brody is Gerber-baby cute. He clocked in 23 hours and 16 minutes after 2001 did, and his arrival, like 2001's, seemed a continuation of the previous year.

He spent the last few months before birth breaking the rules, swimming around in 2 1/2 times the amniotic fluid that most babies have. Unbound by typical tight quarters, he lived in a loft instead of a studio, a condition that Beth's doctor said gave him space to not just kick, but wrestle.

2001's arrival was similar to Brody's. After the controversial 2000 presidential election, and allegations of tampered votes and pregnant chads, 2001 came in as a denouement to weeks of thrashing.

The country was reawakened to the importance of choice and freedom. Through the year, we would be reminded again and again how important freedom is.

Reflection is typical fare at year's end. We cannot help but mull over the best and worst.

But what if this year, instead of just noting celebrity breakups and passings, we look at America and the year 2001 as a life and study it in parallel reflection on the life of Brody.

Brody spent his first three months eating every two to three hours, growing stronger and becoming more aware. But even with increasing strength, he was a delicate blossom opening its petals. "I remember not wanting anyone to hold him," said Ryan, 30, a computer programmer at Hutzel Hospital, where more babies are born than at any other hospital in Michigan, and where Brody was one of 24 babies born Jan. 1.

Brody's mom says he's fearless. "There's nothing that holds him back as far as adventure is concerned," said Beth, 21. "He's a very physical baby."

Brody also became a mini-ambassador whose charm and innocence helped heal old family wounds.

"I noticed that despite my relationships with everyone as a child — we were on the outs with certain family and friends — when they were around Brody, they would be all lovey," Ryan said.

America, too, was forging new relationships, building friendships with old enemies and monitoring adversarial relationships with old friends. We watched our leadership reach out to unite political parties in finding solutions to economic woes.

The U.S. Senate, for the first time, became evenly divided, meaning either working together or standing at stalemate in a year when America would face its greatest crises ever.

By March, Brody began learning that there was more to the world than his bassinet. The brave Blackwells decided to take Brody on his first trip back to central Illinois, where they relocated from in 2000.

Also in March, Brody learned to focus, becoming mesmerized by the twirling blades of the ceiling fan in his room.

America, too, had to focus on new discoveries, albeit more unpleasant ones, discoveries that would reveal themselves through the spring and summer: A spy had been selling secrets to Russia for 16 years in exchange for cash and diamonds, costing American agents' lives and compromising security; faith-based efforts to fill in the social service gaps became suspect because the government responsible for social services was pushing the initiative; a standoff with China over a downed U.S. spy plane led to rising tensions before a moving homecoming.

April news reports on the U.S. plane that went down in China held interest for the Blackwell family. Ryan's younger brother, Brennan, 22, a Marine corporal, was stationed at Twentynine Palms, Calif. He wasn't in danger, but Ryan knew he could be someday.

In June, Ryan and Beth took Brody for bike rides, his rickshaw-style carriage hooked onto the back of Ryan's bike. They also spent time at local water parks, where 5-month-old Brody swam for the first time.

It also was in June that the Blackwells made major decisions after watching reports on the execution of Timothy McVeigh.

"That made me do my will," Ryan said. "It reminded me of my mortality."

In August, Brody got his first crib, moving from the bassinet in his parents' bedroom to his own room, decorated with tiny lights and lemon tulle that makes every moment look like a sunrise.

The Blackwells bought the crib with the $500 tax check they got from President George W. Bush's tax-relief plan, a plan they thought wouldn't work.

In the days leading into September and America's darkest fall, Brody's parents discovered something else: They found that Brody was fearless.

His favorite game is to sit on his dad's shoulders. When his dad says, "Where's Brody" the tyke leans way over toward his daddy's face to answer silently, "Here I am." Then his dad flips him over and places him gently on the floor in front of him.

When terrorists attacked on Sept. 11, 9-month-old Brody wasn't crawling yet, but he was happy and mellow, a baby who rarely experienced crisis.

He was never more symbolic of America, whose goal of a great life for every citizen has come closer to reality than anywhere else.

On Sept. 11, Gary Condit's mixed messages about a missing intern, Dale Earnhardt's tragic death on a race track and Slobodan Milosevic being handed over to be tried for horrific ethnic cleansing in Bosnia were overshadowed by terrorism.

And Brody's uncle, the Marine corporal, got word that he will be deployed to Kuwait to help defend freedom.

So even as Brody was discovering the world around him, the world had come to Brody.

We lost so many people in the first year of a new century, people we thought we knew because our friendship with them was via television or film or words: Carroll O'Connor, Aaliyah and George Harrison.

But it was ultimately the death of about 3,000 strangers that caused us more grief.

There is no way to measure America's loss of innocence or a bliss so great we didn't know how much other strangers hated us. It has overshadowed the typical musings. It was a year that we saw former President Bill Clinton leave the world stage, but still stand at its edge, like an understudy hoping to sneak on.

It was a year that we were forced to learn enough geography to find

Kandahar and Kabul on a map, forced to learn enough about religion to understand that Islam is not to be dismissed.

But it was a year that we finally understood that no matter how much we lost, we still gained because no matter what has happened, we remain free — free to choose and rail against and love, free to not participate in the grief and sadness if we don't want to, free to pretend that nothing happened on Sept. 11, free to sit in a public theater, wearing what we want, laughing in the dark, even while we're at war.

For as much as we lost, we gained, because more potential leaders were born into the world last year here than anywhere, potential leaders like fearless Brody Blackwell.

His parents didn't know that he'd be born in a year that we'd celebrate the 50th anniversary of "I Love Lucy" and the 300th anniversary of Detroit.

But following Sept. 11, particularly in the days following the swearing-in of new leadership in Afghanistan's capital, Brody has continued to grow. On Thanksgiving Day, he crawled for the first time.

Tomorrow, he will celebrate his first year, a year when America not only survived tragedy, but stood strong for freedom.

And, like Brody, we are taking every day, one discovery, one step, at a time.

Dec. 31, 2001

Polanski's Oscar plays badly for America

When Harrison Ford strode onto the stage at the 75th Academy Awards and announced this year's best film director, I sighed.

Why did it have to be Roman Polanski, the director whose fame grew in tragedy (when the Manson family murdered his wife, Sharon Tate), multiplied as he made some of America's best films ("Chinatown") and took a turn to infamy nearly 26 years ago when he raped a 13-year-old at Jack Nicholson's house?

Polanski fled the United States for France in 1978 to avoid at least 20 years in prison and lives in Paris (no French jokes, please)!

Sadder than his name being called was the standing ovation he received from audience members who booed documentary filmmaker Michael Moore for denouncing the president and the war. (Now, to be fair, Moore was using schoolyard bully words inside the classroom, but that was his right.)

Still ...

Polanski's award made me wonder whether we ever really take a good look at ourselves.

In these times when the world is rotating backwards, when down is up and up is down, right is wrong and wrong is popular, maybe it shouldn't seem out of place for Hollywood to celebrate a man who could not come to Los Angeles to accept his award because he'd be jailed. (He pleaded guilty to unlawful sexual intercourse with a minor — statutory rape.)

There was something either defiant and boorish or futile and pathetic about Hollywood bestowing its best on its worst. Even Polanski's victim, now a California wife and mom, said his crime shouldn't affect his career. But as a mom and moviegoer, I want more.

Yes, I know the Oscar contest forms don't say, "Convicted Felons Need Not Be Nominated." But when we celebrate the best of us, it would be nice if it were the best of us, not the best of us who got away with something.

In film, particularly in the director category, the Oscar represents the best effort by an individual to convey a vision. But should the award be only for what was captured on film? Is there any room to honor honor, to express gratitude for persistence, to celebrate integrity and character?

American prisons are full of potential award-winners and Polanski should be the most talented film director behind bars.

Instead, he sits in Paris, the toast of Hollywood. And America looks silly again.

At a time when the world is watching us more than ever, we still thumb our noses at morality, decency and, sometimes, the common good.

I've said it before: America ignores her international reputation. And we let her. We arrogantly live above the troubles that affect everyone else. We don't have to care about the AIDS crisis that will kill millions in Africa. We don't have to care about our government and troops' subsequent involvement in Iraq. (But for a clue, revisit the histories of Korea, Kosovo and Kabul.)

We pay scant attention when the world sees our worst, so a little thing like honoring a rapist doesn't evoke an outcry.

It prompts cheers.

Maybe it's Hollywood. Would he have gotten a business award if he had been an advertising agency president?

For now, he still gets away with rape, and he gets the gold. But no matter how golden it is, his Oscar will be tarnished by his crime.

He may have been voted best director, but I wish the Academy had voted for the best man.

March 26, 2003

Love should rise above the word 'beneath'

My Uncle Napoleon's words slapped me so hard he may as well have thrown them across the kitchen table.

"You know you're not going to find anyone to marry. Black men have a problem with a powerful black woman."

That was 13 years ago, and my power was negligible. I was a low-level editor for a Dallas daily, a rising known-about-town firmly entrenched in a black middle class that included my uncle, the city's most famous principal, whose nationally recognized clean-up of a struggling black high school would have made a great movie, if Joe Clark hadn't done it first, and my aunt, a well-respected school administrator who ranked professionally higher than my uncle.

My uncle's words sounded like those I read in the latest Newsweek on the romantic ramifications of black women achieving at higher rates than black men and whether black women have to "settle for men several steps beneath them."

My question is: Why does love have to be a race?

As a black woman, unmarried and still dating, I've seen the landscape. Oh, the trend is real, and the search is difficult.

But as I read the article, I felt the questions in my heart: "Is this new black woman ... leaping into treacherous waters that will leave her stranded, unfulfilled, childless and alone? Can she thrive if her brother does not, if the black man succumbs, as hundreds of thousands already have, to the hopelessness of prison and the streets? Can she — dare she — thrive without the black man, finding happiness across the racial aisle? Or will she, out of compassion, loneliness or racial loyalty 'settle' for men who — educationally, economically, professionally — are several steps beneath her?"

And there was that word, the one that stung my heart the most: "beneath."

The article cites competent statistics: 25 percent of young black males go to college compared to 35 percent of black women. More black males than females drop out of school; and black women are five times as likely as white women to still be unmarried at 40.

But it's that word "beneath" that should give us pause. Have we, as black Americans, so accepted majority society standards that we can accept only capitalist definitions of compatibility?

My parents, brilliant college graduates of equal stature, split up when I was 3. My siblings both married financially compatible college graduates. Both are divorced.

Now, my grandmother was a college graduate, too. But she had been married to a man with a sixth-grade education for nearly 70 years when they died within months of each other. Together in life. Together in death. What she needed, he got. What she learned, she taught him. They fought hard and loved harder.

When my friend, Toska, tried to set me up with a guy, she called to tell me after the fact: "Don't worry, though. I interviewed him. He's a runner. And he reads the newspaper."

We laughed, but we weren't joking. She knows my needs are simple: a man who takes care of himself and is aware of his location in the world is a man like my grandfather. What I need, he'll get. What he hasn't learned, I can teach.

And if more black women see marriage as a partnership rather than a competition, they may find that there are millions of guys out there between the extremes of ubersuccess and prison. It just takes time to find them.

And you have to look with your heart and hope, not your wallet and a shopping list.

March 7, 2003

Witnesses tell of whistle that cost Till's life

It is as clear in Roosevelt Crawford's mind now as it was 47 years ago, the night Emmett Till whistled outside a store in Mississippi.

"It was seven of us in the car, and we went to Bryant's grocery store in Money to get some drinks and ice cream and candy ..." Crawford, then 15, now 63, recalls.

He got his drink and went outside to watch a couple of kids playing checkers.

"Emmett went in, and he bought what he was going to buy. What he said or done in the store, I didn't hear. But when he got done, he came out and stood beside me."

Suddenly, "this guy made a wrong move and Emmett whistled a wolf whistle. At that time, Carolyn Bryant, the wife of Roy Bryant, who owned the little grocery, came out to her car. Someone in the group said Emmett whistled at this white woman, so right away we broke to the car and we left."

And in that instant, and in the heartbreaking days later, the American civil rights movement got another involuntary martyr. Whether it was at a checkers game or at a white woman, that whistle cost 14-year-old Emmett Till his life.

Two white men led a group to Emmett's uncle's house, pulled him from bed and took him away. He was found less than a week later floating in the Tallahatchie River, beaten beyond recognition.

I learned about Emmett Till the same way Keith Beauchamp did. The New York filmmaker from Baton Rouge, La., was rambling through his parents' study when he came upon the Jet magazine with the photograph of Emmett Till's mutilated face, the photograph taken when Emmett's mother demanded that his coffin be opened to the public so the world could see what Mississippi had done to her son.

"I was 10 years old. It shocked me so much that I ran to my parents right then and there, and they told me the story," he says. "And when I started high school, I started interracially dating, and the first thing my parents told me is, don't let what happened to Emmett Till happen to you."

Beauchamp recalls being beaten up for dancing with a white girl at a local nightclub. He remembered that when he entered Southern University to study criminal justice. After two years, he switched to filmmaking. But his goal for justice was the same.

The 31-year-old's first film is about the Emmett Till case. Beauchamp began researching "The Untold Story of Emmett Louis Till" seven years ago, working with Emmett's mother, Mamie Till Mobley, until her death this year.

It took three years for him to find and persuade witness Simeon Wright to talk. But Wright later introduced him to brothers John and Roosevelt Crawford. The latter, who recently retired from General Motors in Detroit, said it was about time. "It's been 47 years, and nobody ever tried to contact me or get in touch with me, not the NAACP, not the civil rights groups."

Despite testimony from Simeon Wright's father, Moses, and his friend Willie Reed, Carolyn Bryant's husband, Roy, and J.W. Milam were acquitted of murder.

Beauchamp's 90-minute film is to be presented to Detroit, thanks to Tara Young, a local public relations consultant, and the Michigan Civil Rights Commission. Young, 36, says bringing the film to Detroit is her way of honoring those who broke down doors she's been through.

February 19, 2003

Barbie hustles children with sultry persona

It's time to shop for Christmas, and I'm frantically searching for the new must-have doll.

She's called Hooker Barbie and she comes with her pimp, Ken, and her friend, Bambi.

Ken wears a white toe-length leather coat, a lime-green suit with matching lime green shoes, shirt and tie, a waist-length bicycle chain with a bright red faux ruby on it and a white fedora with lime and white feathers. He also has a ring on each of his permanently welded plastic fingers.

Barbie takes the cake, and the corner. She wears black fishnet hose, a mini, cubic zirconia-encrusted Victoria's Secret-knockoff bra and an ankle-length, blue poodle coat.

Her shoes, typically an impossible 3-inch stiletto, are 5-inch black spikes. She comes with three wigs: a waist-length fire-engine red one, a shoulder-length platinum blonde one and a curly black Afro at least 2 inches around.

This Barbie is one of a new variety that speaks when you pull a string attached to the wad of cash in her hand. Her favorite phrase: "Show me what you're working with!"

It should be relatively easy to find the new doll. She's a prototype in a new line of "reality-based" dolls that also includes Dominatrix Barbie, Con Woman Barbie and Lesbian Stand-Up Comedian Barbie. That one looks like Rosie O'Donnell, and her left middle finger is configured into a permanent point.

OK. Before Mattel calls me, the multi-billion dollar toy company hasn't really made a prostitute — yet. But how far should a toy company go in trying to keep up with some people's version of reality?

Mattel wants parents to storm stores for My Scene Barbie, the one with the pouty lips, heavy eyeliner and midriff-baring tops so she can compete with Bratz dolls, who have doe eyes, heavy makeup and platform shoes. But does the toy company really want to copy fads instead of letting Barbie set trends as she's always done?

Barbie has evolved in a changing world to take on new ethnicities to reflect the girls who wanted her.

Barbie taught little girls to see themselves as women did — as successful businesswomen and airline attendants, teachers and a presidential candidate.

She's been Mod Squad and California Girl. She's been '80s aerobics instructor and '90s Women's World Cup Soccer player. She's worn the fashions of 52 real designers. She was a surgeon in 1973, an airline pilot in 1990, an astronaut in 1994 and a dentist in 1997.

Through 80 careers, she has helped show girls that they can be mommies but they also can be doctors. She made $1.5 billion for Mattel in 1999, and more than 1 billion Barbies and friends have been sold since 1959 — not as many as McDonald's burgers, but Barbie's not done yet.

If Mattel wants to stay on that reality road, it might wind up with Hooker Barbie, whose thick make-up hides her tired eyes, and who will show little girls a new way to make money.

Or it could reinvent Barbie the way the movie industry has reinvented James Bond through four decades. She could become a spy or a national security adviser or a rock star who also works for the CIA.

She'll wear a simple black and white, strapless bathing suit and look a lot like she did about 43 years ago.

And little girls' imaginations — and a few nifty spy toys — can do the rest.

December 11, 2002

The interview should have been canceled

The last thing I want, Whitney Houston, is to feud with you.

First, I've admired your God-given talent for too long to just stop caring. Second, even when you were at your nuttiest, with the stupors and strange utterances and concert cancellations, I didn't criticize. I was worried about you.

But after watching your exclusive, all-the-world-has-been-waiting-to-hear-the-truth interview with ABC-TV's Diane Sawyer, all I could think of was: Girl, what were you thinking?

First, you were too hoarse, and I don't care how powerful Diane is, you should have told her to come back next Tuesday.

Second, as a diva, you're entitled to tell all your business on national television. But just remember that when you do, we're watching all your actions, like the way you moved slightly away from your husband when he joined you on the sofa, and how you looked at him when he disputed your claim that he's jealous of your career.

We know he's on drugs and has deluded himself into believing he's still selling records. But girl, you know we both know better.

And another thing. I saw how you yawned when he was talking about how big his talent is. We yawn the same way. So is that why you say you hit him, because every now and then he pretends that he's supporting the family?

Body language is powerful. You know that. You know that surge that goes through your body when you sing. We can see it, the way you lower your head just a little to look right at the audience and then hold your head straight up so that bolt flies right out with those big, high notes.

But the body language that millions of us saw last week was that of a woman in trouble. If you're not on drugs, you shouldn't appear to be. You seemed half asleep, overly defiant, slightly paranoid and quite frankly, a little out of it. At one point, you said you wanted to see the receipts for a drug dealer you paid $700,000 to. Baby, drug dealers don't keep receipts.

And when someone shows you a photo where you appeared to weigh 80 pounds, don't pretend you can't see it. Don't tell her you've always been skinny, as if what we saw on the Michael Jackson special was "skinny." It was skeletal. It was frightening, and we thought we'd be reading your obituary within weeks.

If you're clean, don't be enabled by a husband who says he doesn't smoke pot every day, but maybe "every other day."

And speaking of drugs, when you're trying to convince the world that you understand the seriousness of drug habits, why say you don't smoke crack because "crack is cheap" and beneath you — like cocaine is OK because it's expensive?

Drugs are a serious problem for millions in this country. It costs those of us who don't use them billions in health care and penal hotels. It isn't funny.

And finally, let's talk a minute about marriage vows. I admire that you believe that they're forever. They are. For Diane Sawyer. For your mom. For me when I take them. But that doesn't mean your husband needs to be the monkey on your back.

If you need to live in the Atlanta area and he needs to live in rehab — and I don't mean visit, but reside — that's OK. You're staying true to your vows and he's giving his addictions the actual time they need to heal.

And girl, if any man ever put his hands around my leg and said, "This is mine," referring to me, I'd slap him.

But then again, maybe that's why you did.

December 8, 2002

New citizen takes pleasure in casting first vote

The drive from the American Arab Anti-Discrimination Committee headquarters on Michigan Avenue to John McDonald Elementary School on Warren is only about a mile.

But it took Imad Hamad 22 years to get there.

"As I'm driving to go vote, I just feel this chilling feeling inside me, a mixed feeling, like I'm going to some sort of final exam that will determine my future," he says as he steers his Oldsmobile Bravada toward choice.

Hamad, the 41-year-old regional director of the committee that fights for civil rights for Arab Americans and common ground for all Americans, is a new American.

Tuesday, he drove the mile from his office to an elementary school to vote for the first time.

Hamad was 18 in 1980 when he left a refugee camp south of Sidon in southern Lebanon to immigrate to Louisiana. He and his family lived in one of the largest camps, Ein el Helweh, and although he understood the idea of voting, Hamad says he never understood the freedom of voting.

As he turns off Michigan onto Miller Road, he recalls elections past.

"I always felt like a voter because I always advocated for people to register to vote. I always chased people to get them to vote at every opportunity I had," he says.

He turns right onto Miller. There is sweet irony in the fact that his daughters, Nadeen, 8, and Sarah, 9, are second- and third-graders at this school where he will make personal history. He parks and heads toward a cadre of campaign workers pushing flyers like carnival barkers.

"It's one of those feelings that makes me wonder how people can not vote, not exercise that right, how people can take it for granted. It makes me feel sad because it's in our hands. ... And someday, I only hope that this most precious right that we have, that everyone will take it as serious as it is."

As Hamad walks toward the gym to cast his first ballot, he likens it to taking his final exam on American citizenship after 22 years of hard lessons, perseverance and, always, a love for his new country.

He arrived in America on Nov. 14, 1980, and began college to become an engineer. In 1982, he joined a protest in San Francisco against Israel's invasion of Lebanon. His actions led the federal government to put him on a list of possible terrorist sympathizers.

Hamad moved to the Detroit area in 1987, working from 6 a.m. to 7 p.m. at a produce mart in Eastern Market, making $35 a day.

Hamad later worked for Wayne County and the Arab American and Chaldean Council. Meanwhile, the Immigration and Naturalization Service said he was connected to a terrorist organization, and tried to deport him.

But Hamad, by 1997 the regional director of the anti-discrimination committee, prevailed in court.

Last month he became a citizen, and yesterday, a voter. After leaving the school and his daughters and two ballots (in his excitement, he punched too many numbers on the first), he heads back to work.

"I owe this journey, this passion that I have about civil rights" to the 22-year-old government fight, he says. "I did not reach the role I'm playing today without paying my dues in pain and suffering and without having had a taste of what it means to have injustice be imposed on you.

"Those who are not voting are missing a nice feeling. It's the blessing of democracy, the blessing of freedom and there's no taste better than that."

November 6, 2002

Americans' only voice
is on the ballot

In the end, We the People don't matter.

At least, not every day.

In the end, the decision to go to war against Iraq is not up to parents and grandparents and sisters and brothers of those who will die thousands of miles away from home.

In the end, the decision to rain bombs on Saddam Hussein, second prize in the Terrorist Derby because we can't find Osama bin Laden, isn't ours, mothers who fear for our children.

In the end, the choice to pay Iraq about $28 million a day for crude oil last year wasn't ours, which means we could be funding the weapons that President Bush says Hussein plans to use against us.

In the end, the decision to ignore the warnings of the CIA that Hussein "could become much less constrained" if provoked to terrorism by a U.S. attack, is not our decision.

It was never up to us.

In modern times, we the people are not the ones who choose whether to fight or not, to build up other countries or not, to raise or lower taxes.

We the people did not choose to use force in 1964 in Southeast Asia, or choose to count the 58,000 American dead nine years later. We the people did not choose to attack Iraq on Kuwait's behalf in 1991, leaving 269 Americans dead.

We the people do not decide whether the government should pay attention when an FBI agent expresses concerns about potential terrorists in flight schools.

We the people cannot demand that a Homeland Security Department not be negotiated, but be required and created quickly and quietly in light of what happened in New York a year ago.

We the people sometimes forget that the federal government is not a daily democracy. It is a biennial and quadrennial democracy, and the only time we get to decide whether we go to war or change immigration laws or change the health system that should be a safety net for American families is when we vote for our leaders.

When we choose a president and congressional representatives and governors and mayors, that is when we have the chance to empower those who either share our dreams of prosperity and peace — or don't. It is only then that we have our say.

Sometimes, in the throes of campaign debates over trivia such as whether a candidate has values or is willing to circumvent law for religion, we forget to pay attention to the actual issues that will have greater impact on our lives, such as whether our taxes will make us homeless or our nation will be forever at war.

Sometimes, while marching on federal buildings to demand peace or writing letters to a president who made his decision, his father's decision, long ago, we forget that we chose the poor economy, we chose impending war, we chose the coming darkness.

What we must remember is that if we survive the darkness, if we survive the coming preventive measures that may lead to catastrophic ones, we will have a chance on another dawn to vote.

We will vote whether to resolve differences by war or by negotiation, whether to protect our environment or leave our children with a global mess, whether to protect the public schools that educate the majority of the nation's children or not, and whether to keep the church sacred and the state separate.

When that time comes to vote, we should not pass it up, because if we do, when We The People face another tragic error, such as this war surely will be, we can blame no one but ourselves.

October 11, 2002

Nobody is like Bill
— let's get him back

Two Novembers ago, while politicos and pundits fought back and forth over whether Al Gore got robbed of a presidential election, I wasn't thinking about Gore.

Oh, I wanted the fight to be fair. I wanted all the votes counted until the cows came home because, after all, that's what an election is for. But my first thought was: Wouldn't it have been nice to have Bill back? Wouldn't that have been fun?

Of all the presidents you think you can call by their nicknames — Teddy, Ike, Jimmy — when you say Bill, people know who you're talking about.

And though the media began using the term "Teflon" to describe Ronald Reagan a decade earlier, it never applied more than to Bill, to whom no scandal could stick.

If he had been a lousy president, it would have been easy to send him packing.

Below the whispers was the truth: He was the best.

The Bill Clinton who should be president gave us peace. He gave us economic well-being.

You think that's not possible in times of terror? I say that America has lived in times of terror before. And we've lived in terror for decades, but had the joy of not knowing it until last September.

Now we know.

Still, we don't have to fall apart. We don't have to blow up the world. What we have to do is determine who our real enemies are. And who our leaders are.

What I wanted two Novembers ago and what I want now is Bill Clinton for president.

I want the lowest unemployment rate in modern times. I want the lowest inflation. I want the highest era of home ownership ever. I want lower crime rates, even fewer welfare recipients, a budget surplus. I want to know what's going on in Washington, and I don't want a war that never happened to be used as an excuse for us not knowing.

I want a president who was the first to initiate a national debate on racism.

But can we get him?

It's dang near impossible. Two-thirds of both houses of Congress must agree to change the 22nd Amendment to the U.S. Constitution, which forbids a third term. Three-quarters of all states must also approve the change.

"We've had a lot of constitutional amendments that have been hanging around for ages because it's hard to get them approved," says Brad Roth, associate professor of political science and law at Wayne State University. "There was the equal rights amendment for women, but that failed. And other amendments have stuck around like the balanced budget amendment, the right to life amendment."

The 22nd Amendment came after Franklin Delano Roosevelt's third term.

"You have the people who didn't like him and felt he was around too long," Roth says, "and others who simply saw merit in limiting to two terms to avoid stagnation, to avoid the triumph of personality over policy."

Would America change the Constitution to elect Bill Clinton? Roth laughs heartily. "I would doubt it."

But if anyone could, could Clinton? The Comeback Kid? The man some Americans want to have a talk show because what they really want is for him to be in charge of something again?

Al Gore will never be Bill Clinton, not even with a saxophone.

And Bill Clinton can't run — unless somebody decides that having the right man in the job is worth the trouble.

September 4, 2002

Dear Mr. Heston: Please deliver final message

To: Charlton Heston
c/o National Rifle Association
From: A mom

Dear Mr. Heston:

It was with great regret that I heard the news that you may have Alzheimer's disease and eventually won't be able to challenge and debate in the powerful way you've done in the past.

You've handled this diagnosis with the same grace and dignity you've brought to the big screen, offering practical eloquence at a difficult time.

You'll receive many well wishes. This letter does that, too. But this also is a plea for you to consider saying something while you still have voice.

As the president of the National Rifle Association for so long, you've been a persistent advocate of gun rights. You have stood firm and stood fast.

I don't ask you to change your stance. Let's not debate killing for sport. It's an American right. Let's not debate the American right to bear arms. Those are both duels whose endings will not change soon.

But would you just consider addressing this: We here in Detroit have a serious problem with guns. Kids are dying regularly, either by their own hands or by those of drive-by thugs whom even you'd probably agree shouldn't have guns.

Who, you ask? How about the two guys arguing about a $40 radio who shot up a family's car as they were about to go shopping? Ajanee Pollard was shot in the head. She was 7. Her 6-year-old brother, Jason, lost his pancreas. Her sisters, Aerica, 6, and Alyah, 4, also were injured.

Those guys may not be the responsible gun owners you fight for, but they've got the guns nonetheless, because it's so hard to change the rules.

While you can, would you consider reminding Americans that, while they have the right to bear arms, guns have no other purpose except death?

Guns are not steak knives used to make dinner a little easier until someone misuses them. They are not sleeping pills that can hurt only in certain quantities. The only purpose of a gun is to kill.

Everyone should not have the right to kill, which is a gun's bill of sale.

Could you tell gun owners that when they bring guns into their homes, they bring death into their homes?

Could you remind them that they won't know the day or the hour that death comes, but that the possibility of death is as much a part of the weapon as its trigger?

Could you tell them that death could come as quickly when a burglar breaks a window as when a child gets up unexpectedly for water and breaks a glass in the kitchen?

Could you tell them that every time they put their guns in hiding places like cabinets, but forget to lock the door, their only sad reminder might be the bullet hole in their child's chest?

Mr. Heston, you've won the battle and the fight to bear arms for protection, pleasure or principle. But as one of the nation's greatest fighters for the right, could you, one last time, remind your fellow gun owners that if they want the guns, they have to know where they are? And that they have to take the blame when people kill people with their guns? And they have to, at all times, remember the children?

Maybe they'll listen to you. Maybe they'll be more careful. Maybe they'll keep an eye out for folks who give them a bad name, folks who, unlike them, really shouldn't have guns.

Then, maybe the only gun deaths are the ones that gun owners plan.

Thank you, God bless you, and Godspeed.

Sincerely,

Rochelle Riley

August 21, 2002

Ignored by parents, girl bullies run wild

Trees are falling left and right for a new spate of books about mean girls — 11- and 12-year-old middle schoolers who create entire ecosystems for making other girls feel horrible.

But the interesting thing is that this hate-filled behavior isn't new. What is new and welcome is that folks are finally, finally paying attention to a problem that has caused and can cause lasting damage to young girls.

What psychologists have known for years is that girls can be just as nasty as boys, but in different ways.

A boy will punch you; a girl will declare psychological warfare and not leave you alone until you begin staying home sick just to avoid facing school.

A recent New York Times Magazine article that highlighted the problem mentions girls "leaving nasty messages by cell phone or spreading scurrilous rumors by e-mail, making friends with one girl as revenge against another, gossiping about someone just loudly enough to be overheard."

Researchers have interviewed 11- and 12-year-olds to find where it starts. And the Times found a Washington, D.C., woman holding an Apologies Day in her class at a tony private school.

But what's missing from this picture is parents.

There have always been girl bullies. But what research has been done on the impact of declining parental oversight of children? I want to read a new book about the parents whose daughters are cruel.

Part of the reason it's so easy for mean girls to be mean is parents' lax attitudes about behavior and acceptance of a teen culture where popular girls' cruelty to others has crossed the line to torture.

Some kids don't have parents these days; they have buddies with credit cards who chauffeur them around. And when those kids are making other kids miserable at school, their parents usually are the ones who taught them or who dismiss what they're doing as girlhood pranks.

Girl bullying, or the Art of Middle School Mind Games, isn't fistfights. It's social slaps that make some girls not want to go to school. It has become its own new-age science with categories like Alphas and Gammas.

Yep, everybody's paying attention, except the parents of the girls who are mean.

No one knows the true impact of daily harassment and hate. Who can tell how long it hurts when an innocent victim gets a call, and it's a sophisticated three-way, where the harasser puts her on conference, then calls a third girl she thought was her friend to trash her?

Researchers can do all the studies they want. This boils down to what parents teach their kids. There have always been bullies. There have always been those little girls who were at the center of the circle at recess or at the center seat at lunch. Sometimes, their arrival is serendipitous, sometimes calculated.

But what has always been true is that those who must remain outside the circle or who can't sit at the table suffer lasting loss and pain.

How long it lasts is up to parents who must decide whether their child is dealing in simple meanness that you get over or relational aggression that can do permanent damage. Parents must fix in their children the things they see that they don't like.

How long it lasts depends on parents who take seriously their daughter's grief and teaches that the mean girls are to be avoided.

How well children survive is determined not by the mean girls, but by parents on both sides.

June 16, 2002

A new trial won't repay years lost in prison

How do you pay back 17 years? What do you say to a man who spent all that time in prison for a crime he may not have committed?

"Oops"?

That doesn't cut it, particularly coming from officials in the business of fairness and justice. But it may be the case with Thomas Cress, who at 28 was sent to prison for life for the 1983 murder of a Battle Creek teenager. Cress, a child-like man who possibly was helping to deliver newspapers nowhere near where Patricia Rosansky was abducted on her way to school, has maintained his innocence for 19 years.

But prosecution witnesses at his trial who claimed that he bragged about killing the 17-year-old were able to convince a jury. And that jury ultimately sent him to prison for life.

Ten years ago, a Battle Creek police detective found a suspected serial killer who claimed the crime and told Jon Sahli, then Calhoun County Prosecutor. Not long after, Sahli ordered DNA evidence in the case destroyed.

Sahli told Free Press reporters that he didn't know about the confession (and declined to return calls yesterday), but the appellate court that has ordered a new trial has called Sahli's actions "deeply disturbing."

You know what I call them, if true?

Criminal.

Now Cress might finally have the trial he deserved the first time around, but it won't be fair because the DNA evidence that might have cleared him is gone.

In the scheme of things, law enforcement officials must have the ultimate freedom to do their jobs, for our protection and for truth. But leeway doesn't include bending the law. Those who do for their own personal score cards should be punished as harshly as those who allege false crimes to hurt others.

The Cress case brought to mind the Oklahoma City police chemist,

Joyce Gilchrist, who was fired because she is alleged to have given false testimony in criminal cases, including some that led men to death row. Oklahoma officials are reviewing hundreds of cases from two decades in which her testimony might have led to wrongful prosecutions. One death sentence has been overturned and another death-row inmate has been freed.

But officials also are trying to determine whether her alleged actions led to the execution of an Oklahoma inmate last year. Officials have identified 23 cases in which 11 convicts were executed and 12 are on death row, based on Gilchrist's testimony. They are reviewing the 12 cases where defendants still live. But if there was any illegality about the other 11, well ... oops.

DNA analyses, which weren't available until the 1990s, have helped overturn convictions in courts across the country, in some cases saving lives when used to prove that convicted defendants were not where prosecutors placed them. The Cress case is cited in efforts to pass legislation requiring the preservation of DNA evidence for as long as those convicted are in prison.

Who knows whether Sahli, now a prosecutor in Saginaw, tried to circumvent the law by destroying evidence in the Cress case. But if he did, if he destroyed evidence only after learning that it might free an innocent man and take a notch off his belt, is it possible that other cases he handled should be reviewed as well? And if so, should he be prosecuted?

The real hero in this story is police Det. Dennis Mullen, who risked the scorn of prosecutors to find the truth. Our legal system should not only prosecute those who abuse it, but honor those who uphold it.

March 1, 2002

American cardinals share blame for assaults on kids

A funny thing happened on the way to the Vatican.

Pope John Paul II and America's 12 cardinals met and agreed, in principle, to create a process to defrock any priest who becomes "notorious and is guilty of the serial, predatory sexual abuse of minors." (Since Webster's describes notorious as generally known, that lets the secret predators, meaning those who don't advertise, off the hook).

But what the cardinals forgot to pack for the Vatican trip were responsibility, culpability and guilt. What the cardinals didn't discuss was their own lack of leadership.

On Tuesday, the pope said that many people were "offended at the way in which the church's leaders are perceived to have acted."

Why isn't reality perceived in Vatican City?

Cardinals who paid off families and moved sexual predators from parish to parish did act, and in their action, continued to allow crimes to happen. The pope should have expanded his public scolding of abusive priests to the cardinals.

The leader of an entity is its guiding force. He or she sets the example, charts the path. Catholic cardinals allowed priests the freedom to abuse children over and over, which makes them just as culpable as the sexual assaulters. What consequences await the cardinals?

Moreover, what kind of standards did cardinals set to let priests so easily violate the law?

Whose standards were priests meeting when, having gotten away with emotional murder, they continued to work with other children?

How could these priests allow themselves to remain in the priesthood after committing such grievous sins?

The answer is simple. It is because the leadership of the church demanded no more.

I cannot begin to speak on the issue of forgiveness. It is a God-given right and the most precious gift. How many times do you forgive a transgressor, the Bible asks? Seventy times seven. And then some.

The sexual abuse scandal that has dominated the news is not just a scandal about abusive priests. It is a scandal for leaders, Cardinal Adam Maida included, because they, only men, after all, confused forgiving with condoning.

The saddest thing about the acts that led American cardinals to the Vatican woodshed is that most were against children. Those priests violated God's law as well as man's law.

And, in some cases, they got away with at least one.

I can understand being conflicted. I can understand forgiveness. I can even see a cardinal approving secret payments to families to save the church.

What I cannot understand is why priests who broke God's law were allowed to stay. That is the question that Cardinal Maida, in his near-apologies, has not touched.

In Pope John II's last encyclical, issued in August 1993 and titled "Veritatis Splendor ("The Splendor of Truth") — Regarding Certain Fundamental Question of the Church's Moral Teaching," he wrote, "Truth enlightens man's intelligence and shapes his freedom, leading him to know and love the Lord."

In his next one, maybe the pope should be a little more specific.

Catholics must take a harder look at their leaders, who must also face punishment for complicity.

Any cardinal who allows priests to violate man's law and God's law should be convicted by the former and punished by the latter.

So the Vatican trip aside, the cardinals still have much work to do.

April 26, 2002

Look at Rice for herself, not her party

If she weren't a Republican, we black folks would be praying for her strength and celebrating how happy the elders must be looking down on her.

Just imagine, a little black girl who grew up in segregated schools in Birmingham, Ala., who became provost at Stanford University.

Who became a figure skater.

Who became a concert pianist.

Who speaks four languages, including Russian.

But since she is a Republican, Condoleezza Rice is not getting her due.

We can be so partisan sometimes that we forget to celebrate the monumental.

And Rice's role in government is monumental.

The 47-year-old national security adviser, the first woman and African American ever to hold the post, is a buoy in the middle of a storm — constant, assured and the reason I have been less worried about the decisions that President Bush has had to make since Sept. 11.

It was so easy to be dismissive of Bush and his entire cabinet in the weeks after the November election, an issue that seemed so important then and so incidental now.

November 2000 was a lifetime ago, almost 3,000 lifetimes ago.

Now, we praise Colin Powell as African Americans' greatest hope for a national leader who looks and behaves like us, despite his party. But we forget that Powell isn't the only black person who has the president's ear. As a matter of fact, according to news reports, Rice is closer.

We've paid little attention to the seasoned intellectual, and that's a shame, because she is an expert on the former Evil Empire that we now play nice with and she has the hardest job in the world, according to those who know.

Oh, it's OK to say it. We know how hard it is. She has to explain foreign policy to a former Texas governor whose struggle with global affairs and pronunciation of foreign countries has been the butt of jokes.

Rice has had to synthesize and lay out in layman's terms the crux of centuries-old beliefs and battles. And she's had to do it on the run.

In the weeks since Sept. 11, it has been Rice taking the podium at press conferences to discuss the current state of affairs. Her ability to mold a maelstrom into manageable storms has never been more needed than at a time when its citizens are getting a lesson on foreign terrorists.

Last year, "The Nation" said Rice would be "rock-star big." That she hasn't says more about our inability to let go of politics than her place in history.

A woman called me this week, madder than hell that Bush appointed a homeland security czar when he already had a national security adviser. I shared her thoughts with an insightful colleague who reminded me that the national security adviser's job is bigger than terrorism.

National security is more than making sure we can fly safely and open our own mail.

It has been, since it was created by President Dwight Eisenhower in 1953, the position held by the president's go-to person on global affairs.

If former Pennsylvania Gov. Tom Ridge had been named anti-terrorism czar, much as we've had drug czars in the past, maybe that woman wouldn't have thought Rice was being shafted.

More important, if Rice was working for Al Gore, then the nation's first black national security adviser might be on posters and on our tongues.

Maybe we need to take another look.

And celebrate achievement, not lament defeat.

November 23, 2001

Our America, land of the unbelievable

Two new entries just made the annals of Riley's Believe-It-Or-Not.

At first, both cases seemed to involve government stupidity. But a closer look and a chat with a law professor gave me greater insight into why unbelievable things still happen in America.

I learned about the first late Tuesday as I headed to a place that in my early working days was a regular midnight haunt: the post office just before tax-filing deadline. (The extra day to file didn't help me a bit.)

I was wracking my brain for tax credits I might have missed when my friend Janet called with news. I thought she was joking. But no, it was right there on Page 22 of Sunday's New York Times.

"IRS Paid Millions in False Claims for Slavery Credit."

Apparently, hundreds of people who filed for a slavery credit (which, by the way, doesn't exist) got paid, making the total $30 million that the Treasury Department dispensed without thinking.

The second involves the U.S. Supreme Court, which has refused to hear cases ranging from death penalty appeals to a tribe's fight against neighboring towns to expand on its own land.

But the court DID agree to decide whether a little Kentucky store has caused enough financial harm for the sensual Victoria's Secret chain to sue.

It's all about the 1996 Federal Trademark Dilution Act that protects famous trademarks. The justices will decide whether a plaintiff must show actual financial harm to its trademark before it can sue.

Four years ago, Victor and Cathy Moseley opened Victor's Secret to sell risqué lingerie, sex toys and adult videos in Elizabethtown, Ky. Folks at Victoria's Secret told the Moseleys they couldn't use that name. So they changed it to Victor's Little Secret. Victor is obviously very self-assured.

That still wasn't enough, so the chain sued, saying that Victor's Little Secret (now Cathy's Secret) was taking customers from its 750 stores. The lower court found for the chain, saying the possibility of financial damage is enough.

Now the Supreme Court will decide.

Both cases have a you've-got-to-be-kidding quality, except they will affect future law. For instance, the improper IRS payments, which topped $12 million last year, mean that folks clearly are getting reparations. The IRS didn't want to disclose how the credit was claimed for fear of copycats.

But they won't get to keep that money, and the reparations issue shouldn't be diluted by alleged scam artists taking advantage of the IRS. The lingering damage from slavery is bigger than a phantom tax credit. A $43,000 check won't pay for years of inadequate schools, job discrimination and trod-over spirits. A check for $43 billion might.

As for the Victoria's Secret case? Robert Sedler, a constitutional law professor at Wayne State University, says it's not about underwear. It's about copyright infringement and how the court picks cases.

"The two main considerations are whether there is a disagreement among the federal courts of appeal on the question," he said. "This particular case may seem funny ... but it may be a good vehicle to decide copyright infringement."

The high court might do well to consider just copyright cases, not more serious issues. Its decision to strike down a ban on virtual child pornography because it's free speech and doesn't involve live children is silly.

Allowing virtual child porn is like saying it's OK for a guy to rob a store, as long as his gun isn't real.

Only in America.

April 19, 2002

Marriage incentives miss the point

It wasn't even front-page news.

In the scheme of things, what with war being waged against terrorists and Enron accountants testifying before Congress and intensive debate over what to call captured Taliban fighters and President George W. Bush's first State of the Union address, well, it just wasn't big news that his administration has decided to seek $100 million a year for experimental programs designed to get single welfare mothers to find themselves some husbands.

Initially, I thought I was reading a printed version of a "Saturday Night Live" skit, a transcript of Weekend Update that would go on to say that not only would welfare mothers be offered rewards to get married, but they'd also be rewarded for joining the Republican Party, for becoming Episcopalian and for investing their meager savings in whatever company replaces Enron as the go-to business for Washington bigwigs.

Sadly, the story wasn't a parody but a Bush administration initiative that trumped a conservative push to require single moms to get married to get welfare benefits (as if they would need them if their babies' daddies stayed in the first place).

My first question, no, my second question after "What could they be thinking?" is "What happened to the Republican Party being the party that believed in a smaller, less intrusive government?"

There's something wrong with the government offering to pay women to get married, which is tantamount to bribing some guys who wouldn't otherwise stay to hang around for a little government cash. Marriage is a good thing when it's real and when it's right.

Being married doesn't always mean having a good husband and father. A government coupling just to meet a conservative standard for family values doesn't mean a child will be better off.

Like a domestic green card, the incentives that the government is considering giving to fathers who stay with their children's mothers might become comparable to the cards sought by immigrants who marry Americans just to stay in the States. The card is more important than the marriage license, and the marriages don't usually last.

Considering that half of American marriages end in divorce anyway, what value is being promoted by enticing couples into loveless marriages for money, marriages that, in many cases, don't stand a chance and don't help the child?

Does the U.S. government really believe that all single mothers are single by choice? Nope. Many are single because the fathers leave.

Offering up a little cash might make them stay. But it won't make them better fathers.

Instead of spending $100 million on programs to get single mothers to marry, the government might be better served spending that money on expanding day care, which allows single mothers to work. The government also could emphasize more training so those mothers can work in higher-paying jobs.

Those services, instead of a mating service, would make it easier for welfare mothers to become proud, strong working mothers.

As important as family values are, the most important value is esteem, and the most important esteem is still self-esteem.

And you can't get that from a man.

January 30, 2002

Murderer's execution won't balance the scales

They are strangers to most of us outside of Oklahoma.

Teresa Alexander, 33, was just visiting the Alfred P. Murrah Federal Building in Oklahoma City. Richard A. Allen, 46, was a claims representative. Saundra G. (Sandy) Avery, 34, was a clerk.

But they represent the day America lost its innocence.

Raymond (Lee) Johnson, 59, was a senior volunteer. Derwin W. Miller, 27, was a claims examiner. Julie Marie Welch, 23, was an interpreter. They represent the years that America has waited for revenge. They are the sorrows of families whose souls cry out in anguish every time they hear the murderer's name.

Steven Douglas Curry, 44, was an inspector for the General Services Administration. Harley Richard Cottingham, 46, was a special agent for the Department of Defense. Rebecca Needham Anderson was a 37-year-old nurse.

Now that the legalities are nearing an end, and the FBI's missteps have proved to be nonfatal, revenge is near. But what will it all mean, the making of a martyr?

His execution will not deter madmen intent on changing government by killing innocent people. His execution will not put the Murrah building back the way it was before the disaster, will not stop the screaming in our heads.

His execution will not bring back the children.

Miss Baylee Almon, 1. Danielle Nicole Bell, 15 months. Zackary Taylor Chavez, 3.

They are angels flying higher than his anger can ever touch again.

Anthony Christopher Cooper II, 2. Antonio Ansara Cooper Jr., 6 months. Aaron M. Coverdale, 5.

They might have lived lives to change the world: future presidents, farmers, scientists, teachers. One might have discovered a cure for AIDS.

Elijah S. Coverdale, 2. Jaci Rae Coyne, 14 months. Tylor Santoi Eaves,

8 months.

But what are we teaching other children now, in our anger? They've seen a nation fixate on a pitiful little man whose only claim to fame is changing the way we think about terrorists. We can no longer assume where they live or what they look like.

Tevin D'Aundrae Garrett, 16 months; Kevin (Lee) Gottshall II, 6 months. Blake Ryan Kennedy, 18 months.

Revenge is a hard lesson to teach. An eye for an eye, a death for 168. How can we teach children it is wrong to embrace violence when a nation salivates while awaiting an execution?

Dominique London, 2; Chase Dalton Smith, 3; Colton Wade Smith, 2.

How do we teach children to turn the other cheek, when we are failing our greatest test? Instead of making a man sit in a box for the rest of his life to be visited by the ghosts of the children, America wants to do what he did: Kill.

Anita Christine Hightower, 27, was a secretary for the Job Corps. Kim R. Cousins, 33, was a construction coordinator for the Department of Housing and Urban Development. Carrie Ann Lenz, 26, was a contract employee for the Drug Enforcement Administration. She was pregnant with a son, who was to have been Michael James Lenz III.

Such losses make us want to hate. But when we turn to hate, do we become what we hate? By becoming killers, do we become like the homegrown terrorist who changed our world? Do we really change anything, ensure future safety, achieve true vengeance?

Timothy McVeigh 168, America 1.

Do we really feel better?

June 8, 2001

Remember the man your dad used to be

Hello.

I don't even know your name. But the news of you made quite an impact on the lives of strangers.

You don't know me, either, but more often than not I'm a fan of your father.

This kind of discussion is usually private. But when your father is a national religious, moral and civil rights leader named the Rev. Jesse Jackson and your mother is not his wife, it becomes news.

Children should be born with only joy at their arrival. Your arrival should be no different. So as you travel life, don't be discouraged by this. You can choose not to live in the thin mist of scandal. You can rise above.

As you get older, your friends may ask about your father. If you have a stepfather, it will be that man they ask about. But some may wonder about the father your mother might have explained or that you already know, the one who gave you life but doesn't live with you, the one whose claiming of you made national news.

You can choose to say nothing. Or you can tell them your father was a great man, a leader among men in the 20th Century, a lifelong activist whose crusades made a difference for millions. You can tell them he might have been president in another century or at another juncture in a young country's history.

Tell them he gave his life to America, to its causes and to the least of its citizens, the ones mistreated and dismissed as inconsequential. Tell them he showed up whenever someone was wronged. Tell them he advised presidents and changed Wall Street, that he made the world see people of color with new eyes.

Tell them he was an intellect who spoke about foreign policy as easily as he spoke about basketball.

Tell them he reminded people to "Keep hope alive!" — and they did. Tell them he admitted to being flawed — all great leaders are — and that he always said he was a public servant, not a perfect servant.

And when you have your own questions, when you wonder why your father counseled a president about an extramarital affair while he was having one himself, know that his legacy will rise above that. If the president had been as straightforward as your father, he might not have muddied his political accomplishments.

Your father let the world know that he loved you, was providing for you and was being as good a father as a married public figure can be to a child who faces growing up without him and in the shadow of the spotlight.

It may not be enough. You're entitled to be angry. But never write him off.

He was a good man.

So when you wonder whether his moral horse was too high for someone who was committing adultery, you'll be right.

He let a lot of people down.

But he let them down because he held so many on his shoulders. Many in America looked to your father for guidance, for leadership, for a compass to set them in the right direction. They should have looked to themselves.

When the nation first learned about you, it was a critical time. Your father was trying to ensure that the nation had a fair attorney general and was leading protests about alleged voter fraud in Florida.

The news of you overtook all that. It was numbing, the way you feel upon hearing that someone famous has died. But the only thing that died was the idea of a perfect hero, of a man without spot or wrinkle. No such man exists.

Your father reminded a nation of that, once again.

January 19, 2001

Gore risks it all by flying solo

Somewhere Ken Starr is smiling.

The overzealous independent prosecutor, who dogged President Bill Clinton, spent millions of dollars in public money and treated a naive young woman like a criminal, only to fail to get the president convicted or burned in effigy, has had to wait years to see Clinton punished.

And the punishment is harsh. The affable, public-loving president is being forced to sit mostly on the sidelines while his vice president seeks to replace him.

He is being denied the elder statesman task of handing the presidency to a successor — a job he is suited for, and a job he could do, despite the vice president's misgivings.

While it provides chuckles for Starr, it gives us a clear view of what Al Gore is really doing in this campaign: showing he can stand on his own.

Leaving Clinton on the front porch while he traverses the country could cost Gore some black voters, who are routinely taken for granted by the Democratic Party. No one draws black voters like Bill Clinton — even though 74 percent support Gore, say recent surveys.

Al Gore's biggest miscalculation in this campaign was believing people would care whether George W. Bush was smart enough for the job.

His biggest risk was not using Clinton on the stump because of the Lewinsky affair. Ignoring Clinton's popularity — particularly among black voters, liberal voters, celebrities and young people — Gore charted his own course, making 74 percent of black voters support him. Clinton could have made those numbers higher.

Gore attacked racial profiling and pledged to support affirmative action and a balanced Supreme Court. But Clinton would have made those issues as central to the campaign as health care and Social Security.

It's not enough for Gore to get support from black voters, whom he is counting on and Bush isn't interested in (unless they make more than $75,000 a year). He must get those voters to the polls. And that was Clinton's specialty — firing up the nation's largest minority group, which still fights for every gain and faces discrimination every day.

Clinton, long considered the nation's first black president (or the closest we'll have in the next 20 years), has felt our pain and fought our fights and made mistakes that real people have made.

He not only made the presidency more accessible and human, but he also made it messy, which is the way many Americans live their lives.

At the height of the Starr investigation, so-called pundits expressed incredulity every week that the president could remain so popular despite affairs and lies. They never talked about the fact that when he wasn't showing incredibly stupid judgment, he was an incredible president.

After impeachment, Clinton's approval rating of 73 percent was higher than Ronald Reagan's in his final presidential poll (68 percent).

Heading into the Nov. 7 election, few mention Lewinsky, and Linda Tripp remains a running "Saturday Night Live" joke.

Gore ignored advice I learned as a Southern woman: Dance with the one who brung you. But he's heeding more advice I got: Unless the one who brung you puts his hands in the wrong place. Then get home on your own.

Gore wants to get home on his own, without his date of eight years. It's the biggest risk of his political career. But it shows more courage than debates, stump speeches and kissing his wife on national TV.

October 29, 2000

Only players who cheated should be punished

I haven't been able to keep my mind off the University of Michigan student athletes who are suffering the shame of punishment for past players' deeds.

I'm not a sports expert; I'm a fan who has time and again seen the wrong players punished. It seems so unfair because it is so unfair.

And it made me wonder why the NCAA cannot come up with punishments for universities and cheaters without making future players suffer.

My colleague Mitch Albom rightly suggests that players who violate NCAA rules should be forced to reimburse their schools and be able to be sued.

I think we should go a step further.

Players who cheat should do more than repay their scholarships. They should repay all fines associated with illegal activity, including all university fines.

U-M should forfeit the basketball victories that players who broke rules helped attain, and take down banners connected with that shame.

But I draw the line at punishing current players. If a university discovers a major violation of an NCAA rule, the program should be placed on a multiyear probation. Any future infraction during probation should net a simple version of the NCAA death penalty — prohibition of competition for a year. Shut down the gym. Close the locker room.

There's even one more step I'd suggest: If the NCAA wants its rules taken seriously, it should enlist the NBA's help.

The league should work with colleges, which provide nearly all the human capital for a billion-dollar industry. NBA contracts should include a clause fining players who damage the college that took them to the big show.

The NBA should feel a responsibility to help.

And if they don't? Well, I'm one fan who plans to pick up my pom-poms and go home. As a matter of fact, I won't support any NBA team whose roster includes players who's making millions while their alma maters suffer.

There will be those who ask: Why can't the boys whose families are struggling and who themselves are struggling to make ends meet get a little cheddar for all the glory they bring to their schools?

Because the rules forbid it. Those who need the money should leave school early. Or the university should pay basketball and football players because of the revenue they bring in.

Poor kids can't get the cheddar without a good season. But they can't make it through the season without some financial help here and there.

But it's the same dilemma that student doctors, journalists, biologists, politicians and economists face each year.

I don't know Chris Webber or his teammates personally. I never saw them drive fancy cars or pick up tabs they shouldn't have been able to afford.

But I was a fan. I loved the Fab Five and wanted them to be the Cinderellas they appeared to be.

But now it's midnight and some of those little princes may turn out to be pumpkins.

My disappointment with the university is great: Those responsible for handling the players, and there are many, might have turned their heads from behavior that's been a problem since I attended college.

But my disappointment in the players is greater. Cheating is an individual choice and those individuals should be punished. No matter where they are now.

November 17, 2002

Who needs enemies
when we've got us?

You would think it impossible to find humor in the national debate over gun control.

Gun enthusiasts hitching up their pants and talking about freedom and the Second Amendment while a sniper snatched random victims in the Washington, D.C., area seemed too heinously misguided to be funny.

But as I sat next to Michael Moore and his friend Jeff Gibbs at a Royal Oak screening of "Bowling for Columbine," I laughed involuntarily.

The brilliant and biting documentary has moments so obscenely sad that they are funny: A hunter accidentally shot in the leg after strapping a gun to his dog's back. A kid disappointed that he wasn't first on a list of high school students most likely to make a bomb. He was second.

Moore filmed a National Rifle Association rally in Denver after two students gunned down classmates at Columbine High School in Littleton, Colo., and he filmed parents' disgust with the NRA's presence.

In that darkened theater, while police searched nationwide for a sniper, it became clear why Americans fatally shoot each other more than people in other countries do.

Moore's hypothesis is that there is more fear and hate in America. Because the violence is pounded home in news reports, TV shows, films and video games, dead people can be just numbers to us.

We've watched the sniper's death toll, but do we bother to remember the faces or names of those cut down on their way home, to work, to school?

A coward killed Conrad, Linda, Kenneth, Dean, Pascal, Lori Ann, Sarah, Prem, Sonny and James and hurt a man, a woman and a 13-year-old boy, whose names, gratefully, we don't know.

It is important to realize that this sniper might not be the only one. There might be thousands in waiting, lured by fame, fueled by anger and armed by lax gun control laws.

Talk of gun freedom and the Second Amendment while random shots have broken hearts is laughable. Instead, why don't we focus on the point we've reached in America?

We have known since Oct. 2 what it feels like to be victims of daily terrorism. Sept. 11 introduced us to a level of hatred that we once had the privilege to ignore. But the sniper took us to a different place.

Now we know what Israeli mothers and daughters and fathers and sons go through when they don't know whether the guy beside them has a bomb strapped to his chest.

We don't know how many strangers among us are one personal slight away from the capacity for murder.

America should be at high alert all the time as we battle terrorists from without and within. But because shootings are common in America, we don't notice what Michael Moore's film points out in the simple number of firearm deaths in one year: Germany, 381; France, 255; Canada, 165; United Kingdom, 68; Australia, 65; Japan, 39; America, 11,127. We see news of shootings, watch news reports, then go to work or to dinner.

America is at war as long as any coward in the shadows can hunt innocents like deer. As long as guns are readily available to any nut who wants one, as Moore points out, we are our own worse enemy.

And if the NRA heads to Washington to debate lax gun laws, its members better keep their heads down — just in case neither man arrested Thursday is the sniper.

Or wasn't acting alone.

October 25, 2002

Martha and Rosie reveal their truer selves

Last week saw the unveiling of the true women behind two facades.

Both seemed unable to be themselves because they so differed from their public personas.

Both were caught in glaring spotlights that highlighted their flaws and reminded us once again that celebrities exist for our amusement, not to emulate as role models.

And try as I might, I felt no sympathy for Martha Stewart. But I feel sorry for Rosie O'Donnell.

In the case of America's lifestyle maven, the one Newsweek calls "the Queen of Perfection," who turned housework into a money machine and made millions from embroidering pillowcases and carving cantaloupes into flowers, the curtain was raised on the shrewd businesswoman who may think she's above it all.

After revelations that she sold her ImClone stock (and saved $43,000) one day before the FDA said it wasn't approving the company's new cancer drug, authorities are investigating what she knew in advance.

When Jane Clayson questioned her on "The Early Show" last week, she kept chopping food as if being asked whether she would boil or bake.

She's treating the investigation like an inconvenience, with an aloof arrogance that reeks of elitism.

Maybe the truth will show that she's the luckiest woman on Earth, selling that stock just in the nick of time. But if the truth differs from her story, she might just become the most surprised convict in federal prison.

Rosie, on the other hand, seems to reek of bitterness and anger, maybe because she had to hide her sexual orientation to become a celebrity.

Now she has taken off the mask and gloves, showing America her truer self, a bawdy comedienne, the sassy, irreverent, more-alike-than-different-from-her-old-friend-Madonna Rosie that she was before she became a talk show host.

She skewered fellow celebrities, shunning Michael Jackson at Liza

Minnelli's heralded wedding because she doesn't "speak to pedophiles" and calling the wedding the gayest event since her show's finale.

She is trying to return to herself, or the self she once knew. But no matter what she does from now on, there will be people who no longer like who she is, or was, or wants to be.

Trying to be herself after wearing angel's wings for six years must hurt. And from that hurt, from people not accepting her, from the anguish her children may face by having two mommies, she's lashing out.

That makes me feel for her.

But what I can't figure is why we thought we knew either woman. We read articles and books and watch TV interviews and talk about them like they're old friends. "No, her son's name is Parker!" or "She said you have to braise it first!"

But celebrities create those ideal people who meet our expectations of wonderful. They're not real. But we so buy it that when something happens that forces them to remove their masks, we stand horrified, like learning that a family member isn't family.

The people we want them to be are never who they really are. And after watching two of the biggest remove their masks, I couldn't help but wonder what lies under the others.

Is Katie Couric as sweet as she seems? Is David Letterman as acerbic? What is Oprah like on Saturdays?

Then again, do we really want to know?

June 30, 2002

Catholics struggle with forgiveness

The most amazing thing happened last week: The pope was misquoted around the world, and no one really paid attention.

There, in reports from respected news organizations, were reports claiming that the pope had said habitual sinners could never be forgiven.

That's not what the pope said.

What he actually said was, "It is clear that penitents living in a habitual state of serious sin and who do not intend to change their situation cannot validly receive absolution."

What people took that to mean was that habitual sinners could never be forgiven and that all those sinners except sexually abusive priests are likely to go to hell.

It's an easy mistake to make, but that doesn't mean we should make it.

National outrage over the Roman Catholic Church sex-abuse scandal makes it easy for us to want to throw the church out with the bath water.

But, on behalf of all the good priests in America, those whose reputations and good works are soiled by their deviant brethren, don't judge too quickly.

After all, you don't blame the entire police department when one kills three people and wounds a fourth in nine shootings, as Detroit's Eugene Brown did. You don't blame the whole basketball team when one forward misses a shot in a playoff game. You don't shut a school down when one teacher makes an inappropriate remark to a student.

You find the problems and get rid of them.

The letter from the pope, published May 2, didn't say what should be done with priests who sin. What it did do was return to business as usual.

It was a reminder that the rules of the church still apply, even though some priests have broken them.

Getting back to the basics gives the church something to do while the cardinals and bishops complete their work, which is removing abusive priests as quickly as possible.

In the pope's letter, we might find the answer to the question: Why aren't Catholics streaming out of the church like rats from a sinking ship?

The simple answer is that the ship isn't sinking. Like the White House and its myriad scandals through the years, like Congress and the criminals it has begotten, government is bigger than its individual crooks.

I asked one Dearborn Heights priest about the sanctity and preservation of the church. He explained that the church is struggling with issues of forgiveness and reconciliation.

Everyone in the Catholic Church is forgiven for sins, he says, but not everyone is reconciled. He explained that God forgives all sinners, but whether they reconcile with Him or not is their choice.

Those who want to be absolved of guilt must do so on their own by pledging not to sin again.

Absolution is a technical theological term having to do with change of heart, a blessing for changing one's ways.

So for Catholics who are looking for absolution because what's good for the priests is good for the parishioners, the pope's real message shouldn't be lost.

The rules haven't changed because of what the abusive priests have done. The rules become more important than ever in the cases of those for whom the pope is a spiritual leader.

And for those priests who have violated the law, they are, as a part of church doctrine, forgiven. But they and all who abetted their crimes still need to go to jail.

May 10, 2002

In our rush,
we misplaced humanity

Imagine yourself in their shoes. Put yourself on the Ship Canal Bridge in Seattle last Tuesday morning, late for work and sick of traffic.

Hear yourself muttering under your breath about how long it is taking to clear up an accident just ahead. Hear the occasional shouts from the drivers in front of you.

Near the accident scene, it is clear there had been no accident. There is a car blocking traffic on the other side. And two officers stand 20 feet away from a young woman sitting on the bridge.

Her back is to the passing cars. She is considering jumping. And some drivers are urging her.

Suddenly, the routine of daily traffic was no more. It became one of those moments from TV when you want Superman to come and save the day.

But there were no caped men in tights, only ordinary heroes, hostage negotiators, trying to defuse a bad situation.

By 6:29 a.m., three people had yelled at the woman from the southbound lane, driving by her and encouraging her to drop 150 feet into a thin canal of water with concrete and buildings on either side.

At 7:44 a.m., police had to close the northbound lanes, the opposite lane, because the comments were escalating. They could do nothing about people yelling up from below the bridge.

After about 3 1/2 hours, right at 10 a.m., the woman jumped.

Within 5 minutes, authorities opened the northbound lanes. Ten minutes later, they opened the southbound.

And everyone was on their way. As if nothing had happened.

It isn't the first time, and it doesn't happen only in Seattle. Still Officer Virgil McDonald, a negotiator, was stunned.

"Some were telling her to jump. Some were telling her to jump with a little extra wordage thrown in, a few names."

McDonald doesn't think the comments forced her hand.

"There were things that had happened in her life that she couldn't handle. She actually was quite prepared to do what she did."

But it must hurt to face the hardest decision of your life and get that kind of horrible encouragement.

"It's a very emotionally charging situation for us because we're out there trying to save this person's life and we'll say or do just about anything to save them," McDonald said, "and it's very disheartening to hear somebody drive by or walk by and tell this individual to kill themselves when we're trying very hard to save their lives. These people wouldn't be doing it if it was a member of their family sitting out there on that bridge."

Negotiators, like McDonald, who at 48 has been on the job for nine years, were heartened that the woman survived and is improving in a Seattle hospital.

Meanwhile, negotiators, like McDonald, continue to prepare themselves for the next time.

I like McDonald's shoes. They walk up to a bridge or some other situation knowing their job is to save lives.

As for the motorists so much in a hurry or so keen to see a tragedy that they egged her on, they are the answer to the question: What is wrong with America?

September 2, 2001

Two old soldiers work to lead again

They are friends with much in common.

Their faces are known to much of the world.

Their advocacy has affected U.S. domestic and foreign policy: One accomplished change as a world leader, the other as a leader who galloped the globe.

Their words cost thousands of dollars to hear, except when they're free.

And their lies to their wives revealed them as adulterers.

Their foolishness took the sheen off their celebrity and political futures, so now former President Bill Clinton and the Rev. Jesse Jackson, united in discomfort, must travel the world again to rebuild their public personas.

They were two of the coolest dudes in politics, or so they thought, Bill with his saxophone and Jesse with his rhymes. Did they share locker-room jokes about what they thought they were getting away with?

The national landscape looks barren now that the most virile, handsome, spotlight-seeking buildings marking its skyline have been reduced to doghouses. But after having a skyline like Bill and Jesse, it's no wonder they seem hard to replace.

They were fun before they stumbled and fell. But no one picks themselves up the way they do. So as their forced rehabilitations continue, let's ask ourselves: What do we really want from them?

With Jesse, the answer is simple. Black America doesn't move as a group without someone leading the way, someone the mainstream media can look to for sound bites, someone who'll still stand at the front when everybody else has gone home.

For years, Jesse was at the front of the marches, in front of the cameras. His penchant for being wherever news was became a joke. He could find a crisis faster than a speeding 747.

But he was there. And now he's the only thing that keeps Al Sharpton from assuming the leadership mantle.

Jesse was even charged by some media with setting up his wife's recent protest of military bombings in Vieques, Puerto Rico, in hopes that it would turn attention away from his troubles and Sharpton's own arrest.

Still, spurred to action by celebrity outcry, the U.S. agreed to stop the bombings in two years. So Jesse's in the right place again.

Bill Clinton, who made us believe he felt our pain, or felt it more than any other president, also loved the cameras. In our world of 24-hour news cycles, he strove to be at the top of every hour.

Since leaving office he has traveled faster and more than any previous president, mostly outside America, visiting 17 countries to build global good will and restore the love.

Bill might be criticized for traveling, but he could give lessons on making people believe you care.

And he still knows how to hit a target. Among his trips was one to Africa to help raise AIDS awareness, a crisis that suffers from a lack of urgency on other continents even though it is becoming our scourge.

So both men, Bill and Jesse, still seem to be needed.

Sometimes, the choice is having leadership or not. For all their missteps, Bill and Jesse still elicit visceral loyalty from people.

That says much about them. Unfortunately, it also says much about America.

July 22, 2001

Party switch is one
to be celebrated

As my Aunt Nell would say, it was more than just a notion.

Vermont Sen. Jim Jeffords' decision to leave the Republican Party for independence and to turn the Senate over to Democratic control was the second most important decision of this political year, just behind the U.S. Supreme Court ruling that handed George W. Bush the presidency.

Jeffords' decision is a good thing for everyone, regardless of your party, for bigger reasons than labels and party politics. It affirms one of the most wonderful things about America. We still live in a country where the actions of a single person can change the course of government, and in effect, the lives of its citizens.

It shows that a single leader, as it has been with presidents, civil rights leaders and philosophers, can still make us look at the simplest truth in a simple moment of honesty and integrity.

Jeffords, by honoring his beliefs, honors those who fought for every citizen in this country to have the right to vote and affirmed the meaning of true democracy. He has righted Washington, where the executive and legislative branches are supposed to monitor and check and balance each other. That system of checks and balances once again is in place.

Following his heart means Jeffords has derailed the Bush train that has been rolling through Washington, leaving behind the passenger of bipartisanship that the president promised would get a good seat when the train started rolling just over 100 days ago. Now there will be true bipartisanship.

It would be so easy to say that the Republicans asked for it, because of the arrogance that comes from controlling the White House and the Senate, an arrogance that made conservatives rail against moderate Republicans who didn't toe the party line.

But it's not that simple. Jeffords said he wasn't wounded by a specific slight.

A lifetime Republican because, he said, it was the party of Abraham

Lincoln, moderation and fiscal responsibility, he found that he could no longer attend that party. Its celebrants are becoming more conservative than makes him comfortable and push an agenda he cannot always support.

He said that, in the past, various wings of the party had the freedom to argue and influence and change the party agenda.

"The election of President Bush changed that dramatically," he said.

Jeffords admitted that he would lose supporters and friends, including some Republicans whose lifelong dreams of heading a Senate committee have been dashed and whose leadership of some committees will end.

"Having made my decision, a weight has been lifted from my shoulders and now hangs heavy from my heart," he said. But he was undeterred by personal pleas and party politics.

Jeffords was particularly disappointed by the Bush administration's lack of focus on education.

Bush gave us a promise to give new direction, but new direction without funding is no useful direction at all, he said. The success of American public schools should not be measured by how many children leave them for private education.

All Jim Jeffords did was remind America of how politics works.

And as much as last fall's presidential election shook our faith in our electoral process, a single man may just have restored that faith.

May 25, 2001

'Angels' have their halos on backwards

It says something about my early TV-viewing tastes that I once watched the adventures of a trio of pseudo-superheroes who fought bad guys with their hair as much as with guns.

They reported to a mysterious man they knew only by his voice on an intercom.

And they rarely wore turtlenecks.

It was TV candy, harmless fun. Or was it?

The '70s TV show "Charlie's Angels" made every girl I knew want hair that flipped, swimsuits that clung and the ability to punch guys out. (Of course, that required Ultra Sheen Super, toilet paper in C cups and great imagination.)

But 24 years later, the most popular movie in America is that same TV candy.

Is it progress that a "women's movie" can do great box office only if the actresses are Charlie's Angels again?

I helped opening weekend revenues top $40.5 million because I was among those sitting in the dark, cheering the special effects-laden martial arts.

I wanted to rejoice with producer-star Drew Barrymore for truly cleaning up her life and giving us better movies ("Ever After: A Cinderella Story" and "Never Been Kissed," a comedy about an undercover reporter at a high school who tells it like it always will be).

But her "Charlie's Angels" pulls me in two directions. It was great, great fun! But, like most movies, it sends messages.

It says that a woman can be tough, but should still define her life by the men in it.

It tells young girls that the good life is wet T-shirts, tight clothes and a date on Friday night — and that it's still OK to jump into bed with a stranger.

And, oh, by the way, superheroes must be gorgeous.

"Angels" could never be a chick flick like "The First Wives' Club" or "Thelma and Louise" — movies portraying empowered women thinking for themselves (even if it ends badly). It doesn't break your heart like "Beloved."

Yes, "Angels" is only a movie. But its messages shouldn't go unchallenged, especially for impressionable young girls who will crowd theaters to see it again and again a la "Titanic" and imagine themselves kung-fu fighting in black leather.

The girls belong to Charlie, and they're only as strong as they're allowed to be.

The message for 10-year-olds: I can grow up to kick butt.

The message for 20-year- olds: I can kick butt in tight leather pants and look good doing it.

The message for 30-year-olds: I can kick butt and look good doing it and please a man in the process.

The message for 40-year-olds: Yeah, right, I need a man that I can't see. And tight leather doesn't move like that.

(And 50-year-olds might have a problem fighting bad guys for a boss who's sipping tropical drinks and checking in every now and again to see who's winning. When was the last time you jumped in and helped, Charlie?)

You get the picture.

It's OK to watch fake superheroes as long as young girls know that real superheroes work for themselves, and usually alone.

Real superheroes sometimes run families like small businesses, weathering adversity, juggling schedules and overcoming economic downturns and downsizing while continuing to pay college costs for former company members.

And real superheroes don't have time for movies or tight leather pants. They are the movie, and they might just be wearing tights.

November 8, 2000

CHAPTER THREE

LIFE AFTER 9/11

We'll remember the day when fear came home

There wasn't time. Our throats closed as we watched smoke billowing from a World Trade Center tower, the hole from a plane a surreal scar of terrorism.

We gasped as a nation when a second plane flew into its sister tower, flames blasting into a blue sky.

As reports of further acts of violence came like punches to our stomachs, it was like drowning, coming up for air only to be pushed down again by the news.

All day and all night, we were hammered by reports of injury and death at the hand of an unknown enemy, someone who took away our immunity and our sense of peace.

What united us Tuesday were terror and survival. We feared what we knew, that thousands of people had been killed. And we feared what we didn't know - who did this, how and why? Then after initial paralysis, we rushed to help.

Praying for strangers, we watched as an unknown antagonist shut down our nation. America stopped doing business, and we initially all stopped moving.

When we could move again, we raced to phones to find loved ones and worried for our children sitting in classrooms learning about an America that did not know what we all learned: We are vulnerable.

As night fell, the fear became palpable, the news reports flying like gunfire over our bunkers, the safe havens we created in the world's strongest nation. We struggled with whether to think about a word we didn't want to say aloud: War.

The constriction in our chests grew tighter as the television scrolled bulletins ... U.S. baseball games cancelled. ... All museums and monuments closed. ... All domestic flights suspended. ... Walt Disney World attractions closed.... GM headquarters closed. ... New York City shut down ... Islamic Jihad, Hamas Deny Responsibility ... All Financial Markets in United

States Now Closed. ... Speaker of the House Dennis Hastert Taken to "Safe House."

Someone shackled us to a terrorist nightmare, and we were locked into place, wanting to run but not knowing where, wanting more news, but shuddering at what might come next.

For hours, horror raced against our ability to keep up, to absorb, to respond — and horror won. America isn't used to that.

"Freedom itself was attacked," President George W. Bush said. "... The resolve of our great nation is being tested. But make no mistake: We will show the world that we will pass this test."

America has survived natural disasters. But Tuesday, we experienced first-hand what other countries — Ireland, Israel, Iran, Iraq, Kenya, Eritrea, Somalia — have lived with, a fear greater than that caused by the Oklahoma City and Columbine High School tragedies.

It was uncertainty. By night's end, one fact was clear: America is no longer immune to war on our shores.

Someone attacked our center of commerce.

Someone struck the brain center of our military.

Someone killed innocent people.

And unbelievably, someone, somewhere, was celebrating.

The fear that has ravaged other countries, that scarred other psyches, was now ours.

"This is war," NBC anchor Tom Brokaw announced over and over, commenting on terrorism so great we didn't have to wait for yet another president to declare it. Someone declared it for us.

We watched and said under our breath: "This isn't happening.

"Not to America, not the land of the free and home of the brave.

"Not here."

Yes, here.

Our television images of war, from Vietnam to Bosnia, have been other people's war zones. Now, New York and Washington are war zones. And America shed tears at the casualties: thousands dead.

It was real.

It was live.

We watched people running down real streets in Lower Manhattan, and we yearned for Orson Welles to appear on screen and report that it was only an enactment of something that couldn't happen here.

But this was no "War of the Worlds," Orson Welles' realistic and panic-inducing radio event from 1938.

This was our Pearl Harbor, the worst attack since the day that lives in infamy. The physical and psychological toll will not be known for years.

The images that passed before our eyes over and over Tuesday will remain with us and will become as familiar as the Zapruder film of a Dallas motorcade or the photos of the Alfred P. Murrah building with its side shaved off.

The question of where we were when President John F. Kennedy was shot or when the Oklahoma City federal building exploded is joined by another.

From now on, we'll remember where we were when America faced its greatest challenge to date.

God bless us all.

September 12, 2001

Years change a nation, and a proud citizen

Abraham Turaani recalls seeing the reports about the Oklahoma City bombing six years ago.

He sat glued to the TV, much as he did Tuesday. But six years ago, his first instinct was to be shocked by the magnitude of the tragedy. His second was to pray that the terrorist wasn't Arab American.

"Some major news organizations were jumping to conclusions that this was the work of Arab or Muslim terrorists, and I was in prayer that 'No, it can't be!'"

Tuesday, TV replayed a national tragedy, and he sat horrified again by reports of planes crashing into the World Trade Center.

But six years does something to a man, as the man hopes it does to a country.

This time, Turaani's first and only prayers were for the victims and their families, people who were experiencing unimaginable pain.

"Unconsciously yesterday, I felt a sense of restlessness and overwhelming urgency to do something," he said. "I kept saying, 'There must be something I could do!'"

Turaani, midwest regional coordinator for the American Arab Anti-Discrimination Committee, called other Arab-American leaders to plan a blood drive. He also called some friends who are doctors with another plan.

"We could put them in a van — they're responsible citizens of Arab descent — and just drive to New York and say, 'Here's our contributions as Arab Americans. We are affected! We are harmed! We are grieving with you!'

"I wanted to comfort someone."

Turaani still feels the frustration of being pointed at, of knowing that no matter who he is or what he accomplishes, there are people who will look at him and see a possible terrorist.

But much has changed in six years.

For America, Oklahoma City dispelled the myth that our country is immune to terrorism. It also taught us that terrorists can come in all colors and from all backgrounds. Anger is not genetic.

Every German boy doesn't grow up to be Hitler. Every Ugandan boy doesn't grow up to be Idi Amin. And every Arab boy doesn't grow up wanting to be a terrorist.

Life has given Turaani three lessons since Oklahoma City. They are Kinda, 4, Randa, 3, and Mohammad, who will be 1 next month. He and his wife, Rajah, know what it means to have children you would move Heaven and Earth for.

For the past two months, his wife and kids have been visiting relatives in Syria and Jordan. In two weeks, he will know what it's like to wait at an airport for their safe return.

This week, at the height of terrible tragedy and mayhem in New York, an Arab American in Dearborn said a prayer for the victims, not for himself.

"I'll tell you why. Having my little girls and little boy away for almost two months, I miss them terribly. And not having control of their immediate environment, I oftentimes find myself overly worried about their safety and well-being. You want them here right now. You want to feel their presence ...

"The same thing came over me yesterday when I was trying to put myself in the frame of mind that some of the victims' families were — the husbands, the wives, the daughters, the sons. And it was quite a choking experience."

Six years ago, Abraham Turaani's first thoughts were as an Arab American. This time, this tragedy, his first thoughts were as an American husband and father.

And he sees an America that won't look at him only as an Arab, the way some people did six years ago. This time, maybe others won't be so quick to judge.

Turaani thinks America has grown.

He knows he has.

September 13, 2001

Teach your children love of country

To my darling daughter:

It has been three days since terrorists crashed airplanes into New York's World Trade Center, causing the building to crumble and thousands to die.

You have quietly absorbed the tragedy, asking little except whether there will be more and whether there will be war.

You've watched images of people being pulled from 455,000 tons of concrete, steel and mortar. But you've seen love and anger replace fear.

That prompted me to write this letter about what makes thousands of people get into their cars and ride for hours to help, to explain why firefighters, police officers and paramedics work day after day, with little respite, to explain why I've been walking around singing "America, the Beautiful."

You see, honey, America is a special place. It is a unique entity. In a world full of disparate beliefs and uncertain tomorrows, America is rock solid. It is more than buildings, cities and towns. It is a way of life, an ideal, a democracy where we unite in catastrophe as well as joy.

It is a place built on many concepts, one principal among them — patriotism. To be a patriot is to be considered corny sometimes, but be a patriot, anyway. Until Tuesday, some of us had somehow forgotten that.

Patriotism was something we trotted out only on special occasions, such as the Fourth of July. But patriotism, at the core of our democracy, emerged from the rubble just as miracle survivors did.

It took an act of war to bring it back. But it is back. And it is a sentiment so strong that some passengers on one plane decided to fight the hijackers to possibly save other lives.

There is such outrage and such effort to rescue strangers and clean up a shattered city because a nation's hope hangs in the balance.

We need to act. It was like someone threw a rock at our heads and we are looking for someone to throw a rock back at. We have to be careful not to throw at the wrong people, but we must throw that rock.

The terrorists didn't strike a building. They tried to change the way we dream. When that happens, our extreme love for country makes us strike back.

Love of country was displayed in the large flag that, in the middle of bedlam, workers hung from a broken Pentagon. It is embodied in the smaller flags the government has asked all Americans to display for 30 days.

Love of country can rebuild a broken building and restore our sense of peace. And it will express itself once again in the anthem we sing at baseball games and in the tears we shed for those who fought to keep our country free.

And if we forget, others will remind us. We'll find it in the support other countries are giving us right now.

We'll find it in people who put themselves in boxes or walk across rivers to get here.

Will there be war, honey? I don't know. But if America runs the happiest home in the neighborhood and there's a bully in our block, America will get rid of him.

If there is war, we'll pray it won't last long.

And when you and your peers one day become caretakers of this treasure we call America, you must be equally strong in protecting what we leave you. This is not a place for terrorists. This is a place of peace.

This is a place to love.

Love, Mom

September 14, 2001

Deepest fears are rooted in uncertainty

For 40 minutes, all I knew was that she wasn't there.

I had gone to pick my daughter up from school, and she wasn't in any of the places she should have been — not in the school gymnasium, lingering after basketball practice, not in the school office calling to find out where I was, not in the bathrooms, not in the classrooms.

Not at school.

And for 45 minutes, I couldn't find her.

The bubbling in my stomach and ache in my chest didn't go away until five minutes after I'd learned that she was safely at a friend's house, the victim of a miscommunication between parents.

But for 45 minutes, my greatest fear was not knowing.

For 45 minutes, the ideas of where she might be, the nightmares of what might have happened, the imaginings of what could have been were my only truth.

It was the not knowing that made me crazy.

And it was the second time that it had happened in one day. Earlier, U.S. Attorney General John Ashcroft did the same thing to me, warning that terrorist attacks were coming, but he couldn't say when or where or how.

The nightmares of what might happen, the fears about the possibilities stayed with me. He warned 18,000 law enforcement agencies and about 15,000 times that many residents in America that terror from Osama bin Laden's Al Qaeda network is coming. His announcement was based on the same intelligence that offered an inkling but no details about coming terror in the weeks before Sept. 11.

So all we really know is to be afraid, be very afraid.

At the same time, President George W. Bush was making plans to attend Game 3 of the World Series between the New York Yankees and Arizona Diamondbacks.

I haven't been watching the World Series. I haven't gone bowling or dancing or strolling through the zoo.

And it's even harder to hang out when the federal government tells you something's coming.

The mixed messages aren't helping.

Play ball!

Duck!

It is the not knowing that makes dealing with America's war on terrorism so difficult. If we knew all our enemies. If we knew what they were doing. If we knew what to expect. If we knew where they were ... if we knew more, we would fear less.

Wandering in the darkness takes a great amount of courage. For those soldiers roaming Afghan hills and for the fellow Americans they fight for, it is the darkness before the dawn, the night before a bright sun makes everything clear.

Wandering in the space between Sept. 11 and peace, we live without knowledge. Heroes have given us hope. Soldiers have given us protection. But the terrorists still give us nightmares.

It is the not knowing that is their greatest weapon. They live on the element of surprise. It isn't that they want us to understand their philosophy, their demands. It is that they want us to not question them.

The darkness can either frighten us or can give us time to spend on solving the problems of the day.

But when you're wishing for daylight, trying to solve problems in the dark is a tall order.

I'd rather have fewer vague alerts and more hard facts.

I'd rather have Osama bin Laden in a spotlight and an actual declaration of war than the continuing wandering in the dark, pretending that we can see.

October 31, 2001

Rudy Giuliani shows mayors, leaders how it's done

The men who would be Detroit mayor can learn from a man who, in tragedy, has shown how it's done.

If Rudolph Giuliani could be New York's mayor again, and the law let him enter the race, he might win in a landslide.

For New Yorkers and other Americans who have found reasons in the past to pummel him — the chicken suits, the police problems, the attitude — Giuliani has earned a nation's respect after terrorist attacks on his city.

He was America's mayor, working round-the-clock, shedding tears, walking down the aisle with a bride who lost her father. He showed the mayors of every other city what a good mayor does in times of crisis. He's been so on-target that I privately hoped he was attending those meetings where President Bush is reaching decisions on how to retaliate for an act of war that may have taken more than 5,000 lives.

As a matter of fact, America has seen a triumvirate of leaders on television screens in the past 10 days: Giuliani, Bush and Colin Powell.

Powell — who has faced mounting criticism that he has not been able to be the leader he can be, that he's being overshadowed and outvoted in decisions from the recent United Nations race conference to the way to chase terrorists — still manages to be presidential while talking about our options.

Bush has been involved in matters of war and the politics of garnering support for action that could kill innocents.

But Giuliani has been the guy at ground zero, with updates about the rescue effort, airport travel and pain. He has talked regularly with his constituents and the larger national constituency that has become his during this time of despair. He was the leader that New York had to have.

Dressed casually, like a brother or family friend, he showed that, despite having to deal with illness and a messy divorce, he can still run America's largest city. New York's Sept. 11 mayoral elections were postponed by horror; some New Yorkers want them postponed even further, keeping

Giuliani in office through recovery.

It shouldn't take a catastrophe for a city to see itself. But when disaster strikes, what you see afterwards are the real city and its true leaders.

Detroit has had leaders capable of some great things. But what it needs is someone who can do it all and galvanize a city to finally rise above its own catastrophe, which is now 34 years old.

What Detroit's mayoral candidates can learn from New York and Giuliani, who stood for every victim and every American who worried about victims, is to look out for everyone in their city — the elderly, the children, those angered by blight and those held back by illteracy.

New York, in time of crisis, came together in a hurry and will come back over time. You can see it in the proud faces of those who are cleaning, those who are collecting aid and others who dig through rubble for signs of hope.

When this is over, and it will be over one day, New York will look back with pride at a new legacy, not one that was designed, but one that developed out of pride and resilience.

And in the middle of the mess, in the midst of heartache, someone rose to the challenge and made us all feel a little better.

At the forefront of healing and rebuilding was an outgoing mayor who showed that beyond the politics, beyond the jokes, beyond the criticism, when it was time to be a leader, he showed up big.

In the end, that is a lesson for anyone who wants to lead.

September 21, 2001

There is joy in horror's shadow

It seems we haven't had much to celebrate since the terrorist tragedy.

But consider this: We have the same things to celebrate that we did before. Actually, we have more.

Somewhere on Sept. 11, a baby was born at a time when America was recommitted to maintaining his freedom.

Somewhere, a child took her first steps, an accomplishment that will forever change her parents. She took those steps in an America that has now awakened to the threat of terrorism and vowed to end it.

Somewhere, a young man made his first A on a test, something he never dreamed he could do, but his mom always said he would.

Somewhere a woman learned that her cancer was in remission, and she has been granted the gift of life.

Somewhere someone celebrated 10 years of sobriety.

Somewhere someone got married, pledging to love someone else through times that have become harder since a single smoke-filled morning.

Somewhere someone got a letter from an old friend they thought no longer cared.

And somewhere, a newspaper columnist reached a milestone: her one-year anniversary at a new newspaper.

Tuesday, Sept. 11 was that anniversary for me at the Detroit Free Press. I didn't celebrate. Like everyone else, my life was too full of the shock that turned to fear that turned to despair that turned to resolve.

Tuesday, Sept. 11 also was John X. Miller's birthday. He's the public editor at our newspaper, the one who talks with readers every day about whether the newspaper is doing a good job and meeting their expectations.

It was not a day for him to celebrate the past year and its triumphs.

So last Thursday, exactly one month after horror visited New York, John and I celebrated together over lunch at Pronto. For a few minutes, we put the world aside and talked about our kids.

We wondered whether paying them for grades is an effective tool. (I do; he doesn't.)

We talked about teaching them values. He sends his son off with a "Have a good day at work, son!" I tell my daughter that her grades are her paychecks as well as down payments on bigger paychecks later.

We reminded each other that family remains the most important thing in our lives and pledged to not let the terrorists steal our joy.

Or our reasons to celebrate.

"Every Sept. 11, a lot of prayers will be going up. That's a good thing to have happen on your birthday," John said.

And we vowed to make sure our children always understand the importance of Sept. 11, not the fear and horror of it, but the need to honor ourselves, Americans in all our diversity.

That is the only way to get rid of terrorism in the name of God.

One year, 30 days and 135 columns later, I had a chance to reflect. And I reminded myself that no matter what horror befalls us, we can get through it, with God's help.

And every day, even in grief, we can celebrate, if we count our blessings.

Even in grief, they just keep on coming.

October 14, 2001

Add it up — the terrorists were the ones who failed

You never know where your angels come from. Sometimes they show up because friends' prayers or your own have summoned them. Sometimes they show up because they know it's their time.

I have remained distressed and saddened, along with many other Americans, about what the Sept. 11 terrorist attacks did to our lives. But then a stranger's e-mail, an angelic moment of eloquence, like so many on the Internet, soothed me. I was watching the wrong numbers, the message said.

Instead of focusing on tragic tallies — the growing death toll and rising estimates to repair damage, I should — we all should — remember the other numbers out of New York, Washington and Pennsylvania after the horrible attacks: the survival rates.

The day the twin towers of the World Trade Center fell, newscasters talked about the 20,000 people who might have arrived at work by the time of the attacks. Actually, nearly 50,000 people worked in the center complex, so almost 90 percent of the people targeted by the terrorists survived.

About 23,000 people work in the Pentagon; 125 military and civilian personnel were killed or remain missing. So 99 percent of the people the terrorists targeted survived, something the e-mail called "a statistical failure."

And then there were the airplanes. The terrorists attacked early, so American Airlines Flight 77, a Boeing with seats for 182 people, including crew, had 64 people flying from Washington to Los Angeles.

American Airlines Flight 11, a Boeing 767 with seats for 169, including crew, had 92 people flying from Boston to L.A.

United Airlines Flight 175, a Boeing 757 with seats for 191 people, including crew, had 65 people on board.

United Airlines Flight 93, a Boeing 767 with seats for 175 people, including crew, had 44 people on board. Headed from Newark to San

Francisco, it had the fewest passengers, but they were given the greatest opportunity to show courage. That courage led them to fight the terrorists and help prevent their plane from striking its target, possibly the White House or Capitol.

The heroes on Flight 93 can help us remember how important what we have is. Their deaths can help us remember freedom. Their deaths made it possible for so many others to live.

Of more than 73,000 Americans targeted by terrorists, 92 percent survived or avoided the attacks.

The terrorists, though inflicting lasting damage, really failed.

"The hijacked planes were mostly empty, the Pentagon was hit at its strongest point, the overwhelming majority of people in the World Trade Center buildings escaped, and a handful of passengers gave the ultimate sacrifice to save even more lives," the e-mail read. "Don't fear these terrorists. The odds are against them."

The words comforted me more than many others I'd heard in the past two weeks. They reminded me of how strong our country is and how much we've survived.

It's been three weeks. On Sept. 11, I thought I couldn't see past that day. I thought that every day. But it's been three weeks.

We are surviving. Every one of those nearly 3,000 lives that were taken was important, and America must never forget.

But thousands and thousands more lived and they, joined with 285 million others of us, must make sure that the world never forgets.

October 3, 2001

New normal affects the way we mourn

Three months ago, a plane crash killing nearly 270 people might have been the year's worst catastrophe.

But two months ago, terrorists made nightmares real and a plane crash the lesser of the two evils playing out in our lives. Terrorists led me to pray for mechanical failure instead of a hostile act.

Our numbers have changed, those statistics we use to rank our tragedies. A teen killed by a drunk driver cut through our emotions. Four teens killed by a drunk driver left an open wound. A mail boat sinking rocked us and needled its way into our sleep.

Two months ago, people falling from the sky would have stopped us in our tracks, given us there-but-for-the-grace-of-God-go-I shivers.

But on Sept. 11, a number that used to be unthinkable for a single tragedy became our reality. A cold-blooded act that had not been conceivable on American shores happened in America.

Now, we are no longer who we were.

In America BT (before terrorism), a plane crash was about the worst thing that could happen.

In America AT (after terrorism), a plane crash not tied to Afghanistan is the second-most important story on the news.

Just the idea that the damage in Queens, N.Y., could hardly take my focus away from Afghanistan was enough to wake me from my war-induced catatonia, make me remember that war doesn't have to totally change us.

My prayer for this war, which has not been declared by Congress but mandated by terrorists who cannot be allowed to rule, is that even as we learn to live with war, we don't become so immune that we can walk by death.

This isn't something we're used to. This isn't Vietnam, an 11-year military and emotional conflict, or Desert Storm, a military maneuver fought in a fortnight.

We aren't used to checking the skies before we fly. We haven't had to live with the specter of tragedy dogging our daily decisions.

Our skies have been clear and our lives immune. We aren't used to our streets running with blood.

Americans soon may live the way people have lived in lands of war for decades. We must travel and shop and celebrate the things that are constant — birthdays, anniversaries, first dates — even as shadows cross our paths.

We must forgive television stations for not broadcasting every speech the president makes. We must learn to walk past ruins and not cry, as people in Middle Eastern, African and European countries have done for years.

We must learn not to fall apart at every tragedy because they aren't going to stop now that we're at war.

As painful and unfeeling as it seems, we must gird ourselves to hold it together when the old tragedies happen again. The new normal demands it.

While we're at war, we can't afford not to get up when we fall. Other tragedies will come, not because we earned them, not because God isn't around, because He is. They will happen because they do. And when they do, as one did Monday in New York, we must pray for the dead, help the families recover and fly again.

I did wish that the crash was the result of a mechanical failure.

But even if it wasn't, even if we learn that a monster struck again, the important thing is we prayed.

We fell down.

But we got up.

November 16, 2001

U.S. Taliban's parents let him down

I don't know Marilyn Walker. But I can't help but sympathize with her grief.

I can't help but wonder how she's handling the what-ifs that she surely is asking herself, the woulda-coulda-shouldas that must be haunting her about her son, John, who's sitting in a northern Virginia detention center, indicted on everything but treason.

I can't help but feel her pain, knowing she cannot hug him, cannot take back the years she and her ex-husband, Frank Lindh, let him have total freedom instead of guiding him with stronger hands. I can't help but admire the unconditional love she has declared for him at press conferences.

But what I can't understand is how a parent could let go so easily of a son just because he's becoming a man.

It's just too easy to say Marilyn Walker and Frank Lindh weren't parenting their son, John, but only financing his fantasies and misguided exploration of Islam. It's harder to understand why.

When John rejected his family's Catholicism, they weren't bothered. When he needed more freedom, they sent him to an alternative high school where, according to Newsweek, students shape their own studies and check in with their teacher once a week.

When he embraced hip-hop at 14 and occasionally posed as an African American online, his parents were not the ones he turned to with questions; he asked his online friends.

When he converted to Islam, walking around Marin County, Calif., in long flowing robes and quitting school, his parents did not object.

And when he wanted to move to Yemen to be closer to Islamic purity, his parents paid for it, his father later telling Newsweek he supported his son's "commitment to learning."

But there was more, according to Newsweek. When he e-mailed his father defending the October 2000 attack on the USS Cole that killed 17 sailors because, he said, it was "an act of war" for the destroyer to enter a Yemeni harbor, his father didn't stop funding his descent into hate.

When John came home in 1999, his parents, despite their worries, didn't make the 18-year-old stay home. They let him return to Yemen, which he later left for Afghanistan.

His parents were committed to his learning, but what has John Walker Lindh — I mean, Suleyman al-Faris, — I mean, Abdul Hamid (the name he took when he joined the Taliban) — learned?

For one thing, he has learned that his parents cannot buy his way out of that detention center.

He also has learned that taking up arms with Islamic terrorists against America is serious business.

Some Americans want Lindh tried for treason, something that is not likely to happen to the son of upper-middle class California parents who only wanted to find himself. Others want a trial only if he fought against Americans.

What can a young Islamic convert who bit off more than he could chew do now? He can stand as an example to other teens to be careful of what you search for and what you do with what you find. He is a reminder to parents of all backgrounds that you must parent your children, not just finance their delusions.

If we ever forget, there's a young man who can remind us. He's sitting in a northern Virginia detention center facing a 10-count indictment accusing him, among several things, of conspiring to kill Americans and providing resources to terrorists.

He's only 20 years old. But he'll go to jail like a man.

February 13, 2002

Tribute to dead serves as a testament to life

NEW YORK — Six months ago, two towers stood here, where there is now a cavernous hole in the ground. They stood under a cloudless, clear blue sky, under a golden sun; they stood for capitalism and freedom and America.

On Monday, exactly six months from the moment the world was knocked off its axis, a small gathering of community brothers and sisters from New York's police and fire departments, Port Authority and from its streets and its families, stood on the same spot — testimony that life does go on.

They stood in front of a makeshift altar with the Rev. Brian Jordan, who for six months has walked in the shoes of the Rev. Mychal Judge, the beloved New York Fire Department chaplain who died Sept. 11. Jordan, the interim department chaplain, invited the warriors and saints gathered to join him in reciting the Lord's Prayer and singing "God Bless America."

Everyone knew the words.

At the exact time when a plane flew into one tower six months ago, the bulldozers and workers who were shunting back and forth, turning over earth and digging for souls, all stopped.

There was complete silence as Jordan encouraged the heroes present to call out the names of heroes lost and loved ones killed in the tragedy. The names of the dead hung in the air, the syllables flying on angels' wings to soothe a group of strangers glued by grief to a spot overlooking a hole in the ground.

Among them was Anthony Knowles, a firefighter at Station 17 in the Bronx, who has been digging off and on at the site since Sept. 12.

"It's something that you can never come to terms with that it happened. Every day you look at this and you hope that it doesn't happen again, and if it does, you wonder: 'Are we ready next time?' "

Who knows whether we'll ever be able to answer that question? How can you get ready for horror, for fanaticism so fatalistic that its perpetrators feel justified in taking parents from children, husbands from wives, daughters from mothers?

I went to that cavern, that mass grave where workers have been struggling to free souls, day after day, to find something. Absolution. Hope. Ferocity.

What I found was peace and unity. Jordan told the firefighters and officers to keep their hats on because the service he was conducting was all faiths, all people, all for one. No matter our backgrounds, we said a prayer that many know. No matter our denomination, we sang a hymn we all grew up with.

That is the way with America, only in America. Room is made at the table, at the altar, in our memories, for everyone.

In the 26 weeks since the world shifted and fire lit another cloudless sky, I had felt guilt. Not the guilt of Cantor Fitzgerald survivors who wondered why they lived when more than 650 of their colleagues died. Not the guilt of firefighters who traded shifts with men who went to their graves. I felt the guilt of unfinished mourning.

President George W. Bush demanded that we not only go on with our lives but lift our lives to sustain our economy and show the terrorists we aren't afraid. And we did. Across the country, we've returned to flying. We went back to work, back to class, back to our chores and routines.

But for months, I felt like we hadn't grieved enough, that we had no sustained sense of loss. I felt somehow that the world should have stopped.

But instead, life went on. The victims' names were scrolled on a banner at the Super Bowl as U2 sang. Funds sprang up across the country to help survivors.

And our country embraced our new national agenda of finding out who scarred our country and how quickly we could make them pay. We almost instantly went to war. The targets of our anger have grown, and Osama bin Laden is but one terrorist on our most-wanted list. Did America really take the time to call out the names of the dead?

At the big cross standing at ground zero, erected where it was found with names scrawled and scratched onto it, a small group of Americans stood under a sunny, cloudless sky and called out the names of loved ones.

There in the mourning silence, the simple ceremony was the right one.

With beautiful faces bowed in the sun, these strong men and women did what all the flags and the pomp and the cheers hadn't in the past month.

As we all held hands and sang "God Bless America," you felt that the dead were free. For a moment, you didn't see the damage to surrounding buildings.

I went to ground zero to apologize to the spirits of the dead. But they were too busy to listen. They were preparing for a greater task, holding up a new structure on that site, one built on the souls of the dead, one that will remind us that they lived.

March 12, 2002

We shouldn't have to do the FBI's job

I don't want to be an FBI agent.

I don't want to investigate my neighbors because of their skin color or accent.

And the Bush administration should be ashamed of itself for asking me to.

After being criticized about how much it knew before the terrorist attacks on 9/11, the administration has struck back by giving people the two things that *some* wanted: even more daily warnings of impending doom and carte blanche to mistrust Arab Americans.

The government is asking Americans to look the other way — at our neighbors — instead of question whether 9/11 could have been prevented.

I won't look the other way. Questioning the government is an American tradition. We've questioned whether we could have done more to prevent the Holocaust, whether we should have been in Vietnam, whether we should have let Saddam Hussein stand to fight again.

Now, we're questioning whether our system of counterterrorism is too broken to be fixed.

Those who want to blame President George W. Bush or former President Bill Clinton for terrorist attacks are being viciously political. Those who question why the FBI treated its most important piece of intelligence like a request for a new ceiling fan have their eye on the ball.

I'm talking, of course, about the memo written by Phoenix FBI agent Kenneth Williams warning that some of Osama bin Laden's followers might be training at U.S. flight schools. He urged the FBI to check the visas of foreigners at U.S. aviation academies.

He was ignored.

His memo looks pretty damning in hindsight. It looks like the kind of thing that, if heeded, could have stopped a catastrophe. The problem, of course, is that we'll never know. That memo by itself might have appeared to be like thousands of other terrorist warnings, just another possibility like the Library of Congress report that predicted that an Al Qaeda suicide squad could slam a plane packed with explosives into the Pentagon.

But the Williams memo, written last July, and the report, written in 1999, ARE pieces of a puzzle of terrorism that the American people pay experts to put together.

The current debate shouldn't be over what the president knew and when he knew it. It should be over whether the FBI and other intelligence agencies are so bogged down in bureaucracy and politics that they can no longer do a good job.

The FBI, as the principal investigative arm of the U.S. Justice Department, is charged with protecting the United States from foreign intelligence and terrorist activities. It has 11,000 special agents and more than 16,000 support staff in 400 satellite offices and the headquarters. Its fiscal 2002 budget is $4.23 billion.

That's a lot of money for an agency that until after the attacks wasn't technically able to e-mail photographs to vital satellite offices, and only after the attacks sought volunteers who spoke Arabic.

That's a lot of money to not have a single clearinghouse where someone compares every piece of terrorist information and solves one puzzle.

I don't want to be an FBI agent. I don't want to bog down local police with suspicions that I honed while reading Nancy Drew mysteries or Perry Mason and Nero Wolfe novels. That kind of training isn't adequate.

For $4 billion, someone's training should be.

May 22, 2002

Mark 9/11
by ignoring terrorists

What if we did nothing?

What if, instead of watching nonstop television coverage of the one-year anniversary of Sept. 11, we spent the day in silent introspection?

What if, instead of intruding on what would otherwise be private moments of grief for the families of the dead, we found a quiet place to ponder whether we've individually really changed or learned anything or loved more in the year since our world got turned upside down?

What if, instead of a huge play-by-horrible-play of what happened, we applied quiet grace to our remembrances, took a moment to be grateful for the awesome responsibility and great privilege of living and breathing so free?

Since the day after terrorists flew planes into buildings, I've felt that our daily response to the attack is being charted somewhere on a little terrorist map by little terrorist minds who feed on our fear, on our reaction to their action.

So what if we do exactly the opposite of what they want: What if we ignore them and focus on us?

No, I'm not suggesting that we turn our backs on fanatics. America will never again believe she's so powerful that only fools would dare touch her. The attack made us better, smarter. Sept. 11, and all its accompanying anguish, brought much-needed attention to the inadequate systems protecting us.

But what if we spent the day doing what some of the dead would have been doing — cleaning a firehouse, playing in a park with a child?

We have learned so much about each other in the year since life changed. Some of us chased our dreams, climbed onto roller coasters for the first time, went scuba diving for the first time, got married.

The disaster, with all its hurt and sadness, actually made us better. Toward each other. Toward ourselves.

We should not let the momentum that this attack gave us fall victim to too much reliving of it. It is more than OK to use anniversaries as times to look forward and to remind ourselves of what it means to each of us to be Americans.

We are the top of the heap, still. It is our culture that the world emulates, not just Coca-Cola and jeans, but style and slang. We dominate world music, art and financial arenas. It is to these shores that the world's immigrants still come, yearning to be free.

Entire nations could lose nearly half their populace to AIDS, and it doesn't make our news. For decades, we've lived above the horrors that have been others' daily supper. National magazines try to keep us informed, but they know all we want is to know is who Jennifer Lopez is sleeping with now. We live large.

Should we be complacent? No. Should we grieve those who died? Of course we should.

But should we let terrorists rule the day? No. We should treat terrorists like terrorists, no more or less than dangerous gnats to be swatted before they get into our food, our air and our lives. They don't get to argue a cause. They don't get to make a case. And they don't get to watch me revisit the horror they got away with once.

I won't watch replay after replay of planes flying into buildings. That instant replay is available to me every night when I close my eyes.

I don't want the monsters to see me sad. I don't want my tears to fuel their parades.

I will celebrate the dead by pushing my family to live as if every day could be our last.

But my grief on Sept. 11 will be private. For a day, for me, the terrorists will be smoke, lint, ignored suicide killers whose lost cause has no aim and deserves no mention.

August 14, 2002

Time-out is a chance for happiness

Years from now, I'll remember where I was on Sept. 11, 2001. But I will remember as vividly where I was on Sept. 11, 2002.

Weeks before the media barrage that is just subsiding, I promised my family and myself that we would boycott the reliving of the horror that befell the nation the year before. We wouldn't watch the replays, wouldn't hear the same questions over and over.

We wouldn't attend a funeral that never ends.

Instead, we would devote ourselves to living in the real.

And that's what we did — which meant peeling back 30 years and sliding down a slide. It meant chasing pigeons who swarmed you because you gave one a cracker.

It meant lying beside my daughter on a comforter right in the middle of a sunny-day park, miles from the threat of war, watching white, puffy dogs roam the sky.

We talked about what we liked about ourselves and loved in each other and about my dead grandparents, who brought her joy for too short a time before taking better seats far above us to watch our lives go by.

She blew up a beach ball and we played an odd game of catch. Since we had no control over the ball, what we really played was chase the ball. Eventually the ball was the only thing playing, abandoned near a tall oak, content to just sit until we headed home.

We talked about how much fun "American Idol" had been, understanding that those 15 minutes mean everything to kids who've never had them.

As a news junkie who has spent her entire career chasing people's stories, the latest unknown, the scoop, I thought it would be hard to not be in the know, to not see the scroll at the bottom of MSNBC, to miss the president's State of Terror address.

But it was easy — as easy as reading a murder mystery while children squealed on a nearby playscape, basking in sunshine while laughter erupted at a barbecue across the way. It was easy to push the pause button on what we thought was life so we could live in the real.

For a day, I didn't want to know what has happening in Afghanistan. I didn't need to hear the president use a national funeral to rattle a saber. I didn't want to contemplate the aftermath of striking Iraq, having to spend millions cleaning up the country left behind even as we spend millions repairing the Afghanistan left after U.S. post-9/11 strikes.

For a day, I didn't feel like questioning how the Bush administration lost Osama bin Laden the same way the Clinton administration did by focusing on the enemy they could find — Saddam Hussein — instead of the one terrorizing us on our own soil.

For a day, our most important decision wasn't whether to support efforts to go to war, but whether to have spaghetti for dinner.

For a day, I didn't think about how grateful I am that Gen. Colin Powell is still Secretary of State and among the few keeping a sane lid on the Washington hawks out to settle old scores.

And when 9/11 turned into 9/12 and 9/13, it dawned on me that living in the real wasn't such a bad way to spend time. Knowing all the news doesn't make you smarter. It just means you've spent less time knowing yourself, knowing what your daughter likes about herself and what you want to do with the years you have left.

So as we prepare for the media onslaught that will accompany 9/11/2003, I'm already deciding how to spend my time.

It won't involve a television.

It won't involve news.

And it won't involve hate.

September 20, 2002

Americans must speak out in anger, indignation

What we need right now is the '70s.

I don't mean the music and the bell-bottoms and the big frizzy hair. I don't mean the drugs and the sex and the laissez-faire.

I mean the decade of outrage and protest and the will to disagree.

We have become Stepford America, accepting, complacent, no longer in control and not caring.

Our continued shock over being hated by Islamic extremists has led us to lie down so that a Republican administration bent on war can walk right over us to climb into tanks.

I thought about our new culture the other night as I drove along Jefferson Avenue past the Renaissance Center, past the tunnel to Canada, past Tom's Oyster Bar, past a single line of people on either side of the road, each holding a sign. And each sign held a variation of the same message: Peace Now. No War.

I was glad to see them. It wasn't just because I agreed with their sentiments. I was glad to see protest, even a quiet protest.

America has been absent of protest since terrorist attacks sliced our world open 15 months ago and forced us to look at people who hate us. It is as if the shock stole our voices, and we've stood silently by while our government creates policies for us, mounts campaigns in our name and threatens war on our behalf.

We don't even blink when a president threatens the use of nuclear weapons — a sure path to World War III.

It was pure joy to see those folks holding signs representing the America that we used to be. Seeing them made we wonder how long they could hold out before they joined Stepford America, a nation programmed to agree with what the current Republican administration wants, a nation so in lockstep with President Bush that we stand idly by while he announces that he's hunting for bear.

Even if we don't want bear.

We are Stepford America, a united amalgam of constituencies focused only on the enemy that has been pronounced to us, not the enemy we know. Is anyone looking for Osama bin Laden anymore?

We are so passive about our country's direction that a Senate leader's public longing for the days of segregation had to rise to a storm, instead of sparking instant outrage.

Sen. Trent Lott's assertion was that America would have been better off if Sen. Strom Thurmond had been elected president after his 1948 keep-black-folks-out-of-our-pools-schools-and-churches campaign.

This is the Lott who voted against a federal holiday for Dr. Martin Luther King Jr., voted against extending the Voting Rights Act in 1982 and fought for tax exemptions for a university that outlawed interracial dating.

And it's the same Lott who reportedly made similar comments 22 years ago.

And our so-called leaders? They shuffled, like in a game of musical chairs, to see who had the nerve to stand up first. The best Senate Democratic Leader Tom Daschle could initially do was to accept Lott's explanation that he didn't know his racist statement would be seen as racist.

It took nearly a week for President Bush to speak out against Lott's comments and for Lott's hometown newspaper to call for him to step down.

In the new Stepford America, we follow one leader into a war we don't want and allow another to remind us of the war here at home. Either way, if we sit idly by, refusing to challenge, refusing to question, we're the housewives in Ira Levin's novel: robots doomed to fates not of our choosing.

December 13, 2002

Congress must own up to its role in the war

I love those new TV commercials advertising Las Vegas. They show the aftermath of compromising situations, and the tag line is "What happens here, stays here."

The point: When you emerge from a drunken stupor or the throes of passion, things sure look different in the light of day. That "day after" is where Congress is right now. You know, Congress. Remember them? The men and women elected to serve?

The ones who've been acting more like schoolyard pranksters than leaders?

The ones who've been lobbing rocks at the president from behind trees, instead of standing up to his battle cry?

The ones who've been renaming French fries freedom fries instead of focusing on a postwar strategy?

They are now in the light of a day they created a year and a half ago. They are free of the drunken hate and passion from watching the nation suffer the worst terrorist attack on our soil. And they are wondering: What have we done?

For all those folks who keep asking "How did we get here?" — it's simple. In September 2001, fresh from the scars of 9/11, rubble still heaped on the ground, the search for bodies continuing, Congress was defiant, hunting for bear, determined to right a massive wrong. Its members, in a rare united front, gave President Bush authority "to use all necessary and appropriate force against those nations, organizations or persons he determines planned, authorized, committed, or aided the terrorist attacks that occurred on Sept. 11, 2001, or harbored such organizations or persons, in order to prevent any future acts of international terrorism" against the U.S.

The national news was full of the 98-0 hurried vote that occurred without public debate in the Senate and the 420-1 vote in the House.

The White House wanted even more authority, but Congress rejected a resolution allowing Bush to use force "to deter or preempt any future acts of terrorism or aggression against the United States."

Like what we're doing now.

And few of us minded. We wanted blood. No one was talking about Florida chads or the president's IQ.

But in the weeks leading up to the current invasion, congressional representatives were doing the equivalent of drive-by sound bites, expressing support for the troops while blasting the president for doing what they resolved 18 months ago.

How cowardly.

My opposition to the invasion and criticism of the president for starting what could become a larger war isn't limited to the White House.

Every senator and representative who voted for action should stand by his or her vote and shoulder the criticism, along with the responsibility, regardless of its impact on their political futures.

Sen. Joe Biden, D-Del., speaking on CNN Wednesday, pointed out the error of trying to isolate Congress from the president and reminded his colleagues: "We voted to give him the authority to wage that war ... Now we should step back and support him."

The president appears to be doing more than Congress authorized, but the time to quibble has passed.

All that matters, in hindsight, is first, that representatives admit, in the light of day, that they made a mistake and should have done something way before the train left the track, and second, that we win humanely so we don't gain Iraq but lose America's soul.

March 21, 2003

What the leader said
is not what he meant

The world's eyes are on him. The future of the world may be dictated by his ego. The lives of hundreds of thousands of soldiers depend on whether he will try to prevent a war that could unleash Armageddon.

His public comments are those of a calm leader who feels he has done nothing wrong. His arrogance can only come from living an unquestioned life, one that has made it possible for him to look at the whole world, but see only the subject of his narrow focus, keeping power and having things his way.

His visage is everywhere. His words are inescapable, like the ticking of a clock counting down an imminent attack.

His disrespectful treatment of the United Nations doesn't do justice to an entity whose existence for 57 years has been to promote international cooperation and keep the peace.

His refusal to take seriously the enemy at the gate so he maintains the illusion of power could lead to his downfall and to catastrophe in his homeland.

Yet President George W. Bush remains bent on war.

The Bush administration has spent months using the war on terrorism as an excuse to take on an old enemy. And its leader is putting on a dangerous magic show, a series of illusions and doublespeak the country and Congress seem to accept.

Take, for instance, Bush's prime-time press conference last week, which appeared not only to be scripted but rehearsed.

What he said: "The world is calling for Iraq to disarm."

What he meant: "If I say he has to disarm, that's all that matters."

What he said (about Saddam Hussein): "He's a murderer. He has trained and financed Al Qaeda-type organizations. I take the threat seriously. The price of doing nothing exceeds the price of taking action."

What he meant: "Iraq had nothing to do with 9/11, so far as we know, but they could have, so we need to get Hussein."

When asked why so many countries with access to the same intelligence as the United States were not on the same page, Bush said: ... "we do share a lot of intelligence with nations which may or may not agree with us in the Security Council as to how to deal with Saddam Hussein and his threats."

What he meant: "They read the same thing I did, but I'm discounting their views."

What he said: America "will not wait to see what terrorists or terrorist states could do with weapons of mass destruction."

What he meant: "America will not wait to see what Hussein will do, but we can wait on all the other countries who are firing up their weapons. North Korea didn't try to kill my daddy. I don't care about them."

What he said: "I hope we don't have to go to war. But if we go to war, we will disarm Iraq. And if we go to war, there will be a regime change."

What he meant: "I wish I hadn't gone so far down this road, but if you know anybody from Texas, you know we don't back down. So we're going to get him out, put a guy named Tom in charge and teach Iraq to be more like America."

What he said: "No matter what the whip count is, we're calling for the vote. We want to see people stand up and say what their opinion is about Saddam Hussein and the utility of the United Nations Security Council."

What he meant: "We're going to war no matter what. But we need to take down the names of those who aren't for us, 'cause if you're not for us, you're against us, and we won't forget. And then, we'll take a look at whether that Security Council is even necessary."

What he said he's doing: Chasing the fiends that hit New York.

What he's really doing: Chasing the ghosts of a battle between his father and a despot.

This war will go down in history as Bush's Folly. But while he's focused on Iraq, Bush may be missing one enemy at the gate (North Korea) and creating a larger enemy by rallying rival Muslim sects — and anti-U.S. countries — who never had a cause to unite them.

Until now.

And when that's done, a sly grin and cocky wink and "Oops," ain't gonna do it.

What Bush said: "There are thousands of people who pray for me ... I pray for peace. I pray for peace."

What he meant: I've got plenty of back-up. Let's go to war.

March 9, 2003

Iraqi conflict may liberate people like us

As President George W. Bush issued his final ultimatum to Iraqi President Saddam Hussein, I was driving home to hear it. So I called my daughter and asked her to turn on the VCR.

As he made his final case for a $90-billion war and a possible $100-billion subsequent rebuilding of Iraq, I drove in silence, thinking about plans for my daughter's August birthday party.

As he gave the dictator and his sons until 8 tonight to leave, I pulled into the driveway.

But when I walked in, I didn't rush to the VCR. My daughter was now ready for our time. So we sat in the kitchen, munching snacks and talking about, well, nothing really.

"Did you watch the president's speech?" I asked her.

"No."

"Good. Do you have any questions?"

"No."

Not about war. Not about terror. And that was that. That was the extent to which fear entered our home Monday night. And that was all the difference in an evening chat between an American mother and daughter and an Iraqi mother and daughter.

Here, we could choose to ignore the terror, even if for just a few hours. Here, we had the freedom to sit and talk about everything but war while somewhere in Iraq, a mother and daughter must have wondered whether they'd survive.

It is the human element that makes the spread of freedom so important. Yes, I would prefer that freedom move like an epidemic, with countries liberating themselves from terrorists through sheer will and their own resources.

I read with frustration news reports of Arab leaders' dismay at their own lack of action on Iraq. And yes, I wondered whether the U.S. attack on Iraq would require future attacks on other regimes. Saddam isn't the only terrorist running a country.

But as I tucked my daughter into bed and prayed for the safety of soldiers, all I could think about were a mother and daughter in Baghdad, living where they are voiceless and helpless, where there are no polls to tell us how they feel and where a terrorist president can get 100 percent of the vote in a presidential campaign.

I prayed for every mother and daughter, every father and son, who want only to see their families live without fear. There and here.

Early Tuesday morning, I got up to hear the president's speech. I wanted some sense that he really is in charge, really does see the big picture. I wanted him to speak to the Iraqi people. And he did.

"If we must begin a military campaign, it will be directed against the lawless men who rule your country and not against you," he said to Iraqi mothers and daughters, fathers and sons. "As our coalition takes away their power, we will deliver the food and medicine you need. We will tear down the apparatus of terror, and we will help you to build a new Iraq that is prosperous and free.

"In a free Iraq, there will be no more wars of aggression against your neighbors, no more poison factories, no more executions of dissidents, no more torture chambers and rape rooms. The tyrant will soon be gone. The day of your liberation is near."

And I imagined an Iraqi mother and daughter hearing our president, and I hoped they heard hope. I hoped they'd heard what they could celebrate most when the invasion is over: liberation.

For that mother and daughter, from terror. And for the world, from fear.

March 19, 2003

Fallen children on both sides mark all wars

Marine Pfc. Chad E. Bales, Coahoma, Texas, 20.

Marine Cpl. Mark A. Evnin, South Burlington, Vt., 21.

Marine Pfc. Christian D. Gurtner, Ohio City, Ohio, 19.

The story haunts me. It touches me the way it must have millions of others who read it in their Tuesday morning newspapers.

A 21-year-old coalition soldier, a machine-gunner with the 101st Airborne, makes his way into a neighborhood somewhere outside Karbula in Iraq. They are in combat. They are trading fire.

Suddenly, his fellow soldiers shoot an Iraqi man running with a rocket-propelled grenade launcher in his arms.

He falls to the ground. Marine Cpl. Erik H. Silva, Chula Vista, Calif., 22.

Army Spec. Donald S. Oaks Jr., Harborcreek, Pa., 20.

Army Spec. Ryan P. Long, Seaford, Del., 21. The 21-year-old soldier, barely a man himself, then sees a boy run out of an alley and head for the fallen Iraqi.

The boy grabs the RPG.

And the soldier, Nick Poggs, a private first class from Petersburg, Alaska, shoots him dead. Then he and his fellow soldiers watched as another boy came and dragged the first boy's body away. Army. Pfc. Gregory P. Huxley Jr., Forestport, N.Y., 19.

Army Pfc. Anthony S. Miller, San Antonio, 19.

Marine Lance. Cpl. Andrew Julian Aviles, Palm Beach, Fla., 18. There are moments during the weeks of conflict in Iraq when we've been reminded that war, as ugly as it is, is even uglier when it affects children.

We have seen the faces of Iraqi children slain by mistake as their families rush to freedom, jumping in the streets as they try to determine what every assault means for their lives.

We cry when they die.

But what we tend to forget is that war affects all children.

And every soldier who dies is somebody's child.

Not every military death has been a young one, but too many young lives have already been lost. Though standing tough in their uniforms and shorn heads and military grimaces, some are barely old enough to drink, some are not old enough to have married and left a part of themselves behind. Some took with them dreams of college and careers, maybe teaching or running a company.

Army Pvt. Ruben Estrella-Soto, El Paso, Texas, 18.

Marine Pfc. Juan Guadalupe Garza Jr., Temperance, Mich., 20.

Marine Pfc. Francisco A. Martinez Flores, Los Angeles, 21. They're all, the soldiers on both sides, somebody's children, taught love of country by men and women older and more experienced at death.

I am equally angered by an American soldier who shoots down a boy darting toward a weapon and the boy for grabbing at a weapon.

But I am angry at neither the soldier nor the boy.

Someone taught them that.

Someone else made them enemies.

And as long as they are enemies, they will continue to kill each other.

As long as the war continues, no matter their age, children will be dying. Army Spec. Gregory P. Sanders, Hobart, Ind., 19.

Army Pfc. Wilfred D. Bellard, Lake Charles, La., 20.

Army Pvt. Devon D. Jones, San Diego, 19. As a mother, as a woman who loves her country but hates war, I hunger for peace, because the sooner the battle ends, the sooner the clean-up and political fighting over who's in charge can begin.

Even so, the killing may never stop. So, as long as bodies fall in Iraq, I am not counting soldiers, or enemies.

I'm counting children.

April 11, 2003

War's symphony plays loudly

I woke up with the worst headache. But I got up and marched through my morning, getting the munchkin up, making sure the social studies project was not left behind, and hustling off to school and work.

There I bumped into my office buddy, Rachel, who had just gotten a new tattoo. And we exchanged stories about our aches and pains — her arm, my head. But we both stopped nearly at once, and exchanged good thoughts about our troops.

"How can I complain about a headache when a soldier is sitting in a hot bunker?"

"Every time my arm hurts," she said, "I say 'soldiers in Iraq.' "

And suddenly, our middling problems became dust specks. And I think about the soldiers.

I have not given up my opposition to war, nor my anger at the haphazard and clumsy way it began. I have not lost my disdain for America's arrogant global policy.

But as the protests mount and the criticism of the U.S. administration continues, I found myself thinking about how badly the brave veterans of the Vietnam War were treated upon their return.

And I stopped. Stopped answering the phone. Stopped reading the paper. And I took a moment to review a week of war, to listen and actually hear a symphony of war.

I stopped to hear the voice of a mother worried for her son, to hear an activist demand U.S. withdrawal from the region, to hear the endless streams of information from reporters that don't really tell us where we are in the war: 15 dead in a missile strike, the 17,000-member 101st Airborne Division sent in, 1,000 paratroopers dropped over northern Iraq, seven women assigned to the USS John S. McCain, 10,000 students demonstrating in Madrid.

I hear the dispatches from distant deserts, and the dissent from the streets of city after city. I hear renditions of "God Bless America" and shouts of "No More War" — all part of an American symphony, a cacophony of divergent views and passionate rancor that is part of a larger global concert of power and tragedy.

I stop listening to the mundane score of our existence without war and listen to the pounding rhythms of war.

And the drumbeat that can be heard in every movement, with every chord, is made by soldiers. The notes are played in the faces of young men not old enough to drink, their grim, "I'm tough" visages accompanying stories of their deaths.

The drumbeat can be heard in the matter-of-fact way they describe the sounds of sirens and missiles, and their injuries. "I was shot in the hand ... the bullet's still in there."

The soldiers need us to appreciate that they're on the job, not a job of their choosing but the job they've been assigned. They didn't call this tune, but they're on the floor.

How can I ignore the music? How can I look away when a 30-year-old chef is among those in captivity, and her family is in tears every day?

There are holes in the symphony, silences where context should be. Save for grabbing a map and a compass, we don't really know where Bashur or Diwaniyah are.

"The tree of liberty must be refreshed from time to time with the blood of patriots and tyrants. It is its natural manure," Thomas Jefferson, while minister to France, wrote in a private letter.

That stench coming from the Middle East is the blood of heroes and tyrants. But I can't help but wonder whether it is refreshing the tree of life, or drowning it.

Either way, we must not blame the troops.

March 28, 2003

Success blurs the line
not to be crossed

I felt a little sad for Peter Arnett. For years, I'd watched him cover war, beginning in 1991 during Desert Storm. He became a star, reporting as bombs burst overhead.

But this week, Arnett became a victim of his own success: a prominent reporter whose celebrity pushes him or her to dilute the news with personal views.

Arnett, cornered by an Iraqi TV crew after a government briefing, said the American-led coalition's war plan had failed and that civilian casualties were causing an increase in resistance.

Not only has the success or failure of the invasion not been determined, but it was not Arnett's job, not the job of any reporter, to decide.

Arnett stepped over the line and became a part of the story — and it cost him his job.

The controversy reminded me of a line uttered by William Hurt in the popular film "Broadcast News." Playing a news anchor guilty of his own ethical indiscretion, Hurt tells a colleague that not stepping over the line was hard because the little sucker keeps moving.

It's not the line that changes. It's the status of reporters.

As a young reporter, I justified my tiny paycheck by telling myself my goal was the nobler good. These days, the goal is the paycheck, the glory, the renown, getting famous and getting a book deal.

Problem is, the more fame reporters get, the less they see the line. Some of the country's best reporters have become analysts, commentators, millionaires, not reporters.

It is supposed to work like this: Reporters gather information through interviews and research. They craft a story based on what they learn. Then columnists like me offer our opinions on those reports. Editorial page editors and writers determine newspapers' official stands on those stories. And TV analysts offer context and perspective for those stories.

And the reporters follow up their first story or move on to the next one.

But increasingly, opinion is slipping into stories that read more like columns than reports. And media outlets feel their audiences want to hear more from the reporters working the big stories. So reporters get interviewed on how they got their info. Other times, they're asked to relive their original adventure.

For that Iraqi TV crew, it wasn't enough that the American media reported that the White House may have underestimated risks to American troops. It wasn't enough that American military leaders expressed naive surprise that Iraqis were not greeting coalition troops with open arms.

That Iraqi TV crew, like an American one, wanted more. So they turned to a veteran reporter to get his views. And Arnett, whose job was to interview, not be interviewed, should have said no.

To his credit, Arnett apologized profusely Monday morning to NBC, MSNBC and National Geographic, and to the public. He joked about his plans to leave Iraq and swim to a deserted island.

But he may have done something much greater: to remind reporters that our job is to not become bigger than the story, no matter how much celebrity our jobs afford, no matter how much being on camera feeds our egos.

And no matter how embedded reporters are, how much they want to take that next step toward personal statement or blind devotion to what the government says is true, they should just Joe Friday their findings and offer just the facts, ma'am.

April 2, 2003

CHAPTER FOUR

LIFE WITH CHILDREN

Heroes best found at home

I am my daughter's hero.

It is never more clear to me than when we talk about national leaders, and all the people we mention are dead.

It is never more clear than when we watch 14-year-old boys get sentenced to life in prison for beating someone to death, and people try to raise hoopla about his race and his youth and his naivete, but not about who his role models were (the Rock?) and why.

It is never more clear than when we talk about kids fighting over $125 tennis shoes, which cost more than my biweekly grocery tab. It isn't about the shoes, but what the shoes mean. The kids aren't standing in line for four hours just to buy Nikes. They're standing in line for four hours to buy self-esteem, to buy another step on the ladder of humanity. They're buying heroes based on athletes we put on pedestals. They buy heroes because they aren't seeing them on their streets.

It is never more clear than when we watch time after time as children with challenges shoot classmates. They don't really want to shoot someone who specifically hurt them. If they did, they would find one pistol, find that person and shoot that person, like gang members do.

No, these teens — who are usually white suburban boys — stockpile guns, then head to class and fire on dozens of innocent people, making up for heroes they haven't had, closing a wound that just opened up one day after festering.

At Denby High School, where I volunteer once a week or so, I talk to kids about newspapers. But we spend more time talking about real life, about sex and abortion, adoption, gangs and about living and dying.

These wonderful students are honest and fearless because that's the way many kids have to live these days. These kids are smart, curious and critical thinkers who want someone to know what they're capable of. But they're also in the market for self-esteem. That means they'll get it wherever they can. If they're not getting it at home, they'll look for it in classes full of other kids on the same search. They'll look on street corners or in the backseats of cars.

If they don't get it at home, they look for it in gangs, in cliques, in clubs.

What they're looking for starts at home, even if the home is a mesh of broken dreams that cut like glass and absent fathers who leave holes in abandoned hearts. It starts at home, even if that home is missing a mother's bosom to shed tears on, or a room of their own to dream in.

What they're looking for starts with parents, and when they don't have parents, they must have surrogates, whether it's a teacher or a coach, or a minister or a mentor.

Or just someone who drops by the school every week or so.

For our children, it starts with us. If we aren't willing to be heroes for our children, the ones who show them who they should aspire to be, the ones who give them a sense of importance and worth, the ones who remind them that they can walk out of the house every morning absolutely certain that someone somewhere loves them, then we can't be surprised when we hear that some kid has shot another over a pair of shoes, or taken guns into his school and shot his classmates or driven his car into a crowd of college students.

We shouldn't even be sad.

We should just be ashamed.

I am my daughter's hero.

Whose are you?

March 14, 2001

Teens serve their elders food, fun and frienship

The first thing you notice at the Great Lakes dining room at Henry Ford Retirement Village in Dearborn is that all the waiters are teenagers.

The second thing you notice is that the teens and residents really like each other.

Like an old-fashioned musical, the teens strut quickly from table to table, bearing trays of drinks or rich desserts. They side-step slower-moving friends whose stops and starts are like the winsome notes of a '60s folk song.

Some, like 17-year-old Safaa Chehab, keep one eye on the table they're serving and the other eye on the door watching for their favorites. One of Safaa's is 87-year-old Anna Neal, who shares Safaa's love of pop culture.

"Hey Miss Neal, whassu-u-u-u-u-u-p-p-p-!"

"Whassu-u-u-u-p-p-p-p!" a raspy voice full of vigor responds.

Her other favorite, Dorothy Benson, an 85-year-old fox with perfect hair and nails, approaches and plants a kiss on Safaa's cheek. "Hi, sweetheart. How are you?"

As Safaa and Benson chat on one side of the room, Emanuela Pristavu works the other side like a mother hen, checking on her diners, making sure they have everything they need and entertaining them with stories about school, her family and languages.

"I love it here," says Emanuela, also called Emma. The 17-year-old is a senior at Chadsey High in Detroit.

"Everybody is so sweet," she says. "You have good days and bad days, but I'm always happy."

This job will give Emma a professional future.

"I'd like to go to college," she says, "and be a nurse or pharmacist."

That is the way life should be in America, with teens who represent most teens, who are on the right path, studying in school, working hard, saving money and planning productive lives. Some want to be rich. Some want to be successful. Most just want to have points of pride as they live.

Not a drug dealer or thief among them.

Safaa and Emma are among 180 students who work in dining services at Henry Ford as waiters, servers and busboys and bus girls. They spend their evenings in the Great Lakes and St. Clair dining rooms, fetching coffee, suggesting desserts, carving meat, then cleaning up and heading home to do homework. But the students, all from Detroit-area high schools, do more than serve food part-time. They love full-time.

The students earn about $6 an hour. But some who work at least 1,000 hours during their last two years of high school also can earn a $4,000 college scholarship.

The scholarship fund is a tremendous incentive to get kids hired and encourage them to make a long-term commitment to the village, said Cheryl Presley, its community relations coordinator. The students must work 500 hours in their junior year and 500 their senior year. The money is distributed directly to colleges, $500 per semester. The fund is supported by Erickson Retirement Communities, which developed seven other retirement communities besides Henry Ford, which opened in 1993.

But the residents also support the fund and have donated nearly $300,000 to it since it began in 1995.

Working at a retirement village is something Safaa, a sophomore at Fordson High School, said she never would have anticipated.

"I wouldn't even think of it," says the teen who immigrated with her parents from Beirut, Lebanon, when she was 3. Her father, Adib, used to own a restaurant and her mother, Ibtissam, is a housewife. Work is such an integral part of her day that being at the retirement village is sometimes the most fun she has.

"I work five to six days a week. I get $6 an hour. This is my first job," she says. "I go to school at 7:30. I get out at 2:10. I go to work at 2:30. I get home at 8. I do my homework until 10:30 p.m. and then I go to sleep.

"Work is the best fun I have because I meet new people every day, and I hang out with my friends."

The teens get food for thought from residents who, in turn, savor teen tales of current dating habits and hairstyles.

The teens also manage to get souls to laugh who may have forgotten how.

And they tease men until they uncover boyish spirits that were only hidden, but not gone — like the time a student hid a resident's appetizer while he went to the buffet to get his entree. When the man returned, he couldn't find his food. He was puzzled, but only for a moment. Then he just laughed and laughed as his appetizer was returned.

The kids are walking Benetton ads or fast-moving reminders of the "We Are the World" tune Michael Jackson engineered a few years ago.

"We have Arabic kids, an Asian girl. We have black kids. We have white kids. We have pink kids. We have kids of all colors, and they get along," says Gene Simmons, who has lived for three years at the village, which spans 35 acres and costs residents $900 to $1,500 a month for services that include transportation, outings, home repair, cable, security, exercise facilities, utilities and property taxes.

"We have such a sense of community here between the residents and the staff, particularly the kids," Presley says. "They're like their grandparents. These kids have 1,200 grandparents!"

"The kids get together beyond the workplace, too," she says. "They have basketball games, and they have car washes to benefit the scholarship fund. They show the residents that they care so much about the gifts they've made to the fund that they want to donate as well."

Anthony McCants, who graduated from W.E.B. DuBois Academy in Detroit last year, has been working at Henry Ford since October. Now a student at Wayne County Community College, he will be transferring to the Chicago Institute of Art this year. He wants to be an actor and an artist.

But the popular 18-year-old waiter serves up comedy with every dinner.

"I'm basically the comedian of the place. My dad is a comedian. And when I come in, they expect me to make them laugh.

"I tell them jokes. I do impersonations," he says before becoming, for just a minute, assistant manager Joyce Lynch. "And I laugh when they tell jokes. They want to know who did my hair" — turning so his meticulous cornrows can be inspected. "And I blend into their conversations."

Anthony says he's working to ease the college finance burden carried by his mom, Stasha McCants, who works at Chrysler. (His father is Tony Roberts, a New York comedian who has appeared on "Def Comedy Jam" and "BET Comics.")

"I want to pay for some of the things I do myself."

McCants has a good heart and takes his relationships with his elder friends very seriously.

"My favorite thing about this job is my peers and the residents. If you come to work in a bad mood, the residents understand what you're going through, and you can talk to them."

Most of the students care deeply about the residents and feel comfortable discussing anything.

"Their energy is contagious," says Vera Stapleton, who has lived at the center with her husband, Bruce, for a year. "Just being interested in us makes our day."

The teens and elders get along so well because the elders look past tattoos or nose rings to find great people beneath the decorations.

"Krystal wants to have her navel pierced and she wants one on her tongue and one in the small of her back," Stapleton says, referring to Krystal Clinton, a 15-year-old sophomore at Dearborn High School, who is one of Stapleton's favorites and with whom she has much in common.

"My daughters are 21 and 22. One has a pierced navel. One has a pierced tongue. I always wanted one — a diamond right here!" Stapleton says, pointing to the side of her nose.

Krystal, who hugs Stapleton every time she sees her, plans to attend Michigand State. She says Stapleton and the other seniors "teach me to be a better person."

At dinner, the students seek out their favorite seniors, the ones with whom they share secrets. They chat with each other between bites, the kids sharing tales of dating woes and aced tests, the seniors passing along praise and I-told-you-so's.

"The neatest thing is when the kids go to homecoming or prom or anything like that," said Gene Simmons, who has lived at Henry Ford for three years. "They come and show us their dresses."

"And their date just stands around," Stapleton says.

The teens have typical problems, like one guy who went to five different proms because five girls asked him. The kids not only share stories. They share affection. For residents whose families are constant, it's a bit of gravy. But for residents who don't always get hugs, it's dessert.

"Gabrielle likes to hug," says Simmons, who gets gravy and dessert. "My daughters came to visit one time and they had to stand back and wait until Gabrielle got through hugs.

"You never know the kids' last names. You just know their first names," Simmons says. "We have seven children, so being with kids is something ... I thought I would miss, but I don't because these kids are so wonderful. People talk about special needs kids. These kids are special givers. They give us so much."

The elders are givers, too. But sometimes all they have to give are their memories.

So in addition to these teens learning courtesy, patience and respect for their elders, they learn to say good-bye.

"Once they're gone, they're gone," Simmons says. "They're like the residents. Once the residents die, they're gone. Most often, you know a resident, and you know a resident well. But you don't know the family.

"When a resident dies, that's it. That's the way the kids are, and you adjust. Life is a matter of adjustments."

March 11, 2001

Teacher helps students fathom Santee tragedy

The students in my daughter's class sat up in their chairs Tuesday as their teacher asked about what they'd seen on the news the night before. Eager hands shot up as she wondered aloud whether there was anything that could have changed what they saw in Santee, Calif.

They blamed other students.

They blamed the parents.

The discussion, for just a few minutes, was more important than math or science. When children need to talk about students being murdered at school, it is a wise teacher who stops to listen, who puts everything else on hold and offers an ear.

Sometimes that's all a child needs before becoming a killer.

One child spoke of teachers receiving death threats at her old school. Another questioned how parents could not know their children are hoarding guns or making bombs or getting so mad they could shoot somebody.

And one talked about being picked on and how angry and afraid it made her.

They all talked anxiously about how some children said it wasn't safe to go to school — any school — the day after a teenager walked into a high school and shot 15 people. Two died; 13 will join hundreds of others who will never walk those halls again without sudden noises making the hairs on the backs of their necks stand up.

And somewhere a child is collecting. He has a secret hiding place where he's storing guns and pistols, rifles and anything else that takes away whatever pain he's in. He reads anger on the Internet and he finds a place to vent, but it's not enough. He has to do more to get the attention he so desperately needs or to strike back because he feels the world has been so unfair.

Or maybe he just thinks it would be cool to see blood splatter the way it does in his video games. Psychologists don't really know because they rarely see the children whose anger is rising like a visible plume of smoke that will blow over a school or our homes.

These shooters are always boys and almost always white. They are not usually poor. They have the means to stoke their anger: computers to get information about guns, video games to practice on until they are ready, and parents who work hard, maybe too hard, so they fail to see their son's withdrawal into whatever chamber he must abide in to prepare to kill.

As I watched the innocent 11-year-old hands shoot up and suggest ways to help, I knew they didn't have answers. They just had a need to suggest answers.

They're not alone. We grown-ups don't have answers either. What we have is a responsibility to be a parent. Even if it means we cannot be our child's best friend or bowling partner or movie buddy.

When the fun ends, we have to be the heavy, to ask what they're doing, to demand to know what that thing is on the bookcase that looks like a gun clip.

As I watched the innocent hands shoot up, in a class where there seem to be no problems, I looked again and wondered whether I'd recognize a problem in incubation.

I wondered, as a parent, whether taking away the video games, banning rap or locking your child in his room until it's time for college, will make any difference.

It won't.

Troubled children, the ones who need help way before they begin stealing guns, look just like the children who never have problems and wouldn't think of shooting someone.

The only thing any of us can do is to keep an eye out for that moment when those two children begin to look different, and one looks like he needs help.

It isn't possible to overreact.

So many people knew that Charles (Andy) Williams needed help before Santana High was riddled with bullets police say he fired.

Overreaction might have saved two lives and 13 injuries this week. Overreaction might have saved an additional 32 lives and kept 56 people from being injured in other school shootings in the past five years. It's time for parents, teachers and students to overreact.

If you know, tell. If you hear, question. If you see, ask. If you don't, someone could die.

March 7, 2001

Detroit's children plead for their lives

Walter O'Neal walked up to the news conference microphone and stood before a baker's dozen of teenagers, all with matching T-shirts and grim visages.

He was polite and polished and not just for a 15-year-old. He seemed emotionless as he spoke about nearly being shot. His tone was matter-of-fact, as if he were recounting the plot of a book he'd read.

"My experience with gun violence occurred last year, in the spring of the last school year, when a stray projectile entered our band room during one of our rehearsal sessions," said Walter, who attends Osborn High School. "We almost lost three students that day.

"And it's disheartening to know that we were almost killed doing something that we loved to do, and every day we had to go back and look at the window and look at that bullet hole."

When he abruptly left the mike, unable to go on, it was apparent there was nothing matter-of-fact about the memory of that day. There is nothing matter-of-fact about children growing up having to worry about their safety as much as they do about what to wear to school.

There is nothing matter-of-fact about bullets tearing apart young lives and affecting families across Detroit: at least 23 shootings since January, eight of them fatal.

The news conference was called by teens from the Youth Initiative Project of the Neighborhood Service Organization. They stood behind the so-called Spirit of Detroit statue with their backs against a wall of City Hall. Teens' backs are against the walls in this city, and they want to be heard.

The teens encouraged — pleaded with — metro Detroiters who care about kids to join them Saturday on Belle Isle for a march and rally against gun violence. The march is being held jointly with Million Mom March and the Rehabilitation Institute of Michigan/Pioneers for Peace and True Life Crusaders. The group will meet at 11 a.m. on Jefferson Avenue and walk across the MacArthur Bridge to the park's band shell.

"I want everyone to understand that this is going to be an historical event, something that Detroit has been in need of for a long time," said Londell Thomas, 19. "Once we get on the MacArthurBridge, we're going to launch balloons in the air in remembrance of those young people killed by gun violence. We want everyone to come out. We want everyone to be involved in this great change that Detroit is going to see."

Thomas described the rally as an anti-gun violence peace fest that might recall the '70s when people everywhere "were petitioning to end violence."

But he wants marchers to go back even further in their history books and closets to find their marching orders. "We want to bring back a taste of the civil rights movement," he said.

The rally will feature speakers and several high school bands, including Walter O'Neal's band from Osborn.

These youth are trying to stay one step ahead of the statistics: at least 23 children age 16 and younger shot in Detroit this year, eight fatally.

The numbers are scaring parents and police. But mostly and more importantly, they're scaring our children.

If we won't listen to the experts, and we won't listen to the news reports, and we won't listen to the police department, maybe we'll listen to the children.

May 31, 2002

Teens turn prejudice into peace

Hassanen Al-Hassuni and Danuta Borowska have everything and nothing in common.

Hassanen was born 18 years ago in Iraq. Ten years ago, as the war between Iraq and Kuwait escalated, his family fled the violence, first to northern Iraq and then to Saudi Arabia, south of Riyadh.

Hassanen, his parents and his four sisters and a brother were escorted with thousands of other refugees to the Arabian desert, where they lived in tent camps for two years before immigrating to America. The U.S. troops "would bring water, big trucks of water, and we'd get buckets and have to go grab water," he recalled. "It was hard because we had never lived in the desert before. We were always getting sick a lot. I was the oldest kid, so I had to get the water for my family and the food."

Danuta was born 19 years ago in Poland and lived in rural Krasnik before coming to America in 1992 with her family.

"My father's mother moved here over 25 years ago, and she wanted all her kids to immigrate, so we followed her," she says. Danuta thought she was visiting her grandmother for the summer. She didn't realize her family wasn't returning to Poland until her parents enrolled her in school the next fall. "They didn't want it to have too big an impact," she says.

Before America, Hassanen and Danuta spoke different languages, prayed differently to God and knew mostly their own ways. But America has a way of connecting people who don't let differences get in the way. The teens struggled and spent months learning how to speak English and how to blend into a new culture. But soon they sought ways to honor their own cultures and celebrate their differences.

Those efforts eventually resulted in the United Students Peace Force. Its name sounds military, but the peace force is really a peace-teaching, not peace-keeping, force. The students teach students to celebrate diversity and recognize prejudice. They teach nonviolence; and because they are, after all, students, they work to save the planet. They clean up green space, paint murals, host speakers, travel together and, every now and again, hold a Peace Bash.

The U.S. Peace Force had its beginnings in a multicultural council that used to meet after school at Hamtramck. Its adviser was Nancy Erickson, then the school's librarian.

"I was asked to start it at the high school to help alleviate ethnic tensions in the schools," she says. "The principal asked me to start it to help bring people together more. There was a perception that there were ethnic tensions in the schools."

Erickson says the tensions at the high school mirrored those in Hamtramck, a suburb whose residents include immigrants of Yemeni, Bosnian, Bangladeshi, Polish and Albanian descent.

"We're one of the most ethnically diverse suburbs of Detroit," Erickson says. "Bloomfield and some of the northern suburbs are quite diverse, but they could be second generation. We're known more for our immigrant population as a first stop."

The school's multicultural council had representatives from the diverse cultures, who all worked together on community service projects. "As they worked together, that would improve relations," Erickson says.

Some students on the council successfully pushed to make diversity training a part of the curriculum. It resulted in the peace studies class, which Erickson taught for two years in addition to her library duties. It was discontinued when Erickson began teaching social studies full-time this year. But she hopes at some point that she can teach both.

"When I came to Michigan, I took the peace studies class," Hassanen recalled. He also joined the multicultural council after school.

Some of the people on the council graduated, he says, but they wanted to continue to work with the group. So a half dozen students — Hassanen and Danuta, Amanda Albert, Ema Dzaka, Edin Jakupovic and Melissa Franklin — turned an extracurricular activity into the U.S. Peace Force.

Its most recent event was a Peace Bash, where about 30 teens mingled in the community center. The Peace Force members were identifiable by their camouflage pants and light brown T-shirts.

Hassanen, Danuta, Ema, Melissa and Amanda coordinated games and skits designed to teach diversity and point out ways around prejudice.

In one, the students were separated into five groups, which each got a slip of paper. On each slip was written a word representing what many of the teens say they face: discrimination, prejudice, stereotyping, ageism and scapegoating.

One group pretended they were in a party store. Most of the group, including Amanda, walked around the pretend store while two others stayed near the door. As the student playing the store manager followed Amanda and her group around, the two students who were pretending to be adults cleaned the place out, stuffing a CD player, pens and other items under their shirts.

In another exercise, Danuta asked each of the students in the room to talk about the origin of their names. Only half the students had any idea.

"My father named me Danuta. Danuta was my grandmother's name. It means 'to be blessed by God' in Latin," she says.

Hassanen explained that his first name was the combination of the names of two religious leaders, Hassan and Hussein. "My older sister named me," he says.

Other students shared that they were named for their grandparents, uncles and even a character on "Days of Our Lives."

"Because of our names, we are all unique," Danuta told the students. "Our names unite us."

Hassanen and his fellow peace-teachers hope the lessons learned will show students a better way to see each other and treat each other, and better ways to handle their anger.

"I suffered in the war. A lot of people got killed. I started thinking 'There's better ways. We can control that.' "

The only war Danuta knows is the battle to make people understand that anger and violence are not answers.

"The best way to stop violence is to understand that it is a problem that isn't something only a few of us are facing," she said. "We should try to understand why we're different and look at the things that unite us. We're all human and the fact that we practice different religions and share different cultures unites us, because those are just categories that we all share. We're all a part of each other."

March 23, 2001

Sex with kids illegal for the right reasons

There is a lesson for parents in the case of the Bloomfield Township girl who claimed to have had sex with 22 men and boys and whose escapades led five of them to be charged with criminal sexual conduct.

I don't mean the parents of the girl, who were horrified when they found out. The lesson is for the parents of the guys, who could get 15 years in prison and 25 years on the state sex offender registry.

The lesson is for the parents of any boys who think that girls who say, "Let's have sex," have a legal right to extend the invitation.

In Michigan, if the girl is under 16, she doesn't. No matter how many men she sleeps with, if she's under 16 and you're not, you could go to jail. If the girl and boy are both under 16, they could face charges, but prosecution is unlikely because both would be defendants and neither would be likely to incriminate themselves in court.

Some people say the law is unfair. I say that any law that prevents people older than 16 from having sex with children is not just a good law. It may be one of the best ways to combat a rising tide of teen promiscuity that has led to increased teen pregnancies and sex-related diseases.

I empathize with the parents of those boys who face, but probably won't get, jail time. They were dealing with a girl who had lost her moral center, who bragged in her diary about her exploits.

But boys who want to be men and men who want to be stupid get no sympathy from me for having sex with a girl who was a high school freshman, wasn't old enough to drive or see an R-rated film, and whose phone number they passed around like that of a popular pizza parlor.

The law is not gender-specific, but it's "scarier for people with sons. It means you have to take responsibility and know what your sons are doing and who they're taking to the prom," said Karen McDonald, the assistant prosecutor assigned to the case.

The statute restricts sex between those who shouldn't be having it. And the Bloomfield Township girl, who called herself a sexual predator and victim who had oral and anal sex with nearly two dozen men from October 2000 until June 2001, is a perfect example of a person the law would benefit.

She obviously was in no position to make decisions about her own sexuality. So why would men and boys just a little older than she trust her to make choices for them?

Parents, look at your own ninth-grader. Is she or he ready for sex? Even the best parents, those who tell you they always know where their children are, sometimes don't have a clue.

Parents can't be with children 24/7. As a matter of fact, many kids learn much of their moral attitude away from home, where you might have three to four hours with them each night (while they're awake). They really learn those things on the job — at school. "Look at your kids," Oakland County chief deputy prosecutor Deborah Carley says. "They are no more ready to make those kinds of life decisions than anybody else who's 13, 14 or 15."

Carley says she doesn't think parents don't understand the law. They just might not be explaining it to their children. Oakland County prosecuted 72 criminal sexual conduct cases involving juvenile defendants and victims in 1999, Carley says. The number is closer to 100 annually now, she says.

"I don't know about the kids, what they know in schools and what they don't know. That's why we want to get the word out so they know very clearly what the law is and what they're facing."

The law is to make boys and men — and women and girls — think twice about the consequences of sex with children. That's why former teacher Mary Kay Letourneau sits in the Washington Corrections Center for Women near Gig Harbor, Wash. Six years ago, when she was 34, she said she "fell in love" with a 12-year-old student.

Oh, please.

Just because a girl says yes, doesn't make it right. Just because a boy says he's a man doesn't make him one.

We know kids are having sex. We teach it in schools. We pass out condoms to prevent STDs. But we don't explain that they could go to jail.

I don't want to make it easier for them. I want to shake them — and their parents — and explain the word "consequences." I want to wake them up. I want them to remember that when they decide a good time is better than a good decision, there is a price to pay.

It's a shame about the boys who passed the Bloomfield Township girl around. Their lives will never be the same. But they have done something for society — and their peers.

They are living warnings to other boys and girls who want to have sex with children. Don't do it. You could go to jail.

May 29, 2002

World's kids see a caste system here

We can learn so much from kids, especially about differences.

Take Imdadul Choudhury. He walked into an American school for the first time when he was 11. He did not understand English or American culture.

Thanks to language lessons and caring teachers, he has nearly mastered both, picking up not only the words but the rhythms of his new country.

But what he also learned is that cultural understanding is sometimes a one-way street.

And as we celebrate Detroit and its 300 years of welcoming people from around the world into the fold of city life here, maybe we should consider what some of our children are learning about each other. That's where the lesson may be for the grown-ups.

One of the things that foreign-born teens see is what African-American teens complain about every February: They must learn everything about mainstream American history, but the same isn't true for their own history.

To witness diversity, look no further than Hamtramck High, where Imdadul is a senior. Twenty-eight nationalities are represented in a student body where nearly 2 of 5 students is Arab American. The school is effective, says assistant principal Patrick Victor, because it uses "a little compassion."

"You always think about how would you like to be dropped off in the middle of Russia or Bulgaria. You pick up the language. You pay attention. I've picked up a little Arabic. You have to be able to greet them with 'Salam alaikum (peace be with you).' "

Teaching Arab students is hard, he said, because they read right to left. "To turn a sentence into English, they have to turn the sentence 180 degrees." The school uses English as a Second Language and other programs to help students get acclimated in school. But out of school, the students are on their own.

"Over here, most people care about their culture," Imdadul said. "Back home, it's not like that. Culture is whatever it is, and religion is what it is."

America is a nation of categories, of placement, of a caste system, both economic and geographic, a place where your worth is determined not only by how much money you have, but where you went to school.

That system is not lost on foreign-born youths who face a choice between abandoning their history, weaving it into their lives or being separate — even if it's just over lunch. In the Hamtramck High cafeteria, "you would have an Arab table here and a Polish table next to it and an Albanian table across from it," said Hafzollah Alhalemi (Al) Evaline, a 19-year-old senior from Yemen.

In some cases, the more acclimated students become, the more of their culture they lose. Al has been in America for 13 years. He doesn't remember the name of his hometown in Yemen, and he initially struggled to keep a foot in two worlds.

"At first, I figured what I knew was the same all over the world," he said. "I thought we had the same people all over the world. Communication with people was difficult.

"I was a bad boy. I had to get used to teachers wearing skirts. But as I grew up further, I got to understand the culture. I didn't go by my family. My friends influenced me.

"There were so many temptations. You want to do things, but you can't because of certain rules. For example, friends would go out and have fun or play basketball, and you can't do it because you have to pray or do stuff with family. They understand, but then when you try to explain it to parents, what fun you could have, it's difficult."

Maggie Sokolowska was 5 when her family emigrated from Kielce, Poland, in 1992. Now a sophomore at Hamtramck High, she tries to teach her culture to her American-born friends.

"I always try to keep my background into everything. That's where I'm from. That's where my blood is. It helps me remember where I'm from."

Selman Saleh's family emigrated from Yemen when he was 3. He met his grandparents for the first time in America, and he would run across new family members from time to time.

"One time I was fighting with a kid, and I didn't realize he was my cousin until I looked at his last name," he said.

Selman works with local peace clubs to teach kids to understand one another instead of fighting, and he longs for the day when no one notices differences.

"In some ways, we're all the same. We all have feelings," he said. "If I see somebody wearing something different, I ask 'Why is that?' I try to have more experience so I won't stereotype."

One of the greatest challenges for many Arab teens is teaching their religion. It may be hard for some Christian youth who wear their religion like a Sunday suit to understand Muslims who wear their religion like skin.

For many Muslims, religion is life. Some pray five times a day. That initially proved to be a problem for some teens. But Imdadul and Selman set their schedules to pray before and after school.

"I pray right before dawn, late afternoon, before evening, right when the sun sets and at night," Imdadul said.

The teens are typical in many ways. Imdadul ran track for two years and was the most valuable player last year. Al wrestled. And Selman, who graduated in May, is now looking for a job.

Maggie says her experience has prepared her for life.

"The best thing is you get to experience every culture and when you get out into the real world, you're not going to be confused: 'Why is he doing that? Why does she have a dot on her forehead?' You'll know by the time you graduate. You'll know more about people and you'll understand better. It really helps."

See, we really can learn from kids.

July 24, 2001

A promise commences
a new life for graduates

Under a gleaming sun, on the banks of the Detroit River, a high school held its annual dance between life and students.

The students and life embraced and made promises, then made plans to go their separate ways.

It was Denby High School's graduation, and seated onstage at the Chene Park Amphitheater was senior class president Joleana Wilkins, who searched for weeks to find words that would make a great impact on her fellow students and pass muster with school staff.

She succeeded.

Calling her senior year "the most trying year" of her life, she thanked her fellow graduates for showing her how competitive the real world is. Then she encouraged them to be "responsible, dependable and reliable."

"If we both work at Subway and you can make 40 subs per hour but you goof around on the job, are constantly late, your register comes up short and you don't let the boss know in advance that you need the day off or just don't show up while I only make 30 subs per hour but get to work on time, my register is always balanced and I rarely take off, who do you think the boss is going to keep?"

For weeks as Joleana, 18, toiled, she lamented that she wasn't saying what students needed to hear. "I feel like they need to get over their laziness and realize that no one owes them anything."

But, in the end, her compromise was excellent. As she faced the Class of '01, she did more than throw words. She made them stand up and speak for themselves.

"I ask you now to make a pledge, not to your parents, friends, family or to your classmates, for none of these people will live your life for you. I ask you now on this 11th day of June in the year 2001, after completing four stressful years of high school to stand here before your master and all of these good people who love and care about you to make a pledge to yourself."

And they did.

"I pledge to fulfill my destiny by furthering my education in whatever fields I choose and I look forward to becoming one of the future leaders of the world. I will have pride in my people, my integrity and pride in myself. I will not let others stop me from achieving my goals. I will not let others think for me. I will stand up and fight for what I believe to be true. I will not go quietly into the night. I pledge to believe in me."

Joleana and her sister, Diara, are being raised by their mother, Jerolean Wilkins, a bookkeeper at Cass Tech. She named her oldest daughter for Josephine Baker and Lena Horne, and Joleana's plans for life are as ambitious.

"I will graduate from Wayne State University in four years with a bachelor's degree in both international finance and journalism," she told her classmates. "I will serve my country in the United States Navy as well as in Congress. I plan to work hard and earn my Lincoln Navigator, Chevy Corvette, my motorcycle and my beautiful homes.

"I plan to be somebody ... I realize that my worth is not determined by the car that I drive nor the name on the clothes that I wear. It is more important to have money invested towards my future, so I can live life how I want to live."

Joleana spent weeks preparing a lesson for her classmates. But what she came up with was a lesson for us all.

June 13, 2001

Make some noise now
to save young lives

Someone shot Ajanee Pollard while she was riding in a car on Feb. 25. She was 7 years old.

Someone shot Destinee Thomas while she was watching TV in her bedroom on March 23. It was a drive-by. She was 3.

Someone shot Brianna Caddell as she slept on April 10. More than two dozen shots rattled her house as she died. She was 8.

Someone shot Cherrel Thomas Tuesday as she and her cousin and a friend drove around looking for someone who had stolen some clothes. Cherrel was in the backseat, in the wrong place. She was 15.

Four girls since February.

Four lives lost when they were just beginning.

Makes me wanna holler.

So why isn't somebody hollering? Where's the noise?

Where are the activists who can command thousands to protest a security guard's fatal tussle with a shopper? Where are the civil rights leaders when the enemy isn't a less-than-welcoming mall or a red-lining bank, but hateful young men with semi-automatics?

Where is the massive police presence to prevent gang shootings in the same way that a wave of blue descended on Jefferson Avenue this week to prevent phantom energy demonstrators from getting out of hand? Did you see all the cops downtown, keeping the Renaissance Center safe?

While I care about racism and banks discriminating against minorities and poor people, those should not be the highest priority on this city's agenda. Our agenda must be our children.

Sixteen years ago, when my daughter wasn't even an idea in the back of my head in Texas, the gun toll on children in Detroit was 365 shot, 43 fatally.

One for every day of the year.

The next year — 1987 — 336 kids 16 and under were shot, 37 fatally. In 1988, 308 were shot, 55 fatally.

Down in Ft. Worth, I wondered whether it was possible to live happily in a city where children could be shot to death so often, so easily.

It's past time for Detroiters to treat children as the precious commodity they are.

In some countries, if a man steals, authorities cut off his hand. If you kill a child in Detroit, you get a newspaper story and TV coverage.

What you need to get is caught, thanks to information that someone you know gives to the police. Then you need to be convicted, jailed and look through some bars until you glimpse no more.

The police have their hands full. But their hands aren't the only hands that must shield our children from harm.

If you've ever marched in Detroit about anything, march about children. If you've ever beaten the bushes to raise money or raise awareness, jump on this. If you've ever shouted in a school board meeting about jobs, shout about kids shooting kids.

Children in Detroit are getting killed again. Don't wait for the numbers to surpass those during the city's "killing of the innocents" phase that garnered national news.

Four little girls gone.

Makes me wanna holler. I'm looking for somebody to holler with me.

May 3, 2002

Sometimes, all a kid needs is to be found

It is easy to be moved by sports, not so much by the scores as by the people behind the numbers.

Few stories have moved me as much as that of Greg (Toe) Nash, whose life, at 18, is the stuff dreams want to be.

You could say that some things happen only in America. You could say success comes from whom you know. But nothing is as fitting as saying that life and God find a way.

Nash's story sounds like the movie it will probably become. Benny Latino, a part-time baseball scout for the Tampa Bay Devil Rays who was born and raised in Hammond, La., was hunting talent in rural Louisiana six years ago when he stopped by a Little League game one Sunday. There he saw a 12-year-old with a powerful swing and great potential.

"He was about 5'10" and so much bigger and better and more physical than the rest of the kids," Latino says. "He struck out 17 of 21 batters, and he dominated the game. I grew up in the youth system here and volunteered from the time I was 18 until I was 23, and I'd never seen anything like that."

Latino made a mental note to check back on the kid.

Now, I make mental notes all the time, but I don't remember them a month later.

Latino never forgot. He kept Nash in the back pocket of his memory for six seasons, then went to find him.

"I looked for this kid for a good eight months," he says, detailing a search of local high schools armed with only Nash's nickname, Toe, earned because of big feet.

Nash had dropped out of high school and didn't have a phone at his house. But thank goodness he stayed near the diamond, working with his father as a part-time groundskeeper at the ballpark.

Latino found him — bigger, stronger, better.

And now he's a Tampa Bay Devil Ray. He banked his $30,000 signing bonus, and he got a new full-time friend in Latino. He has been staying in Hammond with Latino, who's guiding his preparation for spring training.

"I wanted to work out with him every day," Latino says. Reporters and fans show up every time Nash works out. "This thing has taken off and changed both our lives," Latino says. "We've both been offered possible movie deals and authors are sending up copies of their books, saying they want to write our stories."

Toe Nash is doing what he loves because a scout with an eye for unpolished jewels found a diamond in the rough.

My question is: How many other Toe Nashes are out there? How many children dream of great things and places, but don't know how to get there? How many children are so near the road to achievement they can see the dust rise from others' travels, but can't get there themselves?

There are millions of children in naked cities so full of ambition, so full of politics, legislation and education that the people in those realms sometimes forget to teach children how to succeed.

At a time when children hear despair as much as encouragement, it is important for them to know they must strive anyway, hope anyway, achieve anyway. And we adults must participate in the success of children.

Sometimes they need us to find them. They're out there, these young people for whom the difference between success and failure is attitude and meeting the right person.

Find them.

And when you do, let's celebrate them.

January 24, 2001

Messages kids send often go unheard

Wasn't it John Lennon who said that life is what happens while you're busy making other plans?

We've been seeing the big stories but missing the individual heartaches. The personal tragedies don't get us until they take all of our attention.

We read about a 12-year-old beating a little girl to death but pay attention only after he's sent to jail for life. We barely pay attention to teens crying for attention, but are horrified when they react to the silence by killing classmates, teachers or themselves. We distance ourselves from songs whose lyrics are the language of anger, then learn too late that most teens are fluent in that language.

Eminem isn't the problem. Marshall Mathers is the messenger. He says what kids say, sharing publicly what kids say in private eruptions. If we don't hear it, we're not listening. Don't blame the music. Hear it.

Aside from the filth and hate, you hear anguish and desperation and decisions coming too soon, as in Eminem's hit "Stan." We need to see what kids see: adults racing to a movie about cannibals, fighting about who's in charge and walking past people with no food or home. Millions of teens look for redemption in the downbeat.

"Dear Slim, I wrote but you still ain't callin'
I left my cell, my pager, and my home phone at the bottom.
I sent two letters back in autumn, you must not-a got 'em.
There probably was a problem at the post office or somethin.
Sometimes I scribble addresses too sloppy when I jot 'em
But anyways; f— it, what's been up? Man, how's your daughter?
My girlfriend's pregnant too, I'm 'bout to be a father ...
I know you probably hear this every day, but I'm your biggest fan ...
This is Stan"

Hear the words as if they're from a son to a father, not a fan to a rock star. In some of the music and the writings — the ones that the police get to after the school shootings, as they did in Pearl, Miss. — you might hear things a kid wouldn't say to his parents. Sometimes, the cries for help are so obvious, we wonder later how in the world we missed them.

> *"Dear Mister-I'm-Too-Good-To-Call-Or-Write-My-Fans,*
> *this'll be the last package I ever send your a—.*
> *It's been six months and still no word — I don't deserve it?*
> *I know you got my last two letters;*
> *I wrote the addresses on 'em perfect.*
> *So this is my cassette I'm sending you, I hope you hear it.*
> *I'm in the car right now, I'm doing 90 on the freeway.*
> *Hey Slim, I drank a fifth of vodka, you dare me to drive? ...*
> *Now it's too late — I'm on a 1000 downers now, I'm drowsy*
> *and all I wanted was a lousy letter or a call*
> *I hope you know I ripped ALL of your pictures off the wall.*
> *I love you Slim, we coulda been together, think about it*
> *you ruined it now, I hope you can't sleep and you dream about it*
> *and when you dream I hope you can't sleep and you SCREAM about it.*
> *I hope your conscience EATS AT YOU and you can't BREATHE without*
> *me ...*
> *Well, gotta go, I'm almost at the bridge now*
> *Oh sh—, I forgot, how'm I supposed to send this s — out?*
> (Tires squeal. Loud crash.)

Slim Shady tells Stan in a letter to get some help. It's more than some parents do. We can run but we can't hide. We can hear kids or continue to be surprised.

March 25, 2001

Child killings demand all our attention

Thugs with automatic weapons have shot and killed five children since New Year's Day.

They have pulled triggers over minor and less than minor grievances and cut short lives that were all special and might have been brilliant. They have either been arrested or are still running. But when they do get caught, others take their place.

Sixteen children ages 16 and under have been shot in Detroit so far this year.

Yet we treat the shootings like reports of traffic accidents. Why aren't we concerned, here in the blackest large city in America?

Is it because the shooters are believed to be black, and that kind of thing just happens here?

What does it take?

What if they had been low-pants-wearing, Eminem-looking, street-talking-so-they-sound-like-rappers thugs, whose bullets pierced angels?

Would we be marching then? Would the NAACP take out a $100,000 reward for information leading to the arrest of?

Would thousands of parents flock to a rally against gun violence?

Why are black lives expendable when black people take them? It is a question as old as studies showing that for decades black-on-black crime has grown to crisis proportions. And, lately, it is one being put to Detroiters.

Why don't we care?

We have to look at the shootings of 16 children for exactly what they are, so much more and nothing less.

For black people to ignore the barbarism of black thugs means that we, more than whites, embrace the stereotypic definitions given to all blacks. Young black men with AK-47s are not me. They are not my brother or my nephew or anyone I know.

If we care we should holler and the din of our hollering should be heard over in Windsor. The fury in our voices should drown out the grieving moans of mothers losing children.

The Detroit Police Department, plagued and nearly outgunned, is at DEFCON 3.

They've taken 2,534 guns off the streets since New Year's Day. Yes, read that number again. Many were AK-47s.

"We need to call together the faith communities, politicians, community groups and, first and foremost, our citizens," says Sgt. Ricardo Moore.

The Neighborhood Service Organization's Youth Initiative Project has already planned a town hall meeting.

But as important, the group has planned a Detroit-area rally when more than 150 youth have committed to gather on Jefferson to march across the MacArthur Bridge to Belle Isle.

La'Risha Sanders, a 16-year-old sophomore at Martin Luther King Jr. High School, wants thousands to come.

Regardless of race.

"We want to talk to youth about gun violence and let them tell us their stories so they can relate to us. We just need to get the message out about guns and how the killing needs to stop."

If 16-year-olds without guns are willing to stand up to the thugs, surely we can stand with them and fight for an end to the killings of children, not black children or white children, but children.

I'll see you there, La'Risha.

May 8, 2002

Sometimes practicality is too cruel

Sometimes people do things without thinking. We have become so focused on being practical that we forget emotion, passion and sometimes common sense.

That's how I felt after reading that the British government, to avoid arguments similar to the ones surrounding Princess Diana's final farewell three years ago, made a special request.

It asked Prince William and Prince Harry to plan their own funerals.

To be fair, the government also asked senior members of the royal family to do the same. But it seemed torturous to ask teens who have yet to chart their courses in life to think about life's end.

They were asked to provide a guest list, to choose the style of music and to decide what kind of service it would be.

How can they suggest what they want the world to remember before they've had a chance to make good memories?

Funerals are not for the buried. They are for those left behind. They allow us to grieve at shared loss and remember that we must complete our work before our own journeys are done.

Princess Diana, in her darkest moments, could not have predicted the tragedy that befell her. She could not have foreseen the international outpouring of love that followed. But if she had been asked, would she have chosen the very public good-bye she was given? Would she have asked her family to remind people that it is the children who matter?

Planning funerals is not a task for boys, whose manhood is so new they haven't yet discovered all its facets. It isn't even a task for the famous because some have yet to realize the lasting impact their lives will have.

If Jackie Robinson had been asked as a teen to plan his funeral, would he have known the impact he'd have on baseball, or would sports have been overshadowed by things with even stronger meaning for him?

If Dr. Martin Luther King Jr. had planned his funeral as a teen, would God have shown him the profound impact his words would have on a divided America?

Can anyone know that soon how long their memory will linger?

The royal teens, who, thanks to international attention, must publicly deal with their mother's death every day, shouldn't be forced to consider their own. Planning one's remembrance is so incongruous to sweet, vibrant life.

No one could have thought to ask Johnnie Walker to plan his funeral. There was no way the bright, 23-year-old Comerica intern could have known what his legacy would be, what people should remember. He had planned to earn an MBA at the time he was abducted from his Sherwood Forest home and shot last year.

Police have not arrested anyone in the case.

Amanda Martin, Jennifer Young and Talia Schiller, the three Chelsea High School teens killed in a car crash last month, could not have foreseen what greatness awaited them. So how could they have known all the things to remind people of at their deaths? No one would have dared ask them to decide on funeral music at a time when they were deciding which prom dress to wear.

Asking any youths to plan their funerals is wrong.

It's like asking someone to recite their life history at 16.

How can you plan a funeral when you're just beginning to live?

December 10, 2000

CHAPTER FIVE

LIFE IN MOTOWN

She polished generations of Motown's brightest

It is one of those undisputed facts of history: Berry Gordy knows music. It is evident in the 69 songs that reached No. 1 and the dozens of young men and women who became worldwide stars during his tenure at Motown, the recording company he founded, initially as Tamla, in 1959.

But in the heady early days of Motown's success, he didn't know much about grooming the rough diamonds he was plucking off the streets of Detroit to create one of the nation's most successful businesses. It took his sister, Gwen, to persuade him to polish the stones. And that's how he met Maxine Powell.

"She's quite a character," says Gordy, who called from Mexico Wednesday to talk about Powell. "She had quite a personality. And she's a star herself.

"She had a finishing school that my sister Gwen went to and that's how we came to know her," says Gordy. "They continued to push me to bring in somebody to groom the artists. They fought hard because I was more interested in hit records and writing songs and music, and this was another side of it that I hadn't thought was as important as it turned out to be."

It was a good thing that family won out. As Gordy developed the Sound of Young America, the woman he calls a "hero" of Motown helped develop the look and style of Young America. Powell taught the stars, including Smokey Robinson and Diana Ross, not only how to carry and express themselves, but how to be themselves, gracefully. She taught them eloquence. She taught them how to be stars.

"What they received from me — help in developing the class, the grace and all of the diplomacies — took time," Powell said. "Four years! It wasn't overnight."

Powell is still polishing jewels in the rough. She lives in a high-rise on the Detroit River, and holds occasional etiquette classes, by appointment, at Wayne County Community College, where she was an instructor of personal development from 1971 until she retired in 1985.

She is in constant motion attending community functions and sometimes traveling with Martha & the Vandellas, one of the groups she helped train and whose lead singer, Martha Reeves, remains a dear friend.

Since Motown, the woman who changed unsophisticated kids into stars still gets interview requests from around the world. No matter how long ago those original Motown days were, people still want to hear her talk about what Diana Ross was like as a teen and whether Marvin Gaye was as smooth when he walked in as when he walked out.

She relives those times, she says, because they were legendary. But these days, Powell wants to talk about much, much more. She wants people to know she existed before Motown.

Meeting Maxine Powell is like traveling back in time. In her world, style and grace are as important as breakfast.

The first time I saw her was the day I picked her up for lunch. As I opened the car door for her, she explained the proper way to enter an automobile, turning her feet just the right way so her ankles were crossed the moment she sat down.

She taught her way through lunch, and by the time we finally got around to discussing Motown, she made clear that she loved the company and the Gordys and was proud of her role in helping to create superstars.

But she made equally clear that she doesn't want to talk so much about Motown anymore. She said she doesn't want her entire life to be defined by a four-year job that paid $110 a week.

"I was here before Motown," she says.

The Maxine Powell story doesn't begin in 1964, when she first assembled Motown's stars in a circle and began teaching them everything from walking and talking to holding a microphone and singing without screwing up their faces.

It actually begins in Chicago where a young girl is raised by her aunt and uncle in a house frequented by painters and sculptors, many from programs at Northwestern and DePaul.

"My aunt did not work," Powell recalls. "She had a beautiful home and she canned everything in the world, she and her daughter — even watermelon rinds.

"We had a big house but this house had a cellar ... and it was a huge, huge room with shelves all the way around it and everything was canned. And she made wine by the barrel.

"When you came into our home, even if you were negative in manners and behavior, we had to treat you with the respect of a king or queen," she recalls.

Powell received charm instruction from the John Robert Powers School and eventually developed an entertainment career with an entrepreneurial spirit.

"I became an actress, a dramatic reader and later on, a professional dancer, producer and director of debutante balls, parties and fashion shows," Powell says. "Then I joined a dramatic league."

Powell remained in Chicago until she visited Detroit one weekend in the middle 1940s. By 1948, she had moved to Detroit. Within two years, she opened the Maxine Powell Finishing and Modeling School in the Ferry Center, a two-story mansion on East Ferry Street that was host to dances, wedding receptions, club meetings and fashion shows, most produced by Maxine Powell.

Her goals were simple: to create the city's first black modeling agency and to train models to be so graceful and poised that their race would not keep them from getting jobs.

She succeeded, and some of her students worked as models for car companies such as Chrysler and Dodge.

"She was very daring about business ventures," said Myzell Sowell, 76, a Detroit attorney who met Powell while she was running her modeling school.

"She never had any reluctance about things she believed in."

Powell took on the daunting task of providing social entertainment for an eclectic black clientele. Most of her functions took place at the Ferry Center.

"I remember when she opened it up and got it going and all that," Sowell said. "She was also interested in charitable endeavors. She was very community oriented, delivering to the community what she perceived that it needed by way of diverse sources of pleasure."

"Anything, pretty much, that was happening socially, Maxine Powell was right out front. Maxine knows so much about Detroit — it's a good thing nobody's asked her to do some kind of expose. She could come out with something wild," he said. "She was a source of inspiration for a lot of people younger than she was at the time. She's an amazing woman."

Powell explained her philosophy in a program booklet for an event at the Ferry Center, a fashion omnibus. She said "... every woman can be beautiful whether she is size 40 or age 60 ... and since no one will stay 18 years of age, and few will remain size 12, it is important to help women achieve the most from their basic beauty assets."

The program outlined her belief that by wearing the right makeup and clothing, any woman could make herself look great. Among her models, who were featured in the program as well, were some of Detroit's most beautiful young women:

Ruby McQuerry, Jean Graham, Frances Gilmore and Ruby Syfax Bruce. They all learned not only about grooming, but also about posture, glamour and grace.

Gwen Gordy wanted that poise and grace for Motown's stars. And she wanted a new role for Powell.

"Gwen Gordy would drag me around every time they appeared somewhere so that I could observe them and see what they needed," Powell said of the stars. "I don't teach puppets. I don't teach and take away people's identities. I have to see what they need to enhance what they have, so they stay unique and become a unique, beautiful human being."

Gwen Gordy convinced her brother that they should hire Powell to teach etiquette to the performers. He approved, so Powell closed her own finishing school and opened a finishing school in Motown called Artist Development.

She initially worked with the artists in one of the storefronts owned by the Gordys at St. Antoine and Farnsworth. (They would later move to West Grand Boulevard, where Berry Gordy was building an empire, contained in houses neighboring Hitsville USA.)

Before her first meeting with the artists, she said Berry Gordy let her announce the new department.

"They left me in charge. So I went downstairs and there was everybody that was in town. There was Smokey Robinson, the Temptations, Martha and the Vandellas, Diana Ross and the Supremes, the Marvelettes, the Velvelettes, and Stevie (Wonder) and Tammie Terrell.

"I put them all in a circle — I do that today. If I have 40 people, we just keep moving and moving until we get everybody in the circle, when I teach a class because I want everyone to come up front because everyone is somebody and I don't want them hiding in the back or feeling left out or feeling shy about who they are and what makes them tick.

"I told them we're going to open up a new department and it has nothing to do with singing because I can't hold a note. That caught their eye. They were all listening. I said, 'This department is going to help you appear in No. 1 places around the country and even before the king and queen.' This was 1964.

"Those youngsters looked at me and at each other and laughed and said, 'That woman's crazy. All we want is a hit record.' They did not have the vision."

The performers attended her class two hours every day, Monday through Friday, for four years, and she traveled the country with them.

"If anyone was on the road — so they did not misunderstand what his intention was with Artist Development — Berry Gordy sent them their itinerary so that everyone knew they had to come through Artist Development," she said.

She taught the performers a new set of ropes: Never turn your back on the audience, don't hold the mike like you're going to swallow it. She taught them how to give interviews, how to conduct themselves with pride and to be cognizant that their every move was being watched. And though she wasn't responsible for choreography, she worked on dance technique, too.

She once happened upon the Supremes doing a dance called the Shake, she told People magazine in 1986.

"You are protruding the buttocks. Whenever you do a naughty step like the Shake, add some class to it. Instead of shaking and acting tough, you should roll your buttocks under and keep smiling all the time. Then I showed them.

"They were shocked that I could do it and how much better it looked my way."

In no time, Powell was part of the Motown machine. As Maurice King taught Berry Gordy's young discoveries the art of singing and famed choreographer Cholly Atkins taught them the art of movement, she taught them the art of grace.

"Besides being one of the most interesting characters in my life and the lives of the Motown artists, she was just a really, really great person and a person who could tell the artists anything in any kind of voice and they would accept it because she was so important to them in terms of teaching them everything there was to know about grooming, how to put on makeup, how to walk in and out of cars," says Berry Gordy, chairman of Jobete Music Co. and West Grand Media.

"And not all of them loved it at that time, but they learned to live with it, and they grew to love it," he says. "She did so much for the artists and so much for all of us, actually."

When you're connected with a legend and living larger than life, the return to real life can be hard.

It seems that life outside the legend doesn't matter as much.

Maxine Powell left Motown in 1968, four years before Berry Gordy moved Motown to Los Angeles. Artist Development continued, as needed, in Detroit and in Los Angeles, but without Powell.

"Most of our artists were on their own. After a while ... they don't need that anymore," Gordy Edwards said.

Thirty-three years after leaving Motown, Powell, a chic, elegant spirit who doesn't so much walk into a room as stride with power, is fighting to reclaim a part of her history that has been living with the ghosts.

After three years of traveling and assessing her life, Powell returned to what she knew, becoming an instructor of personal development at Wayne County Community College, using the philosophies she developed through the years.

Since retiring in 1985, she continues to teach by appointment. She also entertains occasional requests for interviews about working with the original Motown stars. And she's collecting her notes and thoughts to tell her own story. Like Atkins, Powell says she is writing her memoir. It will include her years at the height of Detroit's social and fashion scene.

Telling her own story will help her celebrate the life she had outside of Motown and introduce people to the Maxine Powell they may not know.

"I was swept under the rug from 1968 when I left Motown until 1985 when they gave a tribute for me," she said.

That tribute drew hundreds to the Roostertail in east Detroit, renewed interest in her story and led to a People magazine article and producers calling from England and Australia for interviews.

But the questions are still only about Motown, she said. And she wants the world to see more: She is Maxine Powell, a young Chicago native who moved to Detroit to teach women how to be beautiful.

Even if there had never been Motown, she still might have changed the world.

June 17, 2001

Service, love and laughter fed volunteers' hearts

If you want to have a good time, get some of the silver-haired volunteers from the St. Matthew Meals on Wheels program to tell you about the 425,000 or so hot meals they delivered over a quarter century.

Like the time Janey Quinn littered Eileen Hatty's car. Each team has a driver and a runner. The driver pulls up to the curb and the runner takes the food to the door.

"Janey feeds the dogs," Eileen said of some clients' pets who also need food.

"And she dropped a piece of dog biscuit in my car. My husband picked it up and put it in his pocket because he thought it was my hearing aid. He carried it around for the longest time waiting for me to ask for it. Finally, he said 'Do you need your hearing aid?' And I said 'It's in my ear.' He pulled out the dog biscuit and said, 'Boy, is my face red!' "

Then there was the time that Betty Fennell, 74, climbed out of the car with food, stepped into 2 feet of snow and got stuck. She fell backwards, and all you could see was her knees.

"I couldn't get up," she recalls with a laugh. Not until her husband, John, 77, helped, and they completed their mission.

But there was also the time the Fennells arrived to find a client who had fatally shot himself.

It was more than volunteering that made these angels, these retirees mostly in their 70s and 80s, spend hours a day dropping off meals to people who looked like them. It was out of love that the team — many from the St. Matthew Catholic parish in east Detroit and in the St. Ambrose parish in Grosse Pointe Park — heated and delivered food from St. Matthew.

But on Sept. 30, Meals on Wheels closed its local distribution sites. It plans to make all deliveries from a hub on East Grand Boulevard at Woodward Avenue. The program wants to save money and increase efficiency, but left behind are the elder volunteers for whom the program is now too far away for them to help.

Over the years, the way services are delivered to elderly people has evolved. Meals on Wheels is not immune, said Carla Webb, director of Detroit's program.

She wants to make sure that "everyone is getting the same product with the same quality from the same location." The program still will deliver 2,500 meals every day, she said, and paid deliverers have been trained in customer service.

But that brought little comfort to some of the volunteers.

"It's sad for the people (who get meals) and it's sad for the volunteers," said Dee Clark, the nurse who not only takes care of the parish, but looks out for the volunteers and takes their blood pressure every week.

"The volunteers did it because they wanted to. The paid people will do it because they have to."

She said there was another benefit to having older volunteers visiting older clients.

"They were my eyes and ears," she says. "They'll tell me 'This lady is sick or that lady hasn't bathed all week.' They deliver more than a meal."

As so many of the volunteers pointed out, the meals deliverer sometimes was the only person some clients would see all day.

Betty Fennell recalls the time she visited a man whose son had just mailed him his annual birthday shirt.

"He said 'I don't need another shirt.' I wouldn't be able to do that to my mom or dad."

The senior volunteers will be missed: With age had come dependability and the providing of not just hot food, but comfort.

Eileen Hatty, who has coordinated the food deliveries from St. Matthew for the past 25 years, is 72. She and her fellow deliverers have gotten to know her clients very well — the ones who don't like spaghetti and the ones who think potatoes with the peeling still on are "dirty."

"Nobody has ever quit the program," says Eileen, whose energy and affection for her fellow deliverers is contagious. "People have moved to Florida. They have died. And they have become too ill to work, but nobody said, 'I don't want to do this any more.'"

But when the team got together Friday morning for coffee and cake, it was their last hurrah, a farewell party for workers who became friends.

They greeted each other warmly, exchanged facts about their surgeries (Frank Lewandowski, at 57 the baby of the bunch, has had six). The ladies hugged each other and chatted about family. Eileen brought out photographs from past years, but no one could remember the dates.

"We can't tell from the clothes because we wear things forever," Eileen said. "It must be at least 10 years, because I've got black hair."

Eileen, a 5-foot dynamo who will find other things to do in her neighborhood, was honored Friday with a resolution from her friends and volunteers. In addition to recognizing her dedication and service, volunteer Wendy Hamilton also praised Eileen because she "has consistently given generous raises with her famous phrase '20 percent of zero is still zero' " and she "believed that you're never late until you don't show up."

Father Duane Novelly of St. Matthew said it wasn't a job for the volunteers.

"It was the service of the faithful."

Faith is the evidence of things not seen. Though they may never meet Eileen Hatty, I hope the new deliverers borrow her smile.

October 7, 2001

250 bikes bring kids magic

Yes, Ronald and Jennifer and Nicholas and Dennis and Curtis and Bianca, there is a Santa Claus.

He is as real as when journalist Francis P. Church answered an 8-year-old's doubts about Santa in an editorial in the New York Sun in 1897.

He is as real as the hearts of people who make you happy without knowing you, without wanting anything in return, without asking for a receipt for their good turn.

He is as real as New Hudson businessman Ed Swadish and the joy of a Saturday afternoon Christmas party at St. Hedwig's, where kids who had dreamed of bikes for Christmas saw their dreams come true.

There was so much to do Saturday that there were two Santa Clauses for the 250 children at the 10th anniversary Christmas party. The Renaissance Youth Center hosted the event at St. Hedwig's Catholic Church.

Few of them expressed concern about there being two Santas and whether one was the other one's brother or uncle, or whether everybody at the North Pole dressed like that — because quite frankly, they were wondering about five rows of neatly leaning, shiny bicycles along one whole side of the basement.

The kids were having so much fun hugging 9-foot-tall Woody and Buzz Lightyear and playing games that they didn't swarm over the 250 red, blue, purple and pink bicycles that tugged at them, the ones they figured had nothing to do with them. A few kids asked and were told they were being stored, but not for how long.

But at 1:45 p.m., a booming voice came over the mike and said that Santa, and Santa, were ready for the kids and that every child, every one of them, would get their very own bike — right then, at the party.

There was stunned silence, because it is impossible to talk when you're taking in air. The quiet erupted with oohs and ahhs and a few squeals, but mostly there was longing, a real need among the children to get their hands on a bike.

The children sat as hard as they could, awaiting their turn at a Santa, one by one, and their chance to get their new mode of transportation. But within just a half hour, the St. Hedwig's basement was one big roller derby of smiles and rolling wheels.

For the grown-ups in that basement, the ones for whom Santa is a memory or a friend of their children, Christmas came alive again.

And for the children, especially those who had begun to stop believing in magic, the magic returned.

Many of the children belong to families who are struggling this holiday, children who know that big toys for Christmas are usually just wishes.

Linda Wilson, who is on medical leave from Motor City Casino, said, "Things are kind of tight right now." She added that her 10-year-old daughter, Bianca, who rarely smiles, really wanted a bike but Wilson didn't know how she'd be able to afford one.

Badria Rivera, 37, wasn't sure how she was going to make an exciting Christmas for her three children.

"I've been saving for almost three years to get them bikes," she said. "I knew it wasn't going to happen.

"I bought them used bikes from a garage sale four years ago, but they get so big and the bikes are so small."

Rivera and her husband are both on medical leave from jobs they no longer have. Both worked for Mexican Industries, a Cinderella business story that didn't turn out as well as the original. The company went under as her husband was having two surgeries on his back.

Carol Strawser, 36, is a former secretary at St. Vincent de Paul who had to stop working to spend the months leading into the holiday season recovering from skin cancer. Her son Ronald Rogers, 10, desperately wanted a bike for Christmas. His mom took him to the Christmas party so that he could have some fun, play some games and get a small gift.

But this Christmas party was different. And Mary Swadish, whose husband, provided the bikes, was excited about the moment she had been waiting for — not a moment that honored her husband, but a moment when she could watch children's eyes dance.

"This is Christmas to me," she said just before the children heard about their gifts.

That moment came as quickly as a snowfall that just happens, sometimes if we're lucky, on Christmas Day.

And it came not a moment too soon for some of the children, whose parents are struggling to make ends meet, and who knew this Christmas not to ask for expensive toys.

The bicycles were not just exciting because they're the all-American toy. But who can't remember the first time you sailed along with the wind in your hair, enjoying every moment before you realized that the hand that steadied you was still down the street, attached to a smiling parent who let you know you were OK and that it was all you guiding your bike?

The bikes were important because, as Church told Virginia O'Hanlon — whose friends had stopped believing — Santa reminds us of "how dreary the world if there were no Santa Claus! It would be as dreary as if there were no Virginias. There would be no childlike faith then, no poetry, no romance to make tolerable this existence. We should have no enjoyment, except in sense and sight. The external light with which childhood fills the world would be extinguished.

"Not believe in Santa Claus! You might as well not believe in fairies. You might get your papa to hire men to watch in all the chimneys on Christmas Eve to catch Santa Claus, but even if you did not see Santa Claus coming down, what would that prove? Nobody sees Santa Claus, but that is no sign that there is no Santa Claus. The most real things in the world are those that neither children nor men can see."

Ed Swadish is one of those angels you don't see. Until Saturday, he had never met the people at a center he's been helping since last April. That was when the sponsor of the Renaissance Youth Center's annual Easter celebration backed out at the last minute.

Swadish came through after seeing a plea for help on the TV news. Then he came through again at Halloween to ensure that the kids in the struggling southwest Detroit neighborhood surrounding the center could get treats instead of tricks.

The youth center's staff pulls no punches in getting things for their kids, mostly students from Detroit public schools who come to the center for homework help and to play games in the afternoon. The center is in a neighborhood struggling to reach better days, the kind of place where kids have to be smart to survive. They have to know which side of the street to walk on and which characters to avoid because they're usually peddling drugs.

Program coordinator Armando Armendariz was the one who made the televised plea last spring. And he was the one who called Swadish a week ago

Friday to ask whether he'd buy small gifts to distribute at the annual Christmas party.

"I'd never met Armando," Swadish said. "He's a real good guy and seems pretty concerned about the kids.

"I told him I usually give 15 or 20 bikes a year. He said, 'Mr. Swadish, I've got 250 kids! How could I pick 20 kids? For some of my kids this party is all they usually get. How about getting everybody a $4 board game?' "

Swadish told Armendariz that he'd get back to him. He did.

"I got a hold of Huffy (bike dealers), and they said they'd sell the bikes to me wholesale," Swadish recalled. "So I called him back and said, 'How about I get everybody a bike?' "

Silence greeted him on the phone, and Armando Armendariz, who is rarely speechless, was.

So that's how Ed Swadish went back to the old neighborhood for the youth center's 10th anniversary Christmas party, with family and employees and friends in tow, to meet young children who are just like he was 30 years ago.

He gave each child at the party more than a bike. Hopefully, he gave them a look at what they can be.

Swadish, 39, grew up in Brightmoor, a poor and working-class neighborhood between 5 Mile and Schoolcraft, Telegraph and Lahser, just a few miles from the neighborhood where the Renaissance Youth Center is a safe haven for kids who desperately need one.

"It's always been a kind of poor neighborhood," he said. "I lived there from the time I was 5 until I was 25."

Swadish attended Redford High, where he "was a terrible student. I graduated with a D- average, and right out of high school, I started working at a paper plant. Two years later, they went out of business."

So, at 19 and out of work, he became an entrepreneur.

"I started a paper company right out of my dad's house in Brightmoor, all 600 square feet of it. Customers would pull up in front, and we'd load up on the front lawn. We sold paper rolls, mostly cash register receipt rolls that we manufacture."

Swadish went out of business in a year. "I owed one guy $400 and one guy $200. They wanted to repossess my car, and me and my dad have the same name, so they took his car.

"I said, 'Dad, one day we'll laugh about this!' Every now and again, I say, 'Dad, are we laughing about that yet? And he says, 'No.' "

Swadish, undeterred, started his company, Discount Paper Products, again. The second time took, and now he is president of a multimillion-dollar company with offices in New Hudson and Las Vegas. He and his wife and two sons live in a 7,000-square-foot home in Milford, and he considers himself one lucky man.

He's also a man who believes in giving back. So when he and his wife, Mary, saw the news last April about a youth center in trouble, he jumped in with both feet. Swadish has answered calls from the center ever since. That's why he didn't think twice about taking the call for Christmas gifts.

And that's how the sales room at his company became "the parts department," he said, strewn with screws, wheels, handlebars and seats for 250 bikes that had to be put together in a day.

And that's what led a bunch of elves — employees, family, friends and a few firefighters, a UPS guy named Scott and a proud father whose son bears his name — to the plant on a Saturday to put together those bikes.

(Ed and his dad, "The Wrench," assembled 53 bikes on Friday night. "We had fun," the son said. The proud dad wasn't talking.) Jeff Anderson, a sales rep at the company, worked on a team of engineers and mechanics Saturday morning that put together 42 bikes in 75 minutes.

In total, volunteers assembled 190 bikes between 7:45 and 9 a.m. on Saturday. Then they put them on the trucks and a caravan rolled out of North Pole-New Hudson at 9:54 a.m.

Christmas came not a moment too soon to save the magic for children who don't always see a lot of magic.

As Ronald Rogers — the 10-year-old whose mother is recovering from cancer, the one who hadn't planned to ask for the bike he so wanted this year — maneuvered a brand-new bike around the basement floor, his smile was so big it preceded him and laid down a magic carpet for him to sail around on.

He zoomed over to his mom, who might not have been able to give him that smile in eight days, and said, "Mom, I love this bike. Can I really take this home?"

Yes, Ronald, there is a Santa Claus.

December 17, 2001

A city where angels don't fear to tread

It would be so easy to surrender to Detroit stereotypes, to see only the negative, to ask: What kind of city is this?

But this city I'm growing to love is a place with angels and devils. It deserves to be seen from above and below.

It's the kind of place where someone steals a bank card and PIN number from my mail and goes to 13 ATMs to steal $3,400.

But it's also a place where bank employees feed me Kleenex, fix my problem and send investigators after the thief.

It's a place where some police officers dishonor their uniforms — shooting a man with a rake!?

But it's also a place where two officers stop traffic to help a man in a wheelchair cross the street. Officers Keith Rainer and John Smith (on the force for 14 years, partners for six) see a man with no legs barely making it. So they block the intersection with the squad car and Rainer gets out and walks beside the man, preserving his dignity, not behind him, like he's an inconvenience.

It's a place being deserted for the suburbs, creating a ring around this city that might make metro Detroit eventually touch Lansing.

But it's also a place with reasons to stay — museums, ballparks and proximity to work.

It's a place that invites people to move in without cleaning for company — dirty streets, faulty lights, dilapidated buildings, faulty phone lines.

But it's a place where arts and sports rule (whether teams win or not), where people like Steve Hamp, director of the Henry Ford Museum & Greenfield Village, work tirelessly to preserve the nation's industrial heritage and pieces of history that include Thomas Edison's actual lab and a replica of George Washington Carver's home.

It's a place that fits the stereotypes people threw at me when I announced my move. They suggested I buy a gun, asked how often I would visit my daughter (because surely I would be going alone) and told me how cold parts of my body would be this winter.

But it's also a place where a director nurtures a mosaic of theater students, teachers pay for school supplies and 30,000 volunteers make Angels' Night safe.

It's a place where a thief takes a kid's PlayStation 2.

But it's a place where angels have pounded their stake into the dirt and are getting it together, not just because a Super Bowl is coming.

It's a place where it's possible to envision runners and skaters in a sprawling park in the heart of downtown, where communities and companies turn vacant downtown buildings into shelters, Boys and Girls clubs or high-rise schools.

It's a place where pockets of pride are here and there, struggling to be seen, like flowers blooming through a cracked sidewalk.

It's a place where you can meet the best on the street and you know them. When you speak, they speak back, displaying a gentility that lingers from the times when black folks traveled the Underground Railroad and willing immigrants traveled by boat and wagon to reach a growing port needing workers.

It's a place where angels live in neighborhoods without names, but have clean yards and an eye on each other's children. It is the angels that newcomers move here to meet. It's the angels who make life here worthwhile.

November 15, 2000

History happens at Bethel

We don't always know it when it happens, when history is being made. In many cases, we know a moment is special. But only in the looking back can magic be ranked.

It happened in Washington, D.C., when Dr. Martin Luther King Jr. spoke in 1963 to more than 250,000 souls who endured hot August sun to hear words to help them keep their eyes on the prize.

And, years from now, my daughter and I will be able to say we heard George Shirley, the Grammy-winning, internationally known tenor who was the first African-American tenor to sing a leading role at the Metropolitan Opera House.

Now a professor of music at the University of Michigan, Shirley didn't just sing Friday at Detroit's Bethel A.M.E. Church. He celebrated the legacy of the legendary tenor Roland Hayes, whose pioneering concerts over 50 years paved the way for many of today's black opera stars.

It was Hayes' spirit we heard in Shirley's voice as he sang "L'il Boy," Hayes' signature piece. As Shirley's voice soared, I heard colors, yellows and blues, purple mountains, majesty. I heard a genius interpret a giant.

It was a fitting tribute for Hayes, who from his birth in Curryville, Ga., through his youth in Chattanooga, Tenn., and his college years at Fisk University in Nashville, was undeterred in pursuing vocal achievement.

After college, when he moved to Louisville, Ky., he supported himself by singing arias during silent movies at a local theater. He sang though he had to stand behind a screen to hide his skin color.

Hayes had to become a star in Europe before America embraced him, but he did and America did. And he was the first singer, according to archivists, to include Negro spirituals in his repertoire, ensuring their place on stage forever.

His career was 50 years long, but many people know little about him.

The Detroit Public Library intends to change that. It has obtained Hayes' personal papers — 48 boxes of correspondence, concert programs, recordings, academic stoles representing his honorary degrees, sheet music and hundreds of photographs — from Hayes' home in Brookline, Mass.

The staff is processing the papers for inclusion in the world-renowned Hackley Collection, named for Azalea Hackley, the Detroit singer and choral director who traveled the country conducting community choirs and educating black children about classical music.

The library's director, Dr. Maurice Wheeler, went to Brookline to retrieve Hayes' papers, which will be available to the public within a year.

"At the height of his career, most concert halls in this country were segregated," Wheeler said. "African Americans and many other people regardless of their background could not afford the cost of a ticket to see him. So he spent a lot of time singing in African-American churches."

Hayes's legacy deserves further study, Wheeler said.

"The importance of his career isn't taught as much as it should be. We hear about Marian Anderson and Paul Robeson, but we don't hear much about Roland Hayes.

"I'm hoping that our activities will start to change that."

March 28, 2001

Star shines a light
on Detroit arts

Sidney Poitier going anywhere should be an international event, cause for celebration, cause for watches and work to stop.

Over the top, you say?

Not when you speak of a man who has personified grace, perseverance and elegance in an industry that, until his arrival, couldn't quite bring itself to see that in a black man.

Only a few black men in history have shifted cultural spectrums, turned prejudices upside down, caused people to look at an entire race differently. Poitier did for Hollywood what Arthur Ashe did in changing the face of men's tennis: provided an unexpected and lasting elegance that made people change their values. Both gained global adulation because their excellence was not only gravity-defying but also race-defying.

So why bring up Sidney Poitier three months after his emotional appearance at the Academy Awards, where he stood to watch Halle Berry and Denzel Washington both win a top prize that until that night only he had received?

Poitier is a metaphor for Detroit's arts community, which is full of grace and excellence and surprises, but which people take for granted and no longer shout about.

Sidney Poitier was in town for Bal Africain, the annual fund-raising celebration held by Friends of African and African-American Art and the Detroit Institute of Arts.

It's been a few years since screaming throngs greeted his every move, but why should the screaming stop?

Sidney Poitier is old enough to be my father. Heck, he's older than my father. His legs might be thinner and his hair grayer, but that walk has not changed. His charm, oh, how he charms, is as wonderfully disarming as it was in "Guess Who's Coming to Dinner?"

But we take him for granted as part of the fabric of our history. We know what he's done, so the reverence is implied. That's how we feel sometimes about Detroit's arts. Detroit can get so busy counting its negatives that it forgets its positives.

That may be why Detroit doesn't market itself more. It's too ashamed of the things it hasn't fixed — the dilapidated buildings, its schools — to point out the things that work in the arts: theaters that rival Chicago's, music that was the Sound of Young America and is now redefined in electronic triumph and in festivals big and small.

Detroit has an amazing arts community, one that thrives under the negative spotlight the city shines on itself even more than the world does.

Now, don't get me wrong. Don't think that Mr. Poitier was greeted with anything less than exuberant adoration while here. But no crowds lined the red carpet to scream at him. No TV cameras swarmed to give Detroit a glimpse of the Man Who Did Become King in 1963.

If we cannot celebrate our greatest actor, then maybe that's why we don't celebrate our greatest assets — museums, local talent, concert venues — and our assets with great potential, the Charles H. Wright Museum of African-American History, our youth and the riverfront.

So even as we watch our mayor struggle for change, pushing a boulder of inertia (that has some City Council members sitting on top and is slowed by some residents who long ago gave up), there are positives whose futures we must ensure.

Bal Africain and our arts entities, which stretch from the Detroit River to Troy and from St. Clair County to Dearborn, are some of them.

June 21, 2002

Huge events help us see what can be

In case you weren't looking, Detroit may have just completed a great double play.

The baseball metaphor is appropriate since Detroit is in the middle of extra innings, after a seventh-inning stretch that saw the lights go out, part of the stadium burn down — and some of the crowd leave for good.

But as long and methodical as baseball can be, when greatness comes, you don't want to miss it.

The recent double play consisted of two distinct events that had more in common than organizers might have contemplated.

Last Saturday, 58,000 volunteers — the largest number ever — gathered in spots around Detroit to help with the city-sponsored Clean Sweep, picking up more than 400,000 bags of garbage and sprucing up yards.

Last Sunday, 10,000 went to Cobo Hall for the annual Detroit NAACP dinner, which commemorates victories in the civil rights struggle and encourages the continued fight.

Both events were just that: events. They went off without a hitch. They produced feelings of pride and purpose.

But it is what happens now, after the organized hoopla is over, after the media have gone, that means everything.

Now that the Clean Sweep is over, what Glenn Oliver wants is the Big Change.

Oliver, the city executive assigned to oversee Detroit's makeover, has said he wants Detroit to change the way it lives. Then, instead of having an annual cleanup that lasts one day before the littering and dumping of cars starts again, we can move forward and focus on something besides cleaning up.

Oliver is talking psychological transformation, returning pride to the city. He wants us to get beyond just clean. We need to get to the point where we actually talk about making Detroit beautiful with our own art and aesthetic pleasures similar to those that so define other cities.

In recent months, Oliver has spoken of statues and murals, artistic symbols of Detroit's future and its place in the world.

If we keep working, then weeks after the official cleanup has ended, we'll continue to sweep and fix and maintain, street by street, neighborhood by neighborhood, so we can get to the point of dressing up.

Sitting in a ballroom larger than any I'd been in, watching four giant daises placed around the room (Who says you can't get everybody important onstage?), I watched the most massive undertaking to serve chicken and veggies that I'd ever seen: the annual NAACP dinner.

The political, social and financial power in the room could save Detroit, if that kind of crowd ever got together just to talk about saving Detroit — and brought their checkbooks with them.

But the idea of watching it get done showed me that greater things are possible.

What we have to do is make the one-time events daily missions, make the big deal a daily promise.

Detroit has seen incremental progress in its effort to rise from its own ashes. We may argue about how we get there and disagree about who leads us. But let's not forget that the point is to get there.

And getting there means keeping our eyes on the ball.

Remember what Leroy (Satchel) Paige said in 1920: "Don't look back, something might be gaining on you."

For us, that somebody is Detroit's past. If we keep looking back, we might just miss the future.

May 6, 2001

Archer leaves Detroit a path to prosperity

On the day Mayor Dennis Archer announced that he wouldn't seek re-election, I was standing on a hill nearly 4,000 miles away at the base of the Basilique du Sacre Coeur, which affords one of the best views of Paris.

Throughout Paris, on the streets of Montmartre, in the Latin Quarter, I was awed by how deftly this city has blended its older structures with chic new shops and cafes.

The miles separating me from home were more than linear. Paris is miles from Detroit in celebrating its past without being victimized by it. I pondered this as, an ocean away, Archer planned his exit.

Now Detroit must decide what it wants. Its residents and co-residents, which is what Detroit suburbanites are, must decide whether they want to live in, and be linked to, a failing urban sinkhole or a jewel on the river.

This is a watershed year for Detroit. Historians will look back in 50 years and say: 2001 was the turning point. It was the moment the city reached the fork in the road and decided to take the road less traveled (regional cooperation, legislative respect, intense marketing of Detroit's good points) or the road most traveled (It's impossible. We can't do anything because no one will help! It's bad, but that's just the way it is).

I had intended to ask the mayor to reconsider because he has inspired and accomplished real change and done more to help Detroit than Detroit has done to help itself.

But then I bumped into Archer, who seems at peace.

"No mayor will ever finish the job if he cares about his city," he said calmly, quietly. "If I stayed another four years, I'd be asked to stay another four. The job is never done. The best you can do is hope to leave it in better shape than how you found it."

Detroit is losing a mayor who posed with his white friends and potential investors on the front page of the newspaper, not in a back office like it's wrong to think we can all get along. He helped change this city from a decaying mess into one that will host a Super Bowl. He showed a nation a

221

new vision and made a dent in the entrenched, way-to-look-out-for-a-brother-with-that-job mentality that has been Detroit government.

Now that he's leaving, the work does not fall to one set of shoulders.

So, for each of you who has complained about the City Council, but never attended a City Council meeting,

For each of you who has complained about the school board, but never joined a PTA,

For each of you who has walked past your filthy lawn into your tore-up house, not tending yours or helping elderly neighbors tend theirs,

For those of you who steal from shops and close them so your mama and her friends have no store nearby,

For those of you who have decided you're not going to help Detroit, you're just going to wait until you've saved enough to move to Southfield,

For all of you, consider this: When we do nothing to help our city, we cannot blame others for its demise.

And for those of you who mow the yards and plant the flowers and fight for the schools and create neighborhood watches and join the PTA: You are the future of Detroit, the people that new residents want to have as neighbors and jogging buddies.

One of this city's brightest stars has laid a path. It is up to the city, not just another mayor, to follow it.

April 29, 2001

'American Idol' misses the real Detroit

Some things about Detroit are obvious: the trash, the abandoned buildings.

That is the Detroit the nation is used to seeing, whether it's in the dark despair of Eminem's film "8 Mile" or the loss of a money-making music factory such as Motown to nurture talent.

But the Detroit singers seen on "American Idol" last week in auditions that continue tonight are easy to defend.

It is OK to look at the positive things in Detroit. And one of those is the abundance of musical talent that exists here even without a 21st-Century Berry Gordy to groom it.

That talent exists in church choirs and community theaters, in dozens of clubs whose garage bands are moving more frequently out of the garage and into the national spotlight.

The Motown legacy can be heard in the voices of third-graders who know all the words to "Ain't Too Proud To Beg" and "My Girl." That legacy is what brought me to such frustration over the Detroit auditions.

You saw it, and many of you heard about it. I know because you called me or stopped me with a "Can you believe they said that?"

The "Idol" judges, after surviving hundreds of lackluster auditions, said the "Mo" had left Motown, and that Detroit had lost its edge.

As a matter of fact, the worst of the auditions in the multicity tryout tour that pitted celebrity judges against celebrity wanna-bes came from Detroit. The show's producers really played the Detroit misery card big. The segment featured vignettes of the hopeless struggles of people on the fringe, including a "60 Minutes"-like profile of a single mom-boxer looking for a way out for her son.

The segment left the impression that this city is just one big cesspool that all its residents are trying to escape.

The only problem is that story isn't totally true. Not every Detroiter looks for success in a song.

223

Detroit has enough musical genius to retain bragging rights to creating the Sound of Young America.

Back then, that sound was produced by Hitsville USA and took as its label the name of the city that produced its stars: Diana Ross, Marvin Gaye, Mary Wells and Smokey Robinson. Now, that sound is the White Stripes and Eminem and Kid Rock and the techno-geniuses whose electronic prowess led to the creation of a festival attended by more than 1 million people. About half that many turn out to hear local and national jazz artists during the world's largest jazz festival.

Hitsville USA was the '60s version of "American Idol," except that the talents nurtured there actually could sing and write music.

In Detroit, there are young voices that would have knocked Simon Cowell's socks (and smirky grin) off.

They were performing at Wayne State University during Mosaic Youth Theater Ensemble's annual concert, evoking such emotions during their renditions of spirituals and ragtime that the crowd leaped to its feet.

They sing, but plan to be doctors and teachers and lawyers, not easy-to-heat pop tarts who can be dressed up to look good. It's not that there isn't enough talent in Detroit. The judges left with 22 singers from our auditions.

The "Mo" hasn't left Motown. It just has better things to do.

January 29, 2003

Say something — but what? — about Detroit

The commercial really caught my attention. In it, a thirtysomething woman is outside a wedding chapel, kissing the young stud she has apparently just married. She bids him good-bye and walks away. But suddenly, she runs back, bouquet in hand, for more kisses. Then she leaves again for good.

The commercial's tag line: "What happens here, stays here." It's an ad for Las Vegas. And you know what it means. You can do things you wouldn't want the Sunday School at home to know about.

And it made me wonder: What is Detroit's tag line?

Let me give you a minute to get the jokes out of the way, the ones about crime, guns and carjackings, which happen in all big cities. Don't call me with the road jokes: "Coming to a movie theater near you — 'Holes' — or as we call it in Michigan, Detroit."

Detroit has a catchphrase: "It's a Great Time in Detroit." But what does that mean?

I'm no expert. But I do know what works. So I called the guy who came up with Las Vegas's latest national catchphrase and asked for advice.

"You have to talk to the people who come to visit you," says Randy Snow, vice president and executive creative director of R&R Partners. "What is the essence of Las Vegas that brings you back? We hear the same thing over and over and over. It's this idea that I can do things in Vegas that I wouldn't even think about doing at home."

He suggests that Detroit learn what connects it with people emotionally and reach out to those who haven't written it off.

That sounds like good advice for a city some people still think burns up every Halloween.

I thought about it last year when Detroit Police Chief Jerry Oliver told me that "Normal is the problem here," speaking to our acceptance of a horrible status quo.

It struck me again this week when Chrysler Group president and CEO

Dieter Zetsche said he was "always surprised that people don't understand."

Brad Van Dommelen, the Detroit Metro Convention and Visitors Bureau's senior vice president of strategic business development, wants to make Detroit a destination, but mostly for people within a five-hour drive from here.

The bureau spends zero dollars on ads in the tri-county area and almost none nationally, preferring to lobby meeting planners and influence national travel writers on our music history, sports legacy and automotive prowess. Van Dommelen also wants the media to do more positive stories.

But we forget that when we face out of the city to crow about what's good here, our backs are turned to the city's heart and those here at home who need to hear it, too.

What if the bureau actually marketed Detroit to the residents who live along the spokes of this wheel but abhor its center, as if they are not connected to it?

Detroit's biggest secret weapons could be metro Detroiters, who visit the Detroit Institute of Arts, for instance, at a rate of 2:1 over nonresidents. Detroit should rekindle the romance it once had with them. And instead of just chasing golden strangers, the city could tout itself to those who never left. They could be our best ambassadors and saviors closer to home.

Now about that catchphrase. It hasn't quite the same ring as "I Love New York," "Virginia is for Lovers" and "What Happens Here, Stays Here." If you have an idea for a new one, send it to me.

Detroit thanks you.

April 18, 2003

Detroit lovers everywhere: Advertise your city

You know the old saying: Everybody's a comedian!

In Detroit, everybody's in advertising!

When I recently lamented how poorly Detroit markets itself and wondered aloud why we didn't have a slogan as cool as Las Vegas' ("What happens here, stays here!"), I asked why Detroit's powers-that-be didn't do a better job of making ambassadors out of metro Detroit residents. Who better to get others to visit? I also questioned the effectiveness of our current slogan, "It's a Great Time in Detroit," and whether it really grabs you.

I invited readers to come up with a grabbier slogan, one we could suggest to Brad Van Dommelen, the Detroit Metro Convention and Visitors Bureau's senior vice president of strategic business development, who wants to make Detroit a destination, who gets that Detroit's best marketers may be its residents and who's working on a new campaign.

And Detroit responded.

Some folks came up with entire marketing campaigns. For instance, Bev Clark of Detroit, a freelance writer who spent 20 years in public relations, offered a strategy to speak to the people I mentioned in my column, those Detroiters trying to stone Detroit to death and those who live in a ring around Detroit and throw darts at it, who "live along the spokes of the wheel, but abhor its center as if they're not connected to it."

Clark suggested a photo of Detroit Mayor Kwame Kilpatrick and Wayne County Executive Bob Ficano standing back-to-back, each with arms folded, each smiling with a smirk. The tag line:

"Detroit: Wanna Make Somethin' Of It?"

Clark says her campaign "addresses the concept that the people who live in an area are responsible for supporting it."

She suggests sending new "I Wanna Make Somethin' Of It" kits to metro Detroiters with information on all the programs that they've forgotten about or may not have heard of: Angels' Night, Greening of

Detroit, Blight Busters and Neighborhood City Hall services. The kit also would include schedules for the four major league sports teams, the locations of Parks and Recreation Centers and a "Make Somethin' of Detroit" bumper sticker.

" 'Wanna make somethin' of it' — them's fightin' words," Clark wrote, "and that's the idea. But the little smile on the faces of people who already care make it a friendly challenge, maybe even filled with hope."

Clark wasn't alone in her enthusiasm or suggestions. We expected a few errant rocks thrown from those who can't help it or those who have given up. But the vast majority of possible slogans came from folks who love Detroit's history, music, population, culture, which is among the most diverse in the nation, and its spunk. The best of the rest follow:

Bob Chvala of Farmington Hills offered: "Detroit Driving Our Dreams" — "since 'we suck less than Cleveland' would probably not evoke that sense of purpose that a slogan should provide."

Jean Barnard of Sterling Heights sent: "Detroit: What you'll do here, you'll brag about when you get home!"

Jan Turner of Huntington Woods sent: "Detroit: It's not the greatest, but it's close!"

Dr. Lisa Rogers, a Henry Ford neurologist who lives on Grosse Ile, suggested: "Detroit: It just keeps getting better." She said that, "in a way that could have a negative connotation, but everyone knows that Detroit has had a hard time and this gives it a positive spin.

Georgia Phelan of St. Clair County said: "Come Into Detroit: The Party's Waiting!"

Kathy Forster of Grosse Pointe sent: "We're on a roll, Detroit!" (The ad campaign could feature "the wheels of time, autos, buggies, buses, skateboards, bicycles, and even dice ...," she wrote. "It would be very easy to produce a series of 15-second ads to a Motown beat."

Joie Middlebrook of Northbrook says her favorite sentiment was one she learned from her father.

"My dad, a retired 40-year firefighter (retired Detroit Fire Department senior chief Edward Tujaka Sr.) taught me to always look people in the eye and smile and say hello. ... You wouldn't believe how much Detroiters smile and say hello back."

Her offering: "Detroit: Smile and Say Hello."

Robert Smith Jr. of Detroit offered: "Detroit: A thrill a minute when you're in it!"

And finally, Ann Rock of Livonia, reminded:

"Detroit: The fat lady hasn't sung yet!"

April 27, 2003

CHAPTER SIX

LIFE IN WORDS

(THE CAMPAIGN FOR ADULT LITERACY)

Illiteracy damages all citizens

Here's what some people in Detroit can and cannot do.

They can usually sign their names, but cannot locate their eligibility from a table of employee benefits.

They can usually identify a country in a short article, but cannot locate an intersection on a street map.

They can locate the expiration date on a driver's license, but cannot enter background information on a Social Security card application.

Those things they can't do are impossible because they cannot read or read only at the lowest level of ability.

I've been writing about this problem for more than a year now, since July 2001, and two things are true: Most of the 47 percent of Detroit residents 16 and over who can't read well CAN learn. And most adults who can read don't understand that illiteracy is a problem that affects us all.

Is your interest only in economics? Consider the economic impact of nearly half of a city's adult residents reading at the lowest basic level:

• Unable to understand government so they don't vote;

• Unable to be trained for the jobs that economic development officials want new companies to bring here;

• Unable to understand school work so they can't help with homework;

• Unable to process environmental concerns so they can't support efforts to protect our natural resources.

Is your interest only in making sure that young kids can read? Consider that thousands of Detroit schoolchildren arrive at school unable to read and write. Teachers load them with lessons and send them home to practice with parents who cannot read their child's materials.

The assessment that revealed metro Detroit's problems with literacy revealed a nation's problem. The National Adult Literacy Survey showed that 21 percent to 23 percent — or 40 million to 44 million of America's 191 million adults 16 and older read at the lowest literacy level.

Detroit's biggest problem with illiteracy is admitting that such a basic problem is at the root of nearly every other single problem that the city has, economic, educational and social.

Now consider the fact that it isn't just Detroit's problem. Double-digit illiteracy rates plague Oakland and Macomb counties. And nearly one of five adults across the state cannot read.

So folks, the secret is out and the Metro Detroit Reads campaign to promote adult reading has begun. I'm thankful for the support it received thus far.

Five area literacy centers, joined by the Detroit Free Press, and partners that include the Detroit Pistons, DaimlerChrysler, SBC Ameritech and several elected officials, are making a difference already.

In just a month, the centers have signed up nearly 200 new tutors, one-fifth of the campaign's goal. More than 100 people have sought help to learn to read.

Now the job is convincing others.

It isn't easy.

It requires proud people with secrets to seek help.

If you know one of those people, tell them there's a whole world waiting for them.

September 29, 2002

A reader at last

U.V. Irby decided long ago to put his life on the back burner.

As a child, he helped his family of sharecroppers pick cotton in Tunica, Miss. He quit school in the ninth grade to work full-time. His father made him marry at 16. And when he was 23, his father died, and he became the man of the family, taking care of 10 brothers and sisters and his own children.

His goal: that they all finish high school.

All but one of his siblings did.

All of his six grown children finished high school and attended college.

Now, Irby is married to his second wife, Laura, and is raising his youngest son, the one he calls the "prime rib" — 10-year-old Andre. And he wants to push his dreams to the front burner, for his son and for himself.

At 61, he is learning to read.

But it's not that simple.

He reached the ninth grade back in Tunica without being able to read. With the help of a tutor from Literacy Volunteers of America-Detroit with whom he has worked for nearly three years, he now reads at nearly a fourth-grade level, the same as his son. So guess what U.V. Irby wants: He wants to "go through school" with Andre, learning as his son learns, reading what he reads.

"I'm going all the way," he says.

He wants them to master reading and math and history.

And life.

Together.

Irby's among tens of thousands of metro Detroiters who cannot read or who read at barely functional levels. He is among hundreds getting free, individual instruction from five metro Detroit literacy centers waging a David vs. Goliath battle against a functional illiteracy problem that plagues 47 percent of Detroit's residents 16 and older and 36 percent of Wayne County residents. Functional illiteracy rates in Oakland and Macomb counties are 10 percent and 15 percent respectively.

In the end, U.V. Irby wants to master reading. But before we visit the end, let's go back to the beginning. Irby's story will surprise you.

He was born in Tunica, a tiny town of 1,100 people that eventually would have more casinos (nine) than schools (five).

Irby got his name, as it is, after his infant sister died. Her name was Ula Mae. His grandmother, Hannah Irby, told his mother, Georgia Mae, that she wanted another baby whose name began with a U.

"She didn't never say what U.V. stood for. So my name is U.V. Irby," he says.

Each day, Irby's father, John, would give his children their marching orders.

" 'I want to get a bale today,' he'd say. Papa always kept the pressure on us. But we always came up short, maybe 200 or 400 pounds short. There's 1,200 pounds in a bale. We couldn't get that 1,200 every time. So he said, 'Get half one day and half the next day.' But we'd get the whole thing most of the time.

That was our tradition."

Education was always important in the Irby family, so important that Irby and his brothers and sisters used to trade shoes to attend classes.

"When we were at home, we had to take turns," Irby recalls. "I had to pull my shoes off and let my other brother wear my shoes and go half a day. He'd go half a day, and my sister went all day."

The family efforts were directed by his father, a farmer and mechanic responsible for the entire farming operation until 1958, when one of his mechanics ran over him with a Jeep.

"Papa was at the well, and the mechanic's brakes went out. He was telling Papa to get out of the way, but Papa didn't hear him."

U.V. Irby remembers the man whose farm they worked giving his dad a card to be used like food stamps, to get whatever the family needed.

But what his dad needed was to remain in charge.

"Papa didn't like being in a wheelchair. He preferred his crutches. He never considered himself handicapped, because he worked all his life."

Irby wasn't at the farm when the accident happened. One month before, he had moved to Peoria, Ill., to live with his older brother.

His brother, Joe, told him he'd take him home that weekend. But Irby wouldn't wait, so he began walking from Peoria, Ill., to Tunica, Miss.

His brother took off work, caught up with him and drove him home.

"I didn't go anywhere else for a year and a half," Irby recalls.

With his father's injury, Irby, the sixth of 13 children, took on more work. When his father died in 1961, he became responsible for his younger siblings.

"I put my life on hold, on the back burner because what I had to do was raise my family," he says.

He eventually left the farm and took the entire family to Peoria, working a variety of jobs and pushing them to finish school."He helped us, made sure we all went to school," says his brother, Otis Irby, of Peoria, the only sibling who didn't finish high school, because he quit to work. Otis Irby says he is proud that his brother is learning how to read.

"It's good that he's doing that. I need to go myself. He's a good man."

U.V. Irby moved from Peoria to Detroit in 1964, and worked in construction for 35 years before retiring. He recalls the work he has done in Detroit with pride. He helped build some of Detroit's most distinctive structures, including the People Mover, Harper Hospital and Joe Louis Arena.

During our interview in the Fisher Building, he pointed out the window at New Center One next door.

"I was helping to build that building and couldn't read nothing," he says. He recalled carrying a tape recorder to meetings with the contractor so he could get his his instructions. He'd play the tape back all day.

Irby recalls telling a supervisor on another project that he wanted the company to send him to school.

"I told him, 'You always bring these blueprints in here and you don't know whether I can read them or not.' The man said, 'You look smart.' I told him I look smart on the outside, but I want to look smart on the inside."

The man didn't send him to school, but kept putting him in charge.

"I helped build buildings and couldn't read nothing."

The practice caused some friction.

"The foreman could read blueprints, but he got mad because the contractor let me do all the work," Irby recalls.

"He said, 'That man don't know how to read blueprints, but he's going to tell me what to do?' And the contractor said, 'You're not as smart as that man.'"

Irby also worked on the People Mover. He recalls riding deep into the ground to test the beams that would hold it. And he never feared.

"When you have faith in God, you don't have to be scared."

At an age when many men contemplate the end of their lives, U.V. Irby is at an educational beginning, doing for himself what he made his children do."I always was on my kids about learning because Daddy didn't get his education. I wanted them to have a degree and be something. I was always on them because I wasn't able to get mine.

"My little brother was talking to me just Sunday night and said, 'Brother, remember when you worked in Peoria for the city health department? You know you used to take me to school every morning and I started crying because I didn't want to go because I was new and you told me whenever you get scared or worried, look right out that window, and you'll see my car sitting right down there from you?'

"I would park my truck where he could see it, and I'd go on to work. I'd tell my boss, 'I just brought my brother up here and I'm trying to get him trained in school and he's kind of halfway scared. Can I park my truck where he can see it?' He said,' Yeah.' "

That brother works in Peoria now, designing and delivering furniture.

"I never felt like something was taken away from me," Irby says. "I always felt like mine was on the back burner, and I'd get it sometime."

His time is now, and thanks to his tutor, he has made great progress. Pendora Smith has been working with Irby since 2000 and calls her pupil "an intelligent man."

"When I met him, I was not at all surprised by his accomplishments. He has excellent survival skills.

"He's an inspiration, period."

Smith says that being paired with Irby was as big a blessing for her as for him.

"I met him at a wonderful time in my life," she says. "... I wanted to begin studying the Bible more, and he said it was important for him to read so that he could read his Bible. It was a perfect match."

The pair meet once a week in a quiet spot at the Elmwood branch of the

Detroit Public Library. Like most non- and new readers, Irby's biggest obstacle is to change the way he sees words.

"U.V. has a fantastic memory," says Smith, 46. "He relies on that a lot. He memorizes the words instead of learning them. I have to trick him up. He says he likes that. When I would give him the words in a different context, he wouldn't know them. So I'd change the order. He's a quick study."

Irby is determined.

"This is as real to me as it can ever get," he says. "I want to learn. I have put my life on hold for my family, for me and for them. I watched my Daddy suffer, lost a leg working two jobs. My mother was sick half of her life. Now she's gone, he's gone and my kids are all grown and got their education. Now I want mine.

"I want to learn how to take care of myself. When I went out in the world to make a living, I did construction. I mastered that construction because that was my job. I was married to it. That was my life. It brought me up until now.

"Things have changed. When you get on the phone and you dial the phone number, you've got to punch in a Social Security number and I.D. number or punch in an account number to even get to talk to somebody. I don't know how to do all of that. This is what I'm up against right now."

Irby hopes to move at the same pace as his son is moving through fourth grade, so they can prepare for MEAP tests together. He picks Andre up from school every day. He watches him do his homework. And Andre helps him.

"Every day when he puts his homework on the tape recorder for me," Irby says. "Whatever I'm short on, I get help from Andre. And his helping me means he's going to be brilliant. There's always a way to learn. God will make a way. My shortcomings — Andre's got it covered. We're reading Leviticus now.

"We have to learn first to teach our own kids. This here is Andre's homework," he says, pointing to a folder filled with papers.

"I have to help him with this reading. And he's doing great. And I like that. I've got this plan that I have in my head, some call it a dream, some call it a vision, that God gave me. What I want is to be able to —"

He opens the folder and begins to read.

It is slow and halting and beautiful. He works hard to decipher each word instead of reaching in his memory to find it. When he stumbles, he goes back and tries it again. When he reaches a word he doesn't know, he says, "blank."

He reads the page, deliberately, proudly. When he finishes, he sits back with a smile.

"Now, see what I mean. See how I'm learning. This is my plan."

U.V. Irby began life on a Tunica farm and now lives in Detroit as a man who devoted his entire life to everyone's education but his own.

That is changing, one word at a time.

"I want to be able to pick up a book and read. I want to be able to pick up a book and write. I want to be able to write as fast as you're writing right now," he says pointing to the hasty scribbles in my reporter's notebook.

"We don't realize how great it is that we work all our lives and we learn that we can still learn more."

February 16, 2003

'Holes' hero guides movie with a book

As we drove along Interstate 75, headed for the movie theater, my daughter began reading the book to me. She knows how I like to read a book first in case a movie adaptation ruins it.

She had time to read just the first chapter before we arrived, so I had to take my chances. And like the folks who've bought 3.5 million copies of Louis Sachar's "Holes" since it was published in 1998, I was glad I did.

The themes in "Holes" — the movie and the book — run from self-esteem to love, racism to poverty, homelessness to mysticism. But one particular thread moved me greatly: The main character teaches a young friend to read.

If you haven't seen the movie or read the book, consider yourself truly missing out. Unlike the grand wizardry that surrounds Harry Potter or the epic special effects of "Lord of the Rings," "Holes" is a simple story with even simpler ghosts.

There is a kissing bandit who turns to a life of crime after the love of her life is killed. There is a man who persists in his goal to find a cure for stinky shoes, even if it ruins his family.

And there is a boy, a main character so likable that even the bullies at the camp where he's sent for a crime he didn't commit come to like him.

That character, Stanley Yelnats (Stanley spelled backwards), gets hit in the head by a pair of expensive stolen sneakers thrown from an overpass.

Stanley is found guilty of theft and sent to a camp where the boys dig a hole (5 feet wide by 5 feet deep) every day. They are told it is to build character. But it becomes apparent they are part of the warden's search for treasure.

In Stanley, parents can look for a sense of our children, honor, heroism, loyalty, and other adults can look for glimpses of themselves: a kind heart, a strong spirit, courage. Stanley's heart never wavers, even when life gets tough.

The thing I like about Stanley is what he does for his best friend, Hector.

Oh, he does many things: searches for him in the desert, carries him up a mountain, feeds him to keep him alive.

But what Stanley did that touched me most was teach his friend to read, one day, one word, at a time.

At a time when literacy is finally capturing the nation's attention — citywide reading campaigns are popping up everywhere, school systems are growing programs to make better readers out of kindergartners and communities are increasing tutoring efforts to help adults learn to read — what a wonderful find in the middle of a fairy tale.

I sat in a theater full of adults pretending to be there just to escort their kids and heard sighs as Stanley and Hector went over their lessons. I sat with moist eyes as Hector (who until he learned to read had been called Zero) sounded out his words.

And I cheered when Hector's escape from the camp, which leads Stanley to his destiny, was preceded by a camp counselor declaring him stupid and challenging him to say what "D-I-G" spelled, and Hector cried "Dig!" and popped his tormentor in the head with a shovel (OK. It was violent, but the guy wasn't hurt.)

It is so hard to find positive messages these days, in film, TV or books. I walked out of a movie early for the first time ever when I went to see "Anger Management" the week before.

So it was simple joy to sit in the dark and meet Stanley Yelnats, to see the things in him that I'm seeing in my daughter and to hope that one day, when I grow up, I could be just like him.

April 23, 2003

Fighting illiteracy one word at a time

Derrick Gilford is 39. He lives in Auburn Hills, owns two businesses, and has a drop-dead gorgeous wife who is expecting their first child in October.

Oh, and four years ago, he couldn't read.

He started a janitorial business in 1988, and bought a car wash in 1996, both while not being able to read the contracts he signed.

But six years ago, while watching his attorney speed-read some documents for him, he said enough was enough.

"He caught a lot of stuff they would have gotten me on," Gilford said. "That right then showed me that knowledge is power. I said, 'I need to have this kind of power, this kind of knowledge.'"

He found help through the Oakland Literacy Council in Pontiac, with tutor Margaret Gazette, a 59-year-old Pontiac woman who spends most Thursday nights at the Orion Township Public Library, helping Gilford reconstruct how he thinks.

"She actually took me back to the basics that my parents should have done, ABCs, your vowels, how to pronounce your consonants and syllables," he said.

"It was definitely starting from scratch."

His story is not unique. Hundreds of thousands of adults in metro Detroit cannot read doctor's instructions or prescriptions. An estimated 36 percent of Wayne County residents 16 and older cannot read driving exams or the scroll at the bottom of CNN. About 15 percent in Macomb County and 10 percent in Oakland County cannot read position papers printed by gubernatorial candidates, or canned food labels.

To combat a problem at the root of so many social, economic and educational ills in metro Detroit, the Free Press is joining five literacy groups and state Rep. Mary Waters, D-Detroit, to launch a tri-county campaign to improve reading rates for residents 16 and older in Wayne, Oakland and Macomb counties.

243

As part of the campaign, called Metro Detroit Reads, the literacy centers — Literacy Volunteers of America-Detroit, Macomb Literacy Partners in Clinton Township, Oakland Literacy Council in Pontiac, Downriver Literacy Council in Southgate and Siena Literacy Center in Redford — will work to open 100 reading stations where nonreaders can sign up for help and where tutors and their students can meet for one-on-one sessions.

The campaign announcement comes at a time of renewed interest in reading across the country. The Detroit Pistons Read to Achieve program has garnered national praise. After a near decade absence, the Detroit Public Library's Bookmobile is back on the streets. And Southfield plans to announce itself next month as the Reading Capital of America.

But what does growing interest really mean if huge numbers of people cannot read? Schoolchildren not succeeding? What do we expect if many of them live in homes where their parents can't read? Job layoffs in the tens of thousands leading to lasting unemployment? What do we expect when nonreaders who have hidden their handicap in jobs that didn't require words now can't get jobs?

It is no coincidence that adult reading rates are low as states spend less on adult education. Michigan spends about $113 million a year on adult education, down from $400 million 13 years ago.

"What should be spent is probably at least triple what's being spent now," said Patrick Shafer, executive director of the Michigan Association of Community and Adult Education.

The five Metro Detroit Reads literacy councils, along with smaller church literacy programs, and the Dominican Literacy Center in Detroit, have borne the weight of fighting local illiteracy.

The five partner centers survive on shoestring budgets, headquartered in rented or donated space, using about 1,400 volunteers a year to teach about 1,800 students. But those volunteers donate 141,000 hours of service a year.

If they were paid minimum wage ($5.15 an hour), they'd be paid $726,150 a year. The combined annual budget of the five Metro Detroit Reads centers is $791,500.

Beyond funding, what the literacy center directors say they need most is public awareness and a willingness to get help.

"If people really knew and understood what the problem was, funding would fall into place, volunteers would fall into place and people who needed help would know where to go," said Marsha DeVergilio, director of Macomb Literacy Partners.

Sister Mary Hemmen, director of the Siena center, said we must raise the "willingness to do something about it."

"If you're the one with the need for literacy, the awareness is one thing, but people have to step forward and that's hard," she said. "That is really hard. But we have to get rid of the stigma of 'I'm an adult and should be able to read.'" And Margaret Williamson, executive director of LVA-Detroit, said: "The biggest obstacle is the magnitude of the problem."

Illiteracy is a hidden plague that is rising from secrecy, thanks to some strong advocates in Lansing and Washington. U.S. Sen. Carl Levin, D-Mich., is seeking federal funds for the Metro Detroit Reads campaign. U.S. Rep. Carolyn Cheeks Kilpatrick, D-Mich., has loaned a staff member to the effort. And Waters, the state legislator, got gubernatorial candidates Jennifer Granholm and Dick Posthumus to pledge their support for a state focus on adult literacy last spring. She plans to hold legislative hearings next year on funding for adult education, particularly for nonreaders.

But the best advertisement is Derrick Gilford.

A Detroit native, Gilford had dislocated kneecaps as a child, which made it hard to walk and earned him endless teasing at school. By high school, quarrels with his mother led her to put him out of the house, he said.

Homeless and defiant, he dropped out and began smoking crack.

"I stayed at Belle Isle for about a month in my car," he said.

In 1985, he moved into his grandmother's house in Detroit and began attending church.

"I thought I was fixing to die. She was the only person I knew that was a Christian. I told her I wanted to be saved before I died."

He found God and his future. While working as a dishwasher at TGI Friday's in Dearborn, a staff member said he should be cleaning the whole building. So Gilford started a janitorial service and did just that, not only at that restaurant, but others in Southfield, Utica and Lansing. His business expanded, but on paper, it meant nothing to him. He couldn't read his own flyers about his successful company.

For years, the Auburn Hills businessman memorized hundreds of words, a survival technique used by nonreaders. With his tutor, he had to learn words.

He and Margaret Gazette had something else in common. She, too, was a high school dropout. She married young, raised her children, then returned to school to get her GED, her diploma and a medical assistant's certificate.

The first time they met, he knew he'd found his teacher.

"I knew God sent her to me because she was like a mother," he said." The way she treated me was special. She took time and when I made mistakes, and I mean mistake after mistake, she never got upset. She never got frustrated."

Gazette said Gilford was like family.

"My kids said you must be so proud," she recalled. "I said, I am proud of him.' They said, you must be proud of yourself. But I didn't go into it for the glory. I just enjoy it."

Gilford has begun speaking publicly about learning to read. He can now laugh at himself and share that laughter with others.

"He's just a wonderful human being," said Cathryn Weiss, director of the Oakland County Literacy Council. "He just oozes this wonderful dynamic personality that he has ... Nothing's going to stop him."

Gilford sold his car wash Thursday and plans to focus on the East 7 Mile barbershop he just turned into Detroit's only men's spa. He plans to get his GED, too, so his son, to be named Christopher, can see achievement.

And when he speaks at the Metro Detroit Reads Reading Rally and Festival on Sept. 8, Gilford knows what he'll say to nonreaders.

"It's time to let go, tell the truth, set yourself free and the freeness will get you everything," he said. "Being free means you're not a slave no more. I don't mean that in a race sense. I'm talking about being free to get a job, free to start a business, free to raise your family, free to travel. I mean free to save money. All that takes education."

August 26, 2002

Everyone has a stake in fighting illiteracy

Detroit should have been ashamed of itself long ago. Its leaders have known since 1992, when the Department of Education did a landmark survey on literacy, that nearly half of our city's residents read at the lowest levels of functional literacy or could not read at all.

Yet in the 10 years since that survey, literacy has never been atop a mayor's agenda.

Until now.

Detroit Mayor-elect Kwame Kilpatrick said in an exclusive interview in Lansing this week that he plans to reduce Detroit's illiteracy rate and improve learning by creating an Office of Education and Children. The initiative, a first for the mayor's office, will be overseen by a former teacher, principal or administrator who will serve as Detroit's literacy czar, Kilpatrick said.

"You can't have a strong city if it's not a smart city," he said. "Cities around the country are moving forward because of the people in their cities, families that work who are productive. We will never have the city that we want unless we get people educated."

It isn't rocket science. If Detroit is to succeed, it must have people who can learn and who can lead. If nearly half of the city's adult residents cannot read, why should we expect anything from our children, especially those whose parents cannot read to them, cannot help them with their homework and cannot decipher notes from teachers asking them to help their schools, their children and themselves?

Why are we so surprised by Detroit's lack of progress? In our down-but-not-out, fighting-back city, 47 percent of adult residents read at Level 1 of five levels of literacy or cannot read at all, according to 1992 figures, the most recent available, from the National Institute for Literacy, based in Washington, D.C.

Detroit hasn't made time to care. The city was tied up with racial tensions that never ceased and a suburban exodus that pummeled the tax base. Who noticed that, all of a sudden, Detroit got dumbed down?

After all, Coleman Young was the civil rights and race mayor. Dennis Archer was the bricks and mortar mayor. It is only now that Detroit has a mayor we can judge solely on how he improves Detroit's quality of life.

And we had better.

But we had better help, too.

Because one man cannot pull a city up by himself.

Neither can three men. But three are trying to get it started. Kilpatrick is joining Dr. Curtis Ivery, chancellor of the five-campus Wayne County Community College, and Dr. Kenneth Burnley, chief executive officer of Detroit's public schools, in creating a citywide network of after-school learning programs.

They hope to better organize the array of programs that currently exist into one network of after-school programs that can be used by any Detroit resident to learn reading, computer skills or technology in schools, rec centers and churches.

Kilpatrick plans to pay for the program with foundation grants and state and federal dollars — not city funds, he said. He met Thursday with various foundation leaders seeking funding.

People are willing to "step up to the plate" with funding if there is a specific plan, Kilpatrick said.

He's counting on the business community as well.

"Getting the business community to partner with the school district to provide literacy programs, technology programs, cognitive skills training — that's a big part," he said. "There's been too much of a focus on basketball and football after school but no focus on academics ..." Ivery, who oversees WC3's five campuses, said the problem is bigger than illiteracy.

"Let me go even further," he said. "Only 7 percent of the adult population in Detroit and in other parts of Wayne County own any education beyond high school, and the national average is around 40 percent for communities with similar demographics.

"We have huge issues here around education."

In two years, he said, 85 percent of America's jobs will require some higher education.

Jobs will be "technology-driven and you'll have to have a relationship with computers. Illiteracy is an extremely important piece . . .

"Education is going to be the word of the day," he said. "We talk about the renaissance in this city. If we're not educating our young people, there can be no renaissance."

Burnley, whose emphasis this year has been early childhood education, said fighting the problem early will make fighting adult illiteracy easier. He said the Detroit City Council and several foundations have already provided some money to the cause, some to the Ministerial Alliance.

"We're coming together to talk about what the need is and where the gap is," Burnley said. "The mayor's office wanting to be involved and WC3 being involved will fill the gap."

Burnley said it is possible to teach an entire city "if the entire city unites around it as a major need."

"I'm kind of excited about the conversation around this and the community awareness among the leadership that something has to be done. We're a long way from being where we need to be, but the fact is that our new mayor is interested and Dr. Ivery, likewise. If we put a concerted effort behind this, not only can we help with the literacy issue, but we can do wonders between the hours of 3 p.m. and 8 p.m."

Those are the hours that the superintendent, chancellor and mayor-elect have designated for after-school education.

Three men are committed. The mayor is committed. But it means nothing if Detroit isn't committed.

As I write this, I know that hundreds of thousands of adults in Detroit cannot read it. But illiteracy isn't something that affects only people who cannot read. It affects all of us — our economy, our reputation as a city and our children's futures.

Fight with us.

It's a problem we can solve.

November 30, 2001

How illiteracy devastates city

Sometimes you can't grasp how big a problem is until you say it out loud.

So say this out loud: Nearly half of the adult residents of Detroit are functionally illiterate. That's right — 47 percent cannot use reading as a tool in everyday life. They cannot fill out employment applications or read the newspaper or understand signs that warn of danger in workplaces — if they work.

Some drive, but only because they have memorized the colors and symbols of signs, symbols they cannot comprehend as words.

Some hide it by claiming they've lost their glasses or need an oral synopsis of a report or document.

How does illiteracy affect a city?

Well, consider this: In Detroit's empowerment zone, an 18.35-square-mile region of inner city stretching from Mexicantown near the Ambassador Bridge to the east side, where investors get special incentives to help stimulate growth, more than half the residents do not have a high school diploma.

How does illiteracy affect a school system?

"Kids come home and say, 'Help me with my homework,' but how can parents help if they can't read?" says Margaret Williamson, executive director of Literacy Volunteers of America-Detroit. "That's illiteracy! And that's the problem."

Illiteracy also begets other problems. According to a 1998 Michigan Department of Career Development study, about half of Detroit's working-age men and women were employed or looking for work, meaning the other half between the ages of 16 and 60 did not have a job and were not looking for one. Those figures are from 1998, the last time the department counted. And studies always have margins of error because, like polls, they are based on small samplings of people.

While city government has shone a bright spotlight on new development, new construction and corporate support for the revitalization of a new Detroit — and I'm glad about all that — someone's got to make sure there will be hands to hold up and take care of a new Detroit.

Williamson came home to do just that.

A Detroit native, she graduated from Northern High School and Wayne State University, then began her career at Ford Motor Co. in Dearborn.

"My family is a Ford family," she says. "My father's father came here from North Carolina to work at Ford when my father was 5 years old in 1925. My family has been here ever since."

Ford footed the bill for her master's degree from Central Michigan University.

"It was in the late '70s, early '80s, when we didn't even have a major drugstore chain in the city. I would drive out to Dearborn, and they were building the Hyatt and the Fairlane mall while Detroit was crumbling, and I used to feel so discouraged."

She loved Ford, but watching her hometown fall apart led her to community work. She managed a cultural diversity training program and supervised the reconstruction of affordable homes for low-income families.

In 1995, she was recruited to head the Community Coalition, a social justice agency in Flint.

"I never really left Detroit, because my family is here, so I was back and forth a lot," she says. "But I knew that I was going to come back to Detroit.

"I missed the city."

In March, she started with Literacy Volunteers, fighting one of Detroit's most pressing problems, the lower levels of literacy.

There are five levels:

At least 200,000 people in Detroit are at Level 1, which means they can barely read at all, according to 1997 reports, the latest figures available. The rest of the people Williamson is concerned about are at Level 2, where their skills are limited.

Level 3 is where they comprehend long texts, as would high school graduates. Levels 4 and 5 comprise readers at the college level and above.

The numbers are startling considering it takes $2,800 to $10,000 a year to fund an American student's education, but at least $24,000 a year to fund a prison term.

Yet, prison is where some men and women wind up after they've left high school, still cannot read and can't get a job.

Literacy Volunteers of America works with families, but adults are a special focus.

"I love to read. That is my passion. At any given time I am reading at least two books, newspapers, magazines," says Williamson, the mother of two daughters, one who attends the Detroit High School for the Fine and Performing Arts and one who goes to Wayne State University. "I come from a family of readers, and my aunt had volunteered for Literacy Volunteers 20 years ago.

It's exciting to finally have the opportunity to be a part of something that is so much a part of me."

Her mission is simple: empowerment.

"Every day, I understand to a greater extent the impact illiteracy has on metro Detroit," she says. "How we empower people is through social justice, through housing and giving people the opportunity for home ownership.

"But empowerment also means being able to earn a living and being a productive member of society. Literacy gets to the heart of it, and that's why I'm so excited. When you help open abilities, you provide an opportunity for people to understand who they are and to be more active. It broadens views."

She operates her organization with an office manager and five government-paid assistants from Americorp*VISTA. Each summer, 25 volunteers run summer literacy camps for 400 elementary and middle school students. But her pressing need is more help for clients age 16 and older.

"What I hope to do is recruit 200 new tutors to work with adult learners," she says.

The center has 145 tutors working one-on-one with adults now. But she has 40 people on a waiting list.

And the tutors must be committed. They pay $25 to take the certified literacy training that allows them to work two hours a week with a person who needs them desperately. The tutors and clients usually meet at a public library.

That's where Darline Carter has met her tutor, Judith Stettner, every week for three years.

Carter graduated from Martin Luther King Jr. High School 28 years ago. She remembers standing at graduation and not being able to read her diploma.

Now a desk clerk at the Tip Hotel near downtown, Carter, 46, attends computer classes at night and reads at least a book a week.

She remembers the day her tutoring started in 1998.

"I went to her place and met her by her pool. We got to know each other a little bit and have been together ever since.

"She started me off with some 'Cat in the Hat' books and that's how I got started."

Carter says her later meetings with Stettner at the public library were initially humiliating because the room was full of students.

"Then I said, 'No, I can't be embarrassed. If they see me struggling, they'll further their education.' "

Carter says she was motivated to read six years ago when her only son, 14-year-old Laron, was fatally struck by a car on his way to school. She wanted to read her Bible, something the two of them used to do together.

"When I lost him, I couldn't ask him, 'How do you spell this? How do you spell that?' "

She has worked at the same hotel for 27 years, first as a housekeeper, now on the desk.

"I could read my paycheck. I could read my name and how much I made and how many hours."

Now, Carter loves going to the library.

"I look forward to going to get a book every week and reading it. It might take me longer. I'm trying to read two books at a time."

And what's she reading this weekend?

"Let the Circle Be Unbroken" and "The Well," both by noted juvenile author Mildred D. Taylor.

Oh, one more thing. Knowledge begets knowledge.

Carter is helping to teach her 6-year-old niece, Kamyotta Galmore, to read.

"I can't spell her name. But I started checking out kindergarten books for her and we'd read them together. Now she reads by herself.

"When I get my reading together, I want to help children who are like I was at Martin Luther King. I didn't say anything. I just sat in the classroom and was quiet. My chemistry teacher finally asked me if I was having home problems. I said, 'No, I cannot read.' "

She graduated anyway.

But maybe that won't happen to so many future students, now that Williamson and other literary volunteers are on the job across Michigan, which has an 18-percent functional illiteracy rate.

Or what if everyone who can read just went out and taught someone else?

The reverberations could astound.

July 29, 2001

Schools want readers to feel the heat

Reading isn't baseball. You can't feel the pain of a ball hitting your glove as you catch a pop fly. You can't smell the grass under your feet, grass you think must be growing while you wait for a slow hitter to find one she likes.

Reading isn't swimming. You can't feel the splash of water about your ears or taste the chlorine on your tongue as you keep the water out of your throat. You can't push the water in a perfect freestyle, legs gliding, toes pointed.

Reading isn't basketball. You can't feel the sweat drip from your arms as you dribble and run, dribble and run, shoot and score, the welcome swoosh as familiar as the Nike sign. You can't hear the crowd and look up to see strangers cheering, unable to see any part of their faces but their smiles.

No, you can't slide into home or glide down pools or throw long passes for an alley-oop under the basket. (Trust me, it's a beautiful thing.)

But reading is tangible.

You can't keep your heart from pounding as you read about a murderer trying to catch his next victim.

You can't help but sigh as the Romeo in a love story kisses his Juliet, after pages and pages of twists and turns that kept them apart.

And you can't help but imagine yourself in the shoes of a young boy whose biggest dream is to become a wizard or a girl from Kansas who travels with her dog to Oz.

You can't help but smile as a mean mother and one daughter get their comeuppance after mistreating a second daughter who finds solace in the home of an old woman. You can't keep your eyes from widening as the old woman tells her to return home and take with her some of "The Talking Eggs" in the henhouse, but only the ones that say "Take me." And those give her riches.

Reading takes you places that don't require airline tickets or clothes. It takes only a token of patience to enter a world you've never seen.

And all the people you meet, all the adventures you have, stay with you. You can touch them, whenever you want, in your mind.

It's important for somebody to tell that to our children, to remind them that the most fun they'll ever experience may not be found in a video game.

I haven't seen Huckleberry Finn or Curious George or Kipat from Kapiti Plain in a Game Boy Advantage. I haven't seen Ichabod Crane in a Sony PlayStation.

Somebody in the Detroit Public Schools must know that — because the district, which is trying to introduce children to all the wealth that learning can provide, is kicking off its Warm Up to Reading summer program with a free book.

School officials will distribute free books and food and encourage children to sign up for library cards on the spot.

For the summer program, the school district will provide reading lists of classics for kindergartners through seniors. At summer's end, students who have read the most books will be entered into a drawing to get a prize. The goal is to make sure that all children are reading at grade level by the fourth grade.

Life, school, fun isn't all about the grass and the uniforms. Sometimes the best activities are those that require no uniforms. They require only that you pick up an adventure and open the pages. And sometimes give a mouse a cookie.

Sometimes, reading is a contact sport.

June 5, 2002

Gaines' words open doors to the heart

Nancy Galster has been helping 45-year-old James improve his reading for two years. Among the books she's used is Ernest J. Gaines' "A Lesson Before Dying."

James read it last summer, right after "Huckleberry Finn," and wants to meet the author who wrote so movingly of a man regaining his dignity before being wrongfully executed.

"Because I had read this book with James, I knew that the idea of the book, giving dignity to a young man, is what the literacy effort is about," said Galster, assistant to Sandy Yee, dean of the Wayne State University Library System. Galster works through Literacy Volunteers of America - Detroit to tutor adults to read in a city where 47 percent of adults 16 and over are functionally illiterate.

"The main character keeps a journal in jail," Galster said, "and when his teacher reads his journal after his death and understands the dignity his student gained before dying, that's what I felt.

"I'm opening a door."

Gaines will read from "Lesson" and sign copies today at the Detroit Public Library.

I want to shake the hand of a man whose words, through books such as "The Autobiography of Miss Jane Pittman," "A Gathering of Old Men" and "Lesson" are engraved in my heart. Anecdotes from his books should be as easily plucked and placed into the American lexicon as those from "To Kill A Mockingbird."

The story of Gaines' life is fascinating, and I'll get to that. But first, let me tell you how Gaines got to Detroit.

When Galster heard that Gaines would visit Oakland County, she decided that he couldn't be that close to Detroit and not come here. So she and Jerry Herron, director of Wayne State's honors program, traversed the campus raising funds.

It took a baker's dozen of cohosts: the WSU library system, the departments of English and history and Africana studies, the College of Liberal Arts, the College of Urban, Labor and Metropolitan affairs, the Center for Citizenship, the Academic Staff Professional Development Committee, the Office of the Dean of Students, the Organization of Black Alumni, LVA-Detroit, the Detroit Library and Friends of the Detroit Public Library.

But what pleased Galster as much as the visit was how the campus and community groups came together.

"These are very disparate groups," she said. "Now we have a partnership on campus and can produce other community events."

The partnership can be proud. Ernest J. Gaines is an event.

The author, who was born in 1933 on River Lake Plantation in Pointe Coupee Parish, La., is one of the nation's most celebrated writers. The oldest of 12, he was raised by his aunt Augusteen Jefferson, who would become, in his head and hands, the model for Miss Jane Pittman.

He didn't visit a public library for the first time until he was 16. There, he has said in news reports, he "discovered the Russians: Turgenev, Gogol, who spoke of the peasants. Then the French: Flaubert, Maupassant, Zola. But no one was telling me the story of my people. Thus, a teenager, I decided to write."

Since studying creative writing at Stanford University, Gaines has done just that.

"A Lesson Before Dying," received a National Book Critics Circle award in 1994. It also became an Emmy Award-winning HBO movie in 1999.

April 4, 2003

CHAPTER SEVEN

LIFE MEANS PEOPLE

Love binds couple through ALS

In his mind, he is running. And she is riding her bicycle beside him.

And sometimes, when she comes to visit him and talk about the day, she'll climb onto his lap and lift his arm around her and pull it close. He knows that it makes her feel safe. He cannot hold her, but he can feel her, and she can feel him.

In her mind, he is running. And she is riding her bicycle beside him.

And sometimes when they argue, she sees him the way she met him, tall and strong. Equals. Then they make up like couples do, like they always do.

Love and memories keep Janet and Peter Miesiak close and help them live beyond the truth that confronts them daily, that his body is shutting down in a Farmington Hills hospice, that living happily forever means his forever, not hers.

But this isn't a sad story. This is a lovers' tale about a petite Allen Park woman who met and fell in love with a chiropractor two years before he was diagnosed with ALS.

This is a story about the power of love.

Every Saturday, Janet Miesiak strides into the Hospice of Michigan's Farmington Hills center and signs in at the desk. She heads with purpose down to Room 216, her husband Peter's room.

She conducts business out of her Allen Park home during the week. She sells long-term care insurance, a mission as much as a job, as the result of her experiences with her husband's expensive, long-term care.

But weekends are mostly spent with her husband of six years, her best friend, her soul mate. She's also there to work. That's what it means to be married to someone who is ill, love and work intertwined completely.

On her days with Peter, she does everything for him: bathes him, dresses him, feeds him and makes his coffee, one of his favorite things in life.

They talk in a language that the two of them know best. He struggles to emit broken sounds that she repeats back to him as words. When she's right, he raises his eyebrows. When she's wrong, he tries again. She's rarely wrong, and she interprets for him to visitors just learning their language.

She gets right in his face, and she laughs at his jokes. His boyish charm is evident, even in a face that doesn't move as much as it used to. She hugs his body, remembering what it was like when he hugged back. She knows he's hugging her with his heart.

Peter, even with his room crowded with visitors, looks to Janet for confidence, for acceptance, for understanding. He is still sometimes the man of the family, helping to make decisions, challenging her and starting the occasional fight, not always because he's angry at his illness, but because it's a part of marriage. Their marriage is as real as the day it began, when his brother, Chris, pushed Peter's wheelchair down the aisle as Janet walked beside him.

"We celebrate our anniversary every month," she says, "because at first we didn't know we'd have anniversaries."

It will be six years on Sept. 7. But they celebrated their last one March 7.

"He left me a voice mail message, and I understood every word he said," Janet recalls. "I save it and I listen to it every once in a while."

When things get rough, it is usually Peter who cheers Janet. He uses a computer with an adaptive keyboard. An aide places a small button in his hand, and he can activate it with a slight movement, which, except for his face, is among the few movements he has left.

"Hang in there, sweets!" he recently wrote in an e-mail. "Things are always the darkest before the light shines, and my bulb is burning out (some may say that it burned out long ago, but that is just a ruse), so I have to draw on your strength because you are my sunlight, always have, always will be! I love you!"

And another time:

"Sweets, You know that I couldn't do ANY of this without you and your strength and conviction. I would be pulling a shopping cart full of aluminum cans behind my wheelchair out in the street and I would have a mouse living in my beard and I'd get all of my caloric intake from Mad Dog 20-20. Not a pretty picture!

LOVE, Peter"

When Janet is not able to visit Peter because of work or fatigue, she makes sure he's not alone. She keeps a schedule of family members and friends, all assigned days, so that he always has family with him.

A year ago, Peter entered Arbor Hospice in Ann Arbor. In November, he transferred to Hospice of Michigan in Farmington Hills. And the only part of his life that Janet can control, his interaction with family, she has on schedule.

Wednesday afternoons belong to his mom. And Monday nights and Friday afternoons belong to his younger sister, Lynn.

Mike Harrison remembers getting an e-mail from his sister-in-law asking for help for a friend.

"I thought I'd be doing things like cutting the grass and cleaning gutters. I didn't realize that what she wanted was someone to feed him and keep him company."

Harrison soon realized that it was Peter's company he enjoyed.

"We used to joke about 'Tuesdays with Morrie.' I had Mondays with Peter. I'd bring pizza — it had to be Papa Romano's with ham and mushrooms. We'd eat and talk and often rent movies . . . but the best part was just sitting and talking to him. I think it's been about three years."

Harrison, who at 46 is three years Peter's senior, says he misses Peter when he can't visit.

"It's not quite two guys in a gym, but he's introduced me to things I never thought I'd do, like watching auto racing on TV," says Harrison, who lives half a mile from Janet in Allen Park.

"He's very inspirational. He has changed my perspective on so many things.

Just watching how he's coping with his ALS and watching him and Janet cope with it, when I wake up in the morning and my back hurts ... I realize I have nothing to complain about. ... I know it sounds too lofty, but I think I'm a better person because of him and Janet."

Harrison's visits have been changed to Wednesdays now that Peter is in hospice in Farmington Hills, but the time is the same.

"We can talk about cars or watch movies or talk about anything, like friends, family. We don't get all that deep, because we're guys. But in some of the e-mails he sends me, he's so sharp, smart, witty, funny."

Tuesdays and Thursdays belong to Janet's parents, Mary and Ray

Shomsky, who are 74 and 73.

"There are times when you do crumble, but then you renew your strength again," Mary Shomsky says. "Everybody pitches in and tries to do their part."

She recalls when Janet and Peter met, and she thought, " 'Well, she wants to be an occupational therapist and he's a chiropractor. They can get an office together.' But then we found he would have a problem, so everybody had to rally and help them both, emotionally and physically and financially."

The years haven't been easy, says Shomsky, who's been married to her husband for 52 years, but they have shown her the kind of daughter she's raised.

"It shows that you can survive and be stronger," she says. "There's no way, if somebody's in love, that you can do anything else."

When she looks at her daughter and son-in-law, she sees that "no matter what, they love each other. No matter what. I'm real proud of her."

The schedule Janet maintains keeps the family connected to Peter. It spreads the love and the work that comes with caring for someone with ALS.

Amyotrophic lateral sclerosis, often referred to as Lou Gehrig's disease, attacks nerve cells in the brain and spinal cord.

That sounds so clinical when you're talking about a guy with a smile like Peter Miesiak's.

What ALS really does is stop the brain's ability to control muscles. Patients become totally paralyzed. But the most vicious thing it does is rob the body without robbing the mind, leaving brilliant, funny and wise people trapped in bodies that no longer work.

Early symptoms are so slight, people sometimes ignore them. A person might trip over carpet edges or have trouble lifting.

In Peter's case, eight years ago, it was his alarm clock.

"He happened to mention that he turned his alarm clock off and realized that he didn't turn it off," Janet recalls. "I didn't think anything of it. But about two months later, we were in Ohio at his brother's wedding ... and we were taking a walk, and he happened to mention that he still had it. A weakness two months later? There's something wrong. I said, 'You need to see a doctor.' Then he got scared."

Peter began to do his own research. Inside, he knew what was wrong. The weakness that started in his right hand progressed to his left hand, then his right leg, then his left leg.

"You could tell when he was walking," Janet recalls. "His gait was a little funny. It was all so gradual that it was hard to notice. But by the time he got the diagnosis, yeah, there were a lot of things. His speech was slurred."

Peter called ALS of Michigan Inc., which sent him information.

"I didn't realize until I found it two years later that he'd never opened it," Janet recalls. "I found it sealed. He figured if he opened it and read it, he'd be convinced that's what he had. Until he was sure, he didn't want to see it ... but he thought that's what it was."

It took more than a year, and visits to five doctors, before they got the diagnosis, because the disease has to progress enough to distinguish it from other disorders. But it would be years before the diagnosis really hit Janet, while at an ALS support group.

"It just hit me like a ton of bricks that I'm not going to spend the rest of my life with him. I'm not even going to get to marry him. I wanted to marry him. Marriage is forever. I don't even know how long he'll live. It was just too much to handle."

But the moment passed, as they do every day. Janet placed it away in the same compartment where she keeps the knowledge that Peter's death is imminent.

"Marriage is how long it lasts. That's forever in a marriage. We can still be married forever if we spend his lifetime together," she says.

Half of all people affected with ALS live at least three or more years after diagnosis. It has been eight years for Peter, and 11 since the girl from Southgate and the boy from Utica fell in love.

Janet Shomsky was one of six children born to Ray, a machine repairman at Ford, and Mary, a reading aide in the Southgate Public Schools. Janet ran track and lived in a house full of activity. All her brothers and sisters are married with kids, so she has 17 nieces and nephews.

What Janet remembers most about her childhood is growing up with stability and humor.

"A neighbor got killed in an accident when I had just graduated high school and my dad had always worked midnights and my mom worked days. The neighbor was about his age, and he said he wanted my mom to quit, so they could spend more time together. And my mom said, 'Uh-uh. I need this for my piece of mind.' "

She didn't know it then, but that kind of humor would come in handy years later.

Peter was born in Detroit, but his family moved to Utica, so that's where he went to high school. Just after his high school graduation, his dad was transferred to Ohio. Peter was scheduled to enter the Air Force that August and didn't want to move. His parents let him stay with a friend until he accepted his posts in Italy and Japan.

He returned to Utica and became a chiropractor. He lived with his parents, who had moved back to Troy. His intent was to open his own office and buy a house. He got to do neither, but at a chiropractors meeting in Southfield, he did meet his future wife.

"I was working in a small accounting firm that had started to deal more with chiropractors," Janet says. "My boss wanted us to go to more chiropractic society meetings.

"I was getting ready to leave the office, and my boss said, 'I'm busy. Go and find yourself a nice chiropractor.'"

She did.

She and Peter had been dating for two years when he started getting signs of ALS. She had just returned to school to study occupational therapy. She didn't know what ALS was.

Janet says Peter was adamant about her finishing school. He was living at home with his parents. She was living in Allen Park.

"The whole time I was going through this, I was learning about occupational therapy and working with patients with ALS at Wayne State, and he was going through this."

She spent her weekdays in class and every weekend with Peter. Every Friday evening, she would go to his parents' house and pick him up so he could spend those days with her in Allen Park.

But the disease progressed to the point that he had to stop working.

"Peter didn't realize how many lives he had touched until he quit working, because up until the time he quit working, he didn't tell anyone at work what was going on. Nobody knew.

"He was involved in Kiwanis and the Chamber of Commerce. He quit everything at once for health reasons. When everybody found out what was wrong, daily, he got a stack of mail, cards, letters. He cried every day when he got the mail. He never knew how many lives he touched. The ones he touched most were patients. They just loved him."

Meanwhile, Janet combined full-time school with a part-time job. But "then I realized there was no way we could get married and support ourselves until I started working full-time," she says. "By the time we got married, I didn't know if he was going to live long enough for us to get married."

The couple faced a moment of truth.

"He gave me the option," she says. "He said, 'I will understand if you leave' and I told him, 'Get out of here!' There was never any question in my mind by that time that I was never going to leave him. I wanted to be married to him. Whatever time he had left, I wanted to spend with him. By the time we got married, he needed full care."

After nearly five years of dating and three years of ALS, they married in 1996.

Julia and Conrad Miesiak watched their son go from ladies' man to a loving husband.

"When he was young, the ladies would look at him with his big eyes and that smile and they all loved him," says Julia Miesiak, 75.

She recalls her son being interested in engineering, like his father, Conrad, 75, a mechanical engineer, retired from Chrysler.

But since both his parents made regular visits to a chiropractor, Peter became interested in that.

After Peter was diagnosed, he and Janet dove head first into ALS work. Janet would serve as president of ALS Michigan Inc.

Julia Miesiak says Peter and Janet are their greatest gifts to each other.

"There's always a chance that the girl, knowing there isn't much of a future with that illness, she might have just left. But Janet didn't, and we're thankful every day that she didn't. We love her very much for it."

March 24, 2002

Mr. Begian's opus: Music students return

Fifteen-year-old Harry Begian and a buddy drove from Dearborn to Ann Arbor just to hear the University of Michigan band. It was 1937, and at that moment, all the Fordson High School student knew was that he would never be what he wanted to be: a symphony conductor.

"I couldn't aspire for a symphony orchestra position because I didn't have private lessons. I didn't have training on piano because my father was more concerned about getting bread on the table."

So Begian, who longed to conduct the Detroit Symphony Orchestra, instead became a teacher and eventually band director at Cass Technical High School.

In 17 years, he grew into the job and grew the bands from state renown to international acclaim, developing young minds as well as talent and graduating music stars.

Begian is retired now and lives on Hubbard Lake with his wife of nearly 60 years, Emily, and his memories of teaching. He may have thought his students, some of them, had forgotten him. But this weekend, more than 80 are coming home to Detroit, and they're bringing their instruments. Some are professionals. Some are teachers. They will take the stage Saturday to show their teacher his greatest accomplishment, the symphony of people he helped mold at Cass. They will play a concert.

And Dr. Harry Begian, at 82, will conduct.

Years from now, when historians update American music encyclopedias, there may be a section on cities defined by music: New Orleans, Seattle, Detroit.

And although the Detroit entry will be heavy with lore about Motown and the Sound of Young America, there also will be a spotlight on Detroit's classical and jazz artists, many of them graduates of Cass Tech, many of them taught by Harry Begian, whose band attracted national attention in

1954 when its performance at the Midwest International Band and Orchestra Clinic garnered a standing ovation and an illegal encore. Benjamin L. Pruitt, band director and music department head at Cass Tech (1987-1999), said Begian set the standard for subsequent directors.

"Everyone who followed him had that band to measure up to. I've used the recordings of the Cass Tech bands (under Begian) to hear the interpretation of major works. His presence is still felt because many of the arrangements in the Cass Tech library are ones he performed. His ID stamp is on many of them.

"His personal notes are still on the music, and whenever I perform music I knew he had performed, I would look for those notes to see just how he interpreted the music. There is still a strong presence of Dr. Begian in the music department."

Ten years ago, at the request of the Library of Congress, Begian donated 26 reel-to-reel tape recordings of the Cass Tech band (1954-64) to the Library's Music Division, recordings now on permanent file as part of the Harry Begian Collection. Some of those recordings have been collected on a CD called "Cass Tech: A Documentary," which will be available for $15 at the celebration.

But nothing attests to Begian's influence as much as his students, and none is more famous than Dr. Donaldson Toussaint L'Ouverture Byrd.

"I used to walk home from Cass and look at all the stores along Woodward, and when I got to the library, I'd hang out there and listen to the records on the second floor, and then I'd go home and study," says the man better known as jazz trumpeter Donald Byrd. "That was because of Begian being such a disciplinarian. I better study or else.

"He's the one that set the tenor for our lives, for the rest of our lives," says Byrd, now 70, who lives in Dover, Del., and lectures at the University of Delaware.

Glenda Bolyard Scherf's parents paid tuition for the Royal Oak teen to attend Cass from 1955 to 1958. She says that six of her nine classes were music. And no teacher meant more than Begian, who used to play trumpet duets with her for practice.

"I always thought that was wonderful because he was such a good player. I was cocky. I thought I was good because I was first chair," she says, "and he played circles around me. I had to go home and practice harder."

Scherf says Begian always arrived at 7 a.m., an hour before school started, and stayed after.

"He had a little, tiny office. We called it 1 1/2 N. It was halfway between the first and second floors, just a tiny little thing. . . but we had fun there.

"One time, I wasn't doing well in biology and he made me come there at study hall and study. He didn't help. He just had other kids quiz me to make sure I was ready for the next test."

In December 2001, Scherf and other graduates held a memorial concert for the late Michael Bistritzky, who led the orchestra from 1942 to 1968 and developed a generation of Michigan music teachers.

"It's a shame that we didn't do it for him while he was alive," Scherf mentioned to a fellow graduate. That seed grew into Saturday's concert.

"We're up to 82 and counting (for the band)," she said last Wednesday. "They're calling every day. And a lot of people haven't played since high school and they've gone out and rented instruments or borrowed them."

Scherf said Begian "doesn't realize how much his students really put him as a major factor in their lives.

"Why would students be coming from California, Vegas, New York, just all over the country to see him? A couple have called me from Alaska!"

During his tenure, from 1947 until 1964, Begian became known as the doctor whose medicine was sometimes hard to swallow, but his students loved him.

They, to a person, described him as demanding, excellent, no-nonsense and constantly challenging.

Byrd recalls a rehearsal of Dvorak's New World Symphony.

"I goofed the trumpet part," he says. "Back then, I was damn near first trumpet, and Begian came over and grabbed my trumpet and — he took my horn and played it! — and then said, 'Play that thing right!' "

If Harry Begian was tough, there may be two reasons. First, he loves music. Second, he had it tough growing up.

His parents, Nick and Goldie Begian, were among millions of Armenians caught in the struggle for power between the Ottoman Empire and Russia. His father traveled with a group of friends to America in 1913 and shared a house to earn enough money to send for their families.

But the men didn't foresee World War I or the Turkish deportation of Armenians into the deserts of Mesopotamia. Goldie Begian survived the desert, but it was seven years before she was reunited with her husband. He brought her to Pontiac, where Harry Begian was born in 1921. The family moved to Dearborn so his father could work at Ford, and Begian began playing trumpet in the fourth grade.

His memories of Dearborn are bitter because his family and fellow immigrants were "treated like second-class citizens," he says. He finished high school in two and a half years and earned a bachelor's degree from Wayne State, where he played in the band. It was 1942. His first job was teaching band at Mackenzie High, but he got drafted and spent three years in military bands.

When he returned in 1946, he had a wife he'd met in the Wayne band; he worked briefly at Wayne before studying in Massachusetts for the summer. In 1947, he earned his master's degree from Wayne and became band director at Cass Tech.

"For a professional, it was the best thing that could happen. I learned my craft as a teacher and conductor — and I think of the two terms as synonymous — at Cass Tech."

He remembers the best students, and those better than that. One was Ron Carter, the bassist and jazz innovator, best known for his work with Miles Davis in the 1960s.

"Ron Carter was a cellist in the orchestra, and after his first year, he came to me and said, 'Mr. Begian, I've heard the band in rehearsal and I watched you conduct and I wonder, do you think I could learn enough clarinet to aspire to play in your top band?'"

Begian also remembers Byrd.

"He was a joker. He and I used to have more fun because I used to have to chase him off the Cass Tech stage after the band rehearsal."

Begian accepts his reputation as a tough guy.

"I didn't tolerate any foolishness," he says. "I didn't tolerate any lack of concentration. ... I had every right to expect something from the players because I knew they had the wherewithal to deliver what the music and I asked of them."

Begian completed his music education doctorate at the University of

Michigan. He and Emily had three children, two of them music teachers.

He left Cass in 1964 and became director of bands at Wayne State for three years, then band director at Michigan State for three years. He headed to the University of Illinois, Urbana-Champaign in 1970, from where he retired in 1984. All of us have an opus, the symphony created by our words and deeds, the impact we've had on the lives of others, the score that measures the breadth of our living. For Harry Begian, his symphony lives.

And his boyhood dream did come true. He got to conduct the Detroit Symphony Orchestra, at its invitation, at a special concert at Orchestra Hall in 1987.

June 20, 2003

Family finds peace
where their ancestors slaved

CHARLESTON, S.C. — The family has been chasing ghosts so long, it is hard for the brothers and sister to speak at times as they walk the same patch of earth their ancestors did two centuries ago.

Rose Thompson Morton and her family have spent years searching tax bills, census records and the wills of prominent Southern politicians to find their ancestors. So finally walking the old plantation those ancestors once did is sweet joy.

They've come, Rose, her husband and two daughters, and her two brothers and a friend, to a city they've never seen, to a place that once existed only in her mind, to find names that have been part of the family story for generations.

Her brothers, Charles and Jerry, are joined with her in the search. Their cousin Violetta Harrigan, whose work has been vital in helping them, is there in spirit, but remains in Chicago.

The Detroit-area siblings had hoped to find slave quarters or tree carvings or grave sites. They found none of those. But they did find something they didn't expect.

Peace.

It begins like any family vacation. The Mortons and Thompsons join other tourists walking the grounds of Middleton Place, once the headquarters of a rice empire that, in the beginning, included at least 20 plantations.

The estate was developed by Henry Middleton, second president of the First Continental Congress, and later owned by his son Arthur, a signer of the Declaration of Independence, and later Arthur's son Henry, governor of South Carolina and finally, Henry's son Williams, a signer of the Ordinance of Secession.

The estate's two centerpieces are a restored Middleton residence and the nation's oldest landscaped gardens, which took 100 slaves 10 years to create.

Using a flashlight as a spotlight, a guide invites the family and other tourists into the residence to study artifacts from four generations of a prominent family's exploits at home and abroad. Portraits adorn the walls. Exquisite tea services and china grace the tables. Richly upholstered furnishings, all donated by Middleton descendants, command each room.

After the tour, Rose Morton walks over to the piles of brick that used to be the main house. She bends and picks up a rock, the only artifact she can find that one of her ancestors may have touched.

"I think I'm going keep this little rock. It's not a whole brick, just a rock," she says.

It might seem a small measure of success after a journey that lasted 13 hours and 851 miles, the distance between the Detroit area, where she has spent her entire life, and a Charleston plantation where her family story places its American beginnings.

But that small piece of brick represents a connection between past and present, between a man who might have been a carpenter on these grounds and a Detroit postal worker two centuries later, between the story that Rose Morton and her brother Charles Thompson have researched for years and the story that was passed down through the family since the mid-1800s.

"I never would have dreamed in a million years that I'd be here," Charles Thompson says as he studies the river, the horizon and the trees.

For their brother Jerry Thompson, who endured a 15-hour bus ride and $200 cab ride to join them, the trip's lesson is simple.

"You can say 'I'm from Africa,' but Africa's a big continent. Now I have roots."

A comedian and filmmaker when he's not working 80 hours a week as a Detroit paramedic and EMS technician, Jerry says he plans to make a film about the family's roots. Rose's husband, Clinton Morton, and daughters, Alenna, 13, and Janaye, 16, all of Southfield, finally get to see what has taken her attention for so long.

They walk into the stable yard, made to look as it did in the 18th Century, when the family place had its own blacksmith and carpenter and spinners and weavers and slaves, unpaid laborers to work the rice paddies, milk the cows and tend the gardens. The family visits the small, cramped weaving house where Mary Smalls, another Middleton slave descendant, makes quilts and doilies. In her 70s, she's a charmer. If they cast a movie about the Morton-Thompson trip to Middleton, she would have been played by Pearl Bailey, if Bailey were alive.

Rose peppers her with questions about her family and whether she knows how the slaves were treated at Middleton.

"I don't know. I wasn't here," she tells her matter-of-factly. But Miss Mary shares her own family story as a descendant of Hercules, her great-grandfather who came to Middleton in the 1800s looking for work.

"Miss Middleton wanted a young person to help with the garden. Her husband said, 'If you provide for him until payday, you can have him.' He was one of the ones not punished by beating or being put in a strange place. He would always justify it. He wasn't a person to make confusion."

Miss Mary also says her great-grandfather "would always talk about the coming generation." She named her oldest son for him.

"People should keep a record of things that happened in the family," she tells Rose. And as Rose leaves, she calls out a final piece of advice.

"When you have a boy, name him Hercules. I hope the best for all of this."

Rose Morton and her family gather memories and bits of information that are artifacts as real as the rock she claimed from a pile of bricks. As they walk, she reminds her brothers of the song their mother used to sing to them as children.

I'm from Mi'lton and I'm walking 18 miles
I'm from Mi'lton and I'm walking 18 miles
From Mi'lton, I'm walking, walking to Mi'lton, 18 miles.

The song, the rock, the memories of a spring-like day in February when a great-great-great-great-granddaughter walks under trees that her forebears walked under, those things are all evidence that the study of black history must be the study of the best of us as well as the study of the least of us, a million histories still to be found, stories of those who toiled day in and day out, who suffered heartache and joy and had babies, glorious babies, who would someday come back to find them, to search for their presence, to say hello and good-bye.

The Middleton story is rich and proud South Carolina history. But it also is the untold history of the Middleton slaves, the ones who toiled on those award-winning gardens in winter because they didn't have time during planting season.

The pastoral setting, the peace of sunny skies and the friendliness of everyone, as if the Charleston Chamber of Commerce had sent an emissary, makes the trip seem uplifting instead of heartbreaking.

"You don't feel so bad coming here," Clinton Morton says.

The Middleton gardens were not the refuge of the slaves. On a VIP carriage ride around the grounds in a polished wood and iron buggy, Rose and her family get a view of what the slaves saw. Sitting quietly with her back to the driver, a blanket around her shoulders, she watches expanses of rivers and ponds and acres of unfettered foliage. Later, she will say the ride frightened her.

The guides, Nancy Langston and Jeff Shiflet, are spectacular in their knowledge of history and sensitivity to the family. They offer a little "tour guide embellishment," as Shiflet describes their recollections of past ignorant riders, telling the family about the great grit tree blight of '79 that resulted in a reduction of available grits. (For those who don't know, grits don't grow on trees.)

"We told them how to cook grits, too. You soak grits for 24 hours then cook them for 24 hours," Langston said. (Grits take about five to 20 minutes to cook.)

But aside from the humor, the guides treat the family with respect and awe, astonished to learn how they came to be here and grateful to give them whatever information they can. They guide the carriage down narrow paths choked from either side with 50-foot bamboo shoots. They head to the rice paddies, to areas that aren't a part of the regular tour. This part of the plantation was where most of the work was done. There are no views of enormous landscaped gardens or houses, just the river and the work.

"Even the children worked," Langston explains. "In one tiny corner, the kids were on bird watch. When the crows or rice birds would come, the children would bang the pots and pans. The women did much of the planting."

The carriage heads back to the museum house, past sable palmettos and hundred-year-old oaks. It is like leaving one world for another and returning home again.

Behind the carriage house, Rose shows her brother Jerry the headstones she saw the day before. The names they bear are not a part of the Thompson family story, but they are a part of someone's story.

Edward Brown
who departed this life
Nov. 7, 1851
Aged 22 years 4 months, 21 days
My time was come, my grave you see
Prepare in time to follow me
Go home my friend and shed no tears
For I lie here till Christ appears.

John Johnston
Nov. 24, 1859
Aged 70 years

Sometimes, according to the guides, people sit in front of the stones and rub pencil to paper furiously so they can carry the inscriptions with them. The Mortons and Thompsons touch the stones as well.

Barbara Doyle is the Middleton Place historian. She has spoken with Rose Morton by phone in the past year, but the two don't get to meet on this trip.

She did provide the family a copy of the 1793 inventory of the estate of Arthur Middleton, which lists three slaves named Caesar. She cannot shed more light and wishes them luck in a letter in which she writes, "It is all very puzzling."

It is that puzzle that has driven Charles Thompson for 30 years and Rose Morton for five. Charles was 17 when he rode the bus to Montgomery, Ala., to visit his grandmother, Geraldine Snow. He liked being down South and his grandmother was a lot of fun. And man, could she tell stories.

It was then that his grandmother first gave him the family story about a woman who came over on a ship, shackled to her two children, how they landed in South Carolina, and eventually wound up in Greenville, S.C., on a second plantation Arthur Middleton had there. One of the slaves was sold to Spartanburg, S.C. What happened to the others is unknown.

Rose Morton and Charles Thompson, a dealer at Detroit MGM Grand Casino, each had their own discoveries. For Rose, it was while reading a biography of the late Alabama Sen. William Yancey, to whom her family was passed from the Earles, who got them from the Middletons. She came across a story that sounded familiar, one that she'd heard for years. The author was tagging along with the senator for a day, watched him stop on a downtown Montgomery street and give an old Negress all the money out of his pockets.

"My mother used to always tell that story about how her great-great-grandmother was downtown and Mr. Yancey sneaked her money," Rose recalls. Finding that bit of the family story in an official biography made her chase the ghosts even harder.

She also tackled the song her mother used to sing to her brothers and her when they were children.

From Mi'lton and I'm walking 18 miles
I'm from Mi'lton and I'm walking 18 miles.
From Mi'lton, I'm walking, walking to Mi'lton, 18 miles.
I won't sing the second verse because it sounds so much like the first verse.
I think I'll sing the third verse.
I'm from Mi'lton and I'm walking 18 miles
I'm from Mi'lton and I'm walking 18 miles
From Mi'lton, I'm walking, walking to Mi'lton, 18 miles.
I won't sing the fourth verse because it sounds so much like the third verse.
I think I'll sing the fifth verse.
I'm from Mi'lton and I'm walking 18 miles.

Rose searched the Internet for Middleton Place and found that the old plantation had been partially preserved and was now a tourist attraction, about 18 miles from downtown Charleston. She changed the family vacation destination from Florida to Charleston.

Her brother Charles recalls his excitement 10 years ago while doing research in the Burton Collection at the Detroit Public Library. He found a bill of sale dated May 25, 1820, showing the purchase by George W. Earle of slaves that included Caesar, Phoebe and Agrippa.

He was so excited to see the family names on the document that he "might have yelled out and everybody in the library looked," he says. "Like everybody who studies their genealogy, when they finally find something and yell 'That's it!' — that's what it was like."

He booked a seat in the Morton van to Charleston because of his sister's excitement and because he remembered that whenever his great-great-grandfather John, a blacksmith and carpenter, was asked where he was from, he used to say he was "from Mi'lton to Earle to Mi'lton to Earle to Nabonaparte Snow."

"Somebody was trying to tell him where he originally came from and he was trying to tell us," Charles says. "He wanted it to be known that that was his history." (The family has not discovered what Nabonaparte Snow means.)

The family story is what makes a sister and her brothers climb into a van to reverse the Great Migration and go South in search of home. It makes them fill every seat and drive for 13 hours not knowing what they'll find, Aretha and the Spinners keeping them company.

Rose's husband, Clinton, does most of the driving. Their daughter Alenna, who doesn't quite get her mother's obsession, complains about the cramped quarters, so her mother tells her to sit in her lap and talks to her about how cramped the slaves were who endured weeks and months in the holds of ships to be brought to America as free labor.

When the family finally reaches South Carolina, Rose can hardly wait.

"Hopefully this trip will shed some light on some of the shadows we have in this story," she says.

Over the weekend, the visit sheds light on how brother and sister search for family. Rose is the one who follows her heart while Charles follows a paper trail, throwing out anything he can't prove is connected to the lineage, to the story.

Their brother Jerry, whose comic timing is a constant tension breaker, is usually the referee. He reminds Rose that just because she feels something doesn't make it true. And he reminds Charles not to pick on his sister.

As for Jerry, he needs proof just like his brother.

"I'm a paramedic. I've got to know what it is and what it isn't. Is it red or blue or green or white?"

But Middleton Place changes the brothers some. The lingering, overwhelming need to belong, a longing to connect with distant relatives, wraps Charles in its arms, and for a minute, he doesn't care about documents.

"I'm comfortable here," he says, "like I'm supposed to be here."

And Jerry is content to stand gazing at the river or touching a tree.

He and Charles both decide, whether it's necessary for their hearts or because they have no evidence otherwise, that the Middleton slaves must have been happy. The guides have told them about the task system that existed on the plantation for years. When tasks lasting a quarter-day, half-day or full day were finished, the work was done, some guides said. And since this was the headquarters and the largest job was tending the prize gardens, maybe life wasn't so bad, the brothers decide.

"I get more good feelings than bad here," Charles says. "I know people will be mad at me for saying this, but it's possible that they had a happy and healthy life. I know they didn't have their freedom, but they were free from drugs, free from alcohol. Some people want to be told when to eat, when to sleep.

"They're used to people taking care of them. That's why some of them end up in jail."

You get the sense that Charles Thompson is talking about something other than his ancestors, something closer to an urban plight. But he's emotional and later says he's just talking about people who can't control themselves.

Rose Morton, on the other hand, peppers everyone with questions about everything, as if she finally needs the proof she has let her heart be satisfied without for so long.

On Sunday afternoon, she is looking for a church. She has attended every Sunday this year and today is especially important, so she visits the little chapel on the plantation, a replica of the chapel that stood in that spot 200 years before. She sits in the second row, closes her eyes and prays.

Outside she faces the Ashley River, the sun on her face, and says, "I was praying for those who prayed before. My ancestors, some are in this ground. I can come and remember and speak to them. I'm afraid they'll be forgotten.

"I visit my mother's grave. They don't have any relatives visiting them. I'm visiting their graves."

Her daughter Alenna is as interested as most 13-year-olds in lectures and museum tours and archive papers. She isn't here to chase ghosts. She's more interested in chasing butterflies and milking the cows, which she does with aplomb. She's chasing the chickens in the coop and trying to grab a feather from a proud peacock who is having none of it.

But Rose isn't worried.

"I think it will come to her. When I was younger, my grandmother never knew I would be so interested. I'm planting a seed. If I repeat it over and over and over again, Alenna will have the same knowledge."

Even if Alenna never wants to know her roots or takes up the work of her mom and uncle, it's all right with Rose Morton.

"My brother's son or somebody else will take it on."

As Rose packs her bags to head back to Southfield, she stops a moment to write a letter to the river and the trees and the bricks:

"It is Monday at 7 a.m. As I look outside the window of my room, I see no end to this place. I wonder what my ancestors might have thought as they looked at the grounds. But maybe this early there was no time for thinking, just working.

"I find so many traces of heritage here. I see different things my people might have done. Did my people really, truly think of this place as home? Or were they visitors just like me?"

February 24, 2002

Dedicated siblings continue search for family history

GREENVILLE, S.C. — It is a typical Southern Sunday after church. A blustery chill envelopes Whitehall, the onetime 1800s summer residence of South Carolina Gov. Henry Middleton.

This is Greenville's oldest house, a white two-story that was the main house of a working plantation of 1,017 acres. When Gov. Middleton became minister to Russia, he sold the property to George Washington Earle. Along with it, he sold Earle 26 slaves.

As Rose Thompson Morton of Southfield joins her husband, daughters and brothers to approach the front door of this historic home this cold, damp Sunday, they are excited and curious. Morton and her brothers know that their great-great-great-great grandparents, Caesar and Phoebe, were among those slaves that Earle bought on May 25, 1820.

Charles Thompson, of Detroit, recalls hearing about Whitehall from his grandmother 30 years ago. "I don't know anything about their lives at Whitehall, but I always wanted to see Whitehall since I heard of it as a kid," says Thompson, 48. His brother, Howard Thompson, a 53-year-old boxing coach and hair care entrepreneur, wants more.

The Thompsons are here looking for ghosts. They are looking for answers to questions that haunt their dreams. What they find is real estate appraiser and developer Charles Benjamin Stone, whose family has owned this home for six generations.

It is not historic, the descendants of those who served meeting the descendants of those who were served.

But the wind stops for a moment when Rose Morton knocks on the door, and Stone answers. Both are matter-of-fact, polite. Then Morton says, "Hello. Are you Charles?"

And the scion of one of Greenville's most prominent families says, "Call me Chuck."

And as simple as that, the children of slaves walk into a plantation that once owned their ancestors.

The Thompsons — Rose, her brothers Charles and Jerry, and their cousin Violetta Harrigan of Chicago, have been chasing family ghosts for 30 years, trying to match pieces of documented history with the snippets of the family story passed down from their grandmother, Geraldine Snow.

Armed with abstracts, census records, invoices and copies of pages from prominent Southern biographies, the family has begun making journeys South to retrace the steps of their ancestors. Last February, after learning the location of Caesar and Phoebe's first home, the Thompsons took a road trip to Charleston, S.C. I went with them to visit Middleton Place, Henry Middleton's main home, a rice plantation on the outskirts of town.

When the Thompsons found records showing that Caesar and Phoebe were later sold to Whitehall, here in the heart of Greenville, Rose Morton, her husband, Clint, and daughters, Alenna and Janaye, her brothers, Charles, Howard and Jerry, and his son, Jerry, decided to come here. The family has taken both trips in February — Black History Month — not to study other histories, but to complete their own. Next year, they plan to visit a plantation in Alabama.

Last time at Middleton Place, the Thompsons were just thrilled to confirm some of the family story, overwhelmed to walk land that their family once walked and amazed to hear volunteers dressed in early 19th-Century garb regale visitors with tales of the slave Caesar Carpenter who worked on the grounds.

This time, the trip is more practical than emotional.

Middleton is a tourist attraction. Whitehall is the private residence of a dad, mom and four children, who were pleasant and patient with a family looking for something they couldn't give them.

The Thompsons are disappointed to find that Whitehall is no longer a plantation, but a residence smack dab in the middle of other homes carved out of the plantation's old property.

When the Middletons sold their summer home to the Earles, it became a permanent year-round residence and working plantation. Whitehall was a military hospital during the Spanish-American war and once housed apartments for Greenville families, who sometimes return to see their old homes, Stone says.

Many of the Earle family papers are spread out among the Earle descendants, and Stone suggests that the Thompsons check with those descendants for more information. The home has few original documents, and none pertaining to the slaves that lived there almost 200 years ago.

Chuck Stone, the 48-year-old real estate developer and appraiser whose family history the Thompsons want to plumb for clues, says he was surprised to get the Thompsons' phone call, but wanted to help.

"I'm more than happy to have helped them," he says. "We know how difficult it's been, to trace back your family tree. I'm glad we could be of help. Hopefully, we have."

Stone says this is the first time that slave descendants have come to Whitehall, and he is surprised to learn some things about his family, too.

"It's interesting to me to see," he says. "He (Charles Thompson) had information I hadn't seen before about the purchase of his great-great-great grandfather. I found that interesting. I didn't have a clue. The only thing that I have is the papers, maybe 15 or 20 dating back to the 1840s and 1850s, all for purchase of supplies and things like that."

Stone says he plans to go back through all the old papers to see whether any of the listed property had names.

He says the visit for his children was another Black History Month lesson.

"They're aware of Black History Month and they understand about slavery . . . I think they found it interesting that these folks were able to trace their ancestors back to being slaves working at Whitehall."

As the Thompsons pass through Whitehall's foyer, they sign the guest book the Stones keep. The house is private, but being Greenville's oldest residence, it is open to the public two or three times a year at the family's discretion.

As the Thompsons meander, walking through the living and dining room and heading upstairs to look at the bedrooms, before descending to stand in the family room, remodeled circa 1995, their eyes move over portraits and lamps and furniture. Their unasked questions — where did things come from and was there anything left of the slaves — remain unasked.

In the family room, Chuck Stone suddenly says, "Here's some old papers," and points to framed documents and portraits on a wall. Charles Thompson holds up an abstract he's been carrying around for months. His sheet has portraits of George W. Earle and his wife, Elizabeth Robinson Earle, and Eugene Earle Stone and his wife, Florida Croft Stone.

The portraits are the same as those on the wall.

It is but a brief moment of excitement, but when you're hunting ghosts, every moment counts.

The Thompsons settle in the family room, and Rose Morton asks to visit the nearby family cemetery. Stone agrees.

While he fetches the key from his downtown office, his wife, Rita Stone, serves iced tea.

"This house wasn't meant to be a grand home. It was just a summer place. Like the chandeliers. Those are not original to the house. The plaster and doors are ... "

She tells them about the renovation she and her husband did eight years ago and how the tiny kitchen is now the master bath. The family cemetery, once a part of the property, is 2 1/2 miles away surrounded by a chain link fence next to an empty lot. There are no old slave quarters in this yard near downtown.

Rita Stone married into this historic family and can provide less historic information about slaves than her husband. She doesn't know where the slave quarters once were or who sold whom to whom.

But that doesn't stop Rose Morton from asking.

"So where is the family cemetery?"

"It's not far from here."

"You don't know whether any slaves were sneaked into the cemetery?"

Her brother, Charles, who is sitting at the kitchen counter, buries his face in his hands.

"No. No. No. No, Rose. No."

Stone says nothing, but she offers a shy, slightly uncomfortable smile.

"We found some old Ladies Home Journals upstairs. Would you like to see those?"

The family's excitement is palpable. They think they're going to see diaries. The only word they hear is "journals."

"Yeah! Yes! OK." Their exclamations tumble together.

As Rita Stone returns with the weathered, brownish yellow booklets, the family gathers around frantically trying to get a glimpse.

The books are issues of Harper's Bazaar and Ladies Home Journal from the 1850s. They aren't diaries or records or documents that might give the Thompsons information about their family. Charles Thompson politely thumbs through them and then leaves them on the counter.

He has been one of the linchpins of this search for ghosts. It was to him that their grandmother, Geraldine Snow, told much of the family story. The first to begin the search, he is practical and businesslike. He tosses aside anything that isn't relevant. And while he is not without sentiment, there is no room in historical research for fantasy.

His sister, Rose, is more romantic. There is a quiet desperation in her face. You can see it as she rides in a van through the streets of a Southern town she's never seen. You can see it as she reads documents on a stranger's wall.

You can see it when she's talking to people, watching, hoping that some hint of what she's looking for will fall from their mouths.

It's the desperation of searching for something that might be impossible to find. But she searches anyway, operating on a faith in things unseen.

She watches the Stone children assemble in the kitchen near their mother. They are mostly quiet during the visit, among the most well-behaved children ever. They have few questions because they asked them before the Thompsons arrived.

"They had some of the same questions that the family did: what they would have done, where they would have lived," Rita Stone said.

Chuck Stone has returned, having retrieved the cemetery key. He and his sons climb into his Range Rover, and the Thompson family follows them to the Earle and Stone family cemetery.

There is something peaceful about cemeteries, and it's not just that its occupants are silent. It is because, for them, the journey is over.

As Rose Morton moves among the stone monuments, she knows she won't find her family. But she looks for the names of those who owned them. She recognizes them from her research, and that in itself is a brief victory.

It is those names that will be the starting point for more searches through wills and sales records.

It is through these names that she will find her names.

At some point, her excitement becomes contagious for Stone, who is proud of his heritage and his family's contributions to Greenville and to the South.

Not far from the cemetery is a bronze sign detailing the achievements of Col. Elias Earle, who supplied ammunition to militias in the late 1700s and was the first commissioner of Indian Affairs for the United States.

The Thompsons walk through mud and grass to stand and read it. It is the least they can do for this man who is a link to their past, even if he can't aid their search. But the descendants of the one family and the descendants of the other never talk directly about slavery.

Eventually done with the ghosts of the Stone family, the Thompsons thank their host. And just as quickly as they enter his life, they leave it.

"I'm trying to find our history," Charles Thompson says in the car. They head over to an African-American cultural center run by a woman whose story appeared in the Greenville News the day the Thompsons arrived.

Charles Thompson's latest focus is Phoebe and Caesar's daughter, Judy, his great-great-great aunt. He knows that Phoebe and Caesar's son Agrippa and his wife, Mary, were sold to the Yancey plantation in Alabama, next year's February destination.

But Agrippa's sister, Judy, wasn't sold to Alabama, and was left behind in South Carolina.

"I really want to try to find my great-great-great aunt Judy," he says. "I'm trying to figure out where her kids are. And maybe one of those kids was interested in genealogy. I'm looking for the descendant who's trying to trace his roots."

He pulls up to the center, a two-story house in the heart of town.

"Whoo-oo-ee! You went to visit who?!"

Ruth Ann Butler speaks of Charles Benjamin Stone, the Chuck Stone the family just visited, in the hushed tones reserved for royalty. He is, after all, among Greenville's most prominent residents.

"I'm amazed at that. I applaud them," she says. "I have great respect for the family, and I know of the family, from a distance."

Butler, 59, is a bundle of energy who taught history for 18 years. But, a longtime genealogy bug, she quit teaching to run the Greenville Cultural Exchange Center.

She traced her roots back to Africa and the Thompsons want to get some advice.

"My family came out of Edgefield, about 45 miles from here, and the white side of my family lived in Whitehall," she tells them.

When the Greenville News published a story about her research, she says she got a phone call from a white relative who said, "You are our family."

She has done what the Thompsons are trying to do, so the Michiganders want to see her research, files upon files of notes she has gathered for years.

When the Thompsons first called, she says, "I thought they were going to challenge me in my story. That's when she (Rose Morton) complimented me on the good job I'd done and said she was a descendant, too."

Butler gives the family encouragement, but she also gives them help — a local genealogist named Anne McCuen, who suggests that the family visit South Carolina's capital, Columbia, to look through its census and tax records.

"It's a difficult thing, very difficult," McCuen says. "Here in Greenville County, there once was a record of all the slaves because their masters had to pay taxes on them. But once the Civil War was over, there was no authority over that information. They just threw the records away."

McCuen, 77, says the Thompsons are lucky because their family was owned by wealthy families who were more apt to keep records of land transactions, the goings-on at their plantations and tax records.

That luck is something that Rose Morton and Charles Thompson and their siblings will need as they continue to trace their family's early journey in America.

But they're armed with much more: conviction.

February 23, 2003

FORGED BY DETROIT

Four boys overcome violence, reach their dreams

This is the story of four boys who lived in and around violence, but never let it kill their dreams.

They attended Murray Wright High School back when it was called "Murder Right" and all the nation knew about Detroit was that Motown's youth were being killed left and right.

They were freshmen in 1985 when a shooter pulled into the school parking lot and fired into a homecoming football game crowd, wounding six people.

They were juniors in 1987 when a 14-year-old shot football star Chester Jackson to death in the hall because Chester had pointed a finger at him and bumped him in a hallway.

The four are working to give their hometown a new reputation. It's an uphill battle, but one in which they've already scored: Charles Pugh is a popular anchor at Fox 2 News. Reggie Davis, WJLB's Reggie Reg, is one of the city's fastest rising radio stars. Jamaine Dickens is the mayor's press secretary. And Ricardo Moore is a police officer, his goal since he was 14.

These four achieved despite the likelies they heard like blaring, inescapable radio tunes: likely to drop out of school, likely to have babies before 16, likely to get shot before 18.

Now they've come full circle and have achieved in their hometown. But their success comes as Detroit is once again being defined by the senseless slayings of innocent youth, such as 16-year-old Mario Smith, who was gunned down last weekend while walking home from work.

Their success comes as the 2002 death toll for Detroit youth nears 30.

Two escaped the violence, one skirted it, and the life of another could have been devastated by it. But all four survived and have become what they told classmates 13 years ago that they would be.

They want to be role models for youth who need someone to look up to besides Ja Rule and DMX. They work with young people and preach the values of hard work and nonviolence. They, more than concrete and steel, should represent Detroit's true renaissance.

They — and the tens of thousands like the boys they once were — are the human capital that Detroit must focus on as much as buildings and business.

"My success is possible for a young person who goes to any Detroit high School, even Murder Right. You have what it takes to make it. You have what it takes right now." — Charles Pugh

"God is very influential ... without Him, it can't happen. Young people, you got your DMXs and Ja Rules and Cam'rons ... You can call them your heroes but then you can call us your heroes!" — Reggie Reg

"If you're from Detroit, you're going to make it. No matter what your social status is, no matter what school you're in, you can make it happen. You just have to want it for yourself." — Jamaine Dickens

"Everyone has problems, and it's how you get rid of your problems that determines whether you rise to the top or sink to the bottom." — Ricardo Moore

CHARLES PUGH: THE ANCHOR

The violence struck Charles Pugh when he was 3.

The skinny, smart kid was born on Aug. 3, 1971 to George and Marcia Pugh. But his parents divorced when he was 18 months old, and soon after, his mom began dating a drug dealer.

"She knew too much about his drug cartel, and he was abusing her, so she was killed," Pugh says, not matter-of-factly, but with the resignation that comes with years of accepting the Thanksgiving Day 1974 tragedy.

He moved in with his father, and was living there when, depressed and out of a job, his father killed himself on Friday, Oct. 13, 1978.

"Before I heard the gunshot, he came in my room, took me downstairs and put me on the couch," Pugh recalls. "Then he was taking my stuff, sheets and things, so I went back to bed. We went back and forth, back and forth to the living room and the bedroom. He did that two or three times.

"So finally, he left me in my bed. And he said, 'This is the last time, son.'

And I was thinking, 'Well, I hope the hell so, because you've been putting me back and forth on the couch and the bed.'

"That wasn't the last time he was talking about. That was the last time he'd see me alive. So he kissed me. I kissed him. He said, 'I love you,' and I said 'I love you, too.' He went back in his room, which was right across the hall."

The second-grader heard the shot and ran to the phone and dialed 911.

"There was blood everywhere," Pugh recalls. "I'd seen CPR on TV, so I put my mouth on his mouth and blew."

His father's death left him to his grandmother, Mary Pough, who raised him on Social Security and a lot of love. He attended Murray Wright because it had a TV station, and he had a dream.

"I always wanted to be on TV," he says. "It was confirmed when I saw the Oprah Winfrey show, and I said that is the baddest woman ever. She's smart. She's savvy. She's beautiful. She's funny. And she's so rich that she has such a great influence on the world. . . . I said, I want to do that."

When he graduated, Pugh used a Ford Motor Co. scholarship to attend the University of Missouri. He began his professional TV career in Fort Wayne, Ind., three hours from Detroit.

"It was so nice. It was the first time in five years that I was able to get home," he says.

He next worked for the NBC affiliate in Norfolk, and his career really took off. He became the 5 p.m. weekday anchor and had his own talk show.

He was 26, and the timing was significant.

"My mom was 26 when she died. My dad was 32 when he died, and God promised me that I would be able to live the rest of their lives for them," Pugh recalled. "When I turned 26, I was promoted to be the 5 p.m. anchor in Norfolk. At that time, I was the youngest and the first black person to co-anchor the news with another black person."

In December 1998, producers at WJBK-TV saw his tape and called him home.

"I had told my classmates that before our 10-year reunion, I was going to be on TV at home. So there was my opportunity."

The class reunion was in August 1999, two months after his June 21 debut on Fox.

He was 27.

You would think the violence in Pugh's younger life might have dictated the direction of his future. But his salvation, he says, came in two words:

"My family."

"Because I had such tragedy, my uncles became my fathers, my aunt became my mom and my older cousins became the older brother and sisters that I never had. They would not let me fail. They would not let me feel like I didn't have any love."

REGGIE REG: THE DJ

He was 14 when he learned that his father had been labeled as one of North America's top drug dealers.

He was 16 and a sophomore at Murray Wright when his father, Reginald Gary Davis, was sentenced to 45 years in prison for cocaine trafficking.

But Reggie Davis, the small guy with the great voice, decided to chart his own path, and that road led to radio.

He was born and raised in Detroit by his mother, Bambi, and her mother, the late Hattie Mae Booth, a native of Rome, Ga. It was his grandmother who provided the spiritual grounding that would lead to his success as a DJ.

Davis, known to his legions of fans as Reggie Reg, who turned 32 on Sunday, which means he has loved radio for a quarter century.

He grew up in Palmer Woods and spent most of his early years in parochial schools. But he chose Murray Wright for high school because it had a radio station and he wanted to be in a public school, to be around what he called "real people."

His first time on the air was at age 12 on a teen talk show on WGPR. In high school, he did a teen rap show for WDTR, the Detroit Public Schools' radio station.

He's been Reggie Reg since 1985 when, as a high school junior, he began working at any radio station that would have him.

But he also was skirting the edge of Detroit's youth violence. He partied. Hard. And he had an obsession with guns.

"I had two 9-millimeters, a .45, a sniper rifle and a double-barrel sawed off," he says. "On New Year's I'd shoot them. I got in trouble with the police for excessive loud noise during New Year's. They called me a trigger-happy guy."

Staying on the straight and narrow "was definitely a major struggle for me," he says. "My grandmother, Hattie Mae, would sit me down and talk to me and encourage me and make sure I stayed on the right track because all of that was so close to me.

"There were times where I came close, extremely close," he says. "Violence was more of an obstacle for me than anything,"

He had stopped attending school regularly because radio and "the life" had become everything. But all that changed on Feb. 10, 1987.

It was a Tuesday. The WJOB-FM intern and his sister and her boyfriend were headed to his house.

"We're flying down the street! We get to Seven Mile and Wyoming on the way to Palmer Woods, and some man in a van was driving drunk . . . and hit us. We hit a curb and a light. I flew out of the car and hit my head."

He was in the hospital for six weeks.

"Before that, I was devoting too much time to radio and to my dreams. I had a talk with God and what came out of that was I needed to get back and understand right and wrong," he says.

The accident and the things his grandmother had always told him straightened him up.

"If it wasn't for my grandmother, I'd be dead or serving time, or doing something wrong," he says.

He returned to school and graduated with honors, earning a four-year scholarship to Wayne State University. He skipped college to work full time, initially in Flint, later in Tulsa and Los Angeles.

In 1998, station owner Terry Arnold was changing WCHB 105.9 from jazz to hip-hop, and wanted Reggie Reg for the new format.

"They flew me in," Reg recalled. "We met on a Saturday, and the station was playing jazz. On Monday, there was no more jazz. We went from Earl Klugh to LL Cool J overnight."

He eventually wound up back at WJOB and has been there ever since. Now he co-hosts "Sports Wrap," a sports and entertainment show that airs on CBS on Saturdays, is a reporter for a cable news show, and is penning his autobiography. And if all that isn't enough, he's been approached about a possible film on his life.

RICARDO MOORE: THE COP

Ricardo Moore's life was that of a typical middle-class boy. The son of Delores and Edward Moore, a warehouse manager, he grew up in northwest Detroit. The youngest of five kids, he knew what he wanted to be.

"When we played, everybody wanted to be the robber," he says. "I wanted to be the cop. I was a big fellow, which was strategic in playing cops and robbers."

At 14, he joined Detroit's Junior Police Cadet program.

"I was transformed," he says. In his years at Murray Wright, Moore, like his friend Jamaine Dickens, was an enforcer who kept bullies from picking on their skinnier and smaller buddies, including Charles Pugh and Reggie Davis.

He steered clear of the violence that plagued some kids for two reasons:

First, in his mind, he was already a law enforcement officer. Second, his father was 56 years old when he was born.

"Because I had older parents, I had a structured lifestyle," he recalled. "My father was 72 when he died, and I was 16. My mother will be 71 in April.

That's why I wasn't able to get into those things that the average person was doing, kids with youthful parents who let their kids run up and down the street. I was very fortunate."

After graduating from Murray Wright, he earned a bachelor's degree in criminal justice from Western Michigan University. He says he was mentored into the department." I had been around police officers since I was 14. I understood leadership. I understood rank structure. It was comfortable."

He initially worked as a security director for a downtown apartment building before joining the department in 1995.

Moore also grew up in Central Christian Methodist Episcopal church. But away from church, he listened to the Isley Brothers and was a budding rapper.

Moore's friends call him a kind spirit sure of his soul.

That certainty of spirit is something he'll need now. He was transferred from communications to the 13th Precinct as a patrol supervisor after he criticized Police Chief Jerry Oliver's decision not to promote officers currently eligible because some had past disciplinary problems. Moore went from speaking for the chief to working midnights covering midtown Detroit. On his last day in communications, he issued a press release outlining the exchange of opinions he'd had with the chief. He was suspended, and the chief has ordered that he undergo a psychological evaluation.

In battles between an officer and a chief, the chief usually wins.

But officials at the Lieutenants and Sergeants Association say the union will fight Moore's suspension vigorously.

And Deputy Chief Gary Brown of the department's professional accountability bureau says the investigation is simply to check Moore's fitness. He said he expects Moore to be with the department "for a long time."

"I see him as one of the leaders of the department. The goal is to return him to work. That's our goal — absolutely."

Moore's lesson for youth might be how to survive adversity.

"This is a perfect example of times in your life that aren't going to be perfect, regardless of what you know or who you know," Moore says. "You just have to stand up."

JAMAINE DICKENS: THE WRITER

Unlike his friends Charles Pugh, Reggie Davis and Ricardo Moore, who knew they wanted to be a TV anchor, a radio DJ and a cop, Jamaine Dickens knew only that he loved writing.

The youngest of nine boys and the first in his family to go to college, he knew one other thing: "I wanted to wear a suit and tie and carry a briefcase."

The violence was always close to Dickens, but his family kept him a step away even as they got involved with drugs themselves.

"I had eight older brothers," Dickens says, "and a lot of them had been involved in 'activities,' and I saw where it landed them.

"I had two brothers on drugs. One is in prison for double life. I never even met him. I just heard stories about him. And one drank himself to death.

"I looked at the things they were doing and not doing and decided to do things they were not doing," he says. He avoided Detroit's late '80s mayhem, he says, by using the violence "as motivation to succeed."

Despite their penchant for trouble, his brothers loved and protected him, Dickens recalls.

"They didn't show me violence," he says. "It was drugs and drinking. I pieced it together later in my life. They tried hard. My oldest brother told me in later years, 'We didn't take you with us, let you hang out with us because we didn't want you to do what we were doing, be what we were.' "

Dickens graduated from Murray Wright intending to enlist in the Air Force. But after a visit to a college fair, he wound up applying to Jackson State in Mississippi.

"I got a letter saying I'd been accepted, and Jackson State came through (on funds)," he says. But "I got there still not knowing what I wanted to do."

He worked as a DJ at the campus radio station, WJSU, making $200 a month playing jazz. Between the money and his easy-listening voice, he became a babe magnet.

But those weren't the girls who interested him.

"I walked out of the station one day on my way to class and saw a beautiful woman," he recalls. "I followed her down the hall to this door. It said Student Newspaper. I went in. It turned out that she was an editor, so I told her I wanted to do a story."

The editor, LaWanda Black, assigned him one. He turned it in, and she marked it all up in red ink.

"I reworked it and gave it back to her and said, 'I dare you to put a red mark on it.' She later became my wife."

Dickens had found a way to do what he always wanted: write. He joined the staff of the city's black newspaper, the Jackson Advocate, making $25 a story and $15 per photo. He did internships in Jackson and Memphis.

"All that time, I wanted to get back home," he says. "I wanted to work at the Free Press or the News."

After graduation, he worked for newspapers in Alabama and Florida, before changing careers to become the public affairs director for the Leon

County (Fla.) Board of Commissioners.

He was 26.

He was in Detroit on Christmas vacation in 2000 when a friend of Kwame Kilpatrick, who was Democratic leader of the Michigan Legislature, told him he'd put his name in the hat to be Kilpatrick's communications director.

"I called him out of courtesy," Dickens says. "I had just bought a house and had started my own PR company. I thought he would be a good contact to make."

Kilpatrick invited Dickens to Lansing. When they met, Dickens was Kwamied — so moved by what the future Detroit mayor said that he couldn't say no.

"I called the people at the county (back in Florida) and told them I wasn't coming back," he says. He was on the job two days later. Three months after that, his new boss decided to run for mayor of Detroit. Dickens became his press secretary last summer.

As for his ambition of writing?

"I get to write all the time," he says.

December 6, 2002

DORIS BARKSDALE

Score an assist for 'Canes' motivational counselor

Few people outside Detroit have heard of Doris Barksdale.

But on the day of what might be the final game in this year's fight for the Stanley Cup, it's important to know this woman whose role with the Carolina Hurricanes makes her unique to hockey.

Barksdale, a lifelong learner who has counseled hundreds of people, from corporate executives to city officials to NBA stars over the past 15 years, is the spiritual adviser and motivational counselor for the Hurricanes.

That means that in one of the whitest sports around, the guiding spiritual force behind a team in the Stanley Cup spotlight is a black woman from Georgia who spent most of her life in Detroit — and wasn't a hockey fan.

The Lord works in mysterious ways.

Barksdale doesn't talk to Hurricane players about icing or being more aggressive at the net; she talks to them about feeling good about themselves.

The amazing life of Doris Barksdale is one for the books, or a book or a TV movie about a Douglas, Ga., girl who survives racism, moves to Detroit after the grandmother raising her dies and makes, instead of finds, a life for herself.

But what matters now, as the Hurricanes head into a must-win game tonight against the Red Wings, the NHL's most talented team, is that they better bring gale forces and all that Doris has taught them.

Her influence is unparalleled. She counsels the players and the staff — from general manager Jim Rutherford to coach Paul Maurice, who said her job is not to be a coach, but to build self-esteem.

"We use her in a motivational manner, not in terms of coming in and giving the Gipper speech, but on an individual basis for players throughout our system," Maurice says. "She has a great way of helping players develop game plans in terms of their individual goals and team goals, helping them really see clearly that the two are intertwined."

Barksdale, reached at her three-bedroom condo five minutes from the Entertainment and Sports Arena in Raleigh, N.C., said she's been counseling Hurricanes since some were tiny storms, playing junior hockey for the Windsor Spitfires and the Junior Red Wings. She met the team through Rutherford.

"A couple of my clients were NBA players who were playing for the Pistons," Barksdale said. "They were playing golf and somebody . . . wasn't playing well, and he said, 'I need to talk to Doris,' and Jim said, 'Who's Doris?'"

Rutherford called her.

"He said he understood that I counseled people, and he'd heard my name and he wanted to talk to me," Barksdale said.

Rutherford vividly recalled their first conversation and her first hockey client.

"I had a player who was having some personal problems, and he was really down. It was affecting his life, affecting his play, so I set up an appointment and I drove him to her house," he said. "I remember so clearly how he was depressed. I dropped him off. He met with her for an hour, or hour-and-a-half.

"I came back, and he came out, and it wasn't the same person I dropped off."

When those players moved from Windsor to Hartford and then to North Carolina, Barksdale still counseled them.

Then five years ago, Barksdale relocated from Detroit to Raleigh to work full-time as the team's sports counselor and community relations director, working on projects that included the area's bid for the 2007 Pan American Games.

She counseled the committee both before its big presentation in San Antonio, and after its bid was beaten.

"There's just a sort of get-on-with-it thing with her," said Jim Goodmon, president of WRAL-TV and a member of that committee. "She reminded us that we did the best we could, so what's next? She told us that the fact that all of us went through that together was more important than whether we won or lost.

I was ready to shoot somebody, but she got us looking at the positive."

Since a mild heart attack last year, Barksdale has relinquished such community duties to focus solely on counseling.

"What I do is I keep telling them (the players) how good they are, how great they are, and they are great because everybody is great!" she said. "One of the things that's wrong with the world is we're not told often enough that we're OK or more than that, that we're special."

Maurice, 35, the youngest coach in the NHL and one who has sought her counsel, says her lack of formal training is a plus. Barksdale didn't graduate from high school, but earned a GED, took some college courses and participated in dozens of YMCA-sponsored workshops.

"In some ways, it's an advantage that her training is through life experiences," Maurice said. "She's not structured to the point of theories and approaches. The human approach is the right approach."

After attending years of workshops, she created her own program, which she presented most recently in April at the Detroit Unity Temple.

"She's gifted," says the Rev. Argentina Glasgow, senior minister, who attended high school with Barksdale. "I think she's able to touch people at a level where we all need to be touched, and that's our inner self. When you do that, we're able to find our own power."

Barksdale said her lack of a degree will not hinder her.

"I'm not going to live on this Earth with these gifts that flow through me and not validate the divine plan for my life," she said.

The irony of her joining a hockey club is that, even after 40 years in Detroit, she was never a Red Wings fan.

"I knew they existed. I was glad that they won a Stanley Cup. But I didn't feel them," she said. "I didn't have the association. I didn't feel weaved into their fabric. They were not weaved into mine."

Barksdale said she loves working with her boys, attending their games and enduring their teasing when she tells other players, "Get off of him!" And it is her work with the Hurricanes and their junior teams, in Massachusetts, Florida, and in Plymouth, that fuels her life now — that and expanding her counseling.

Her modesty has kept her job hidden from public view, and she says she's "just glad to be a dot on the paper they write all this stuff on."

And though she won't reveal her age, she reveals her love of life every day.

"I'm 60-plus and I've got a whole lot left to do," she said. "I don't count numbers. I'm grateful for the numbers. But I count the joys."

June 13, 2002

The champion steals the spotlight at 'Ali' premiere

LOS ANGELES — Outside Mann's Chinese Theater on Hollywood Boulevard on Wednesday, celebrities command the red carpet that covers the sidewalk for nearly a block. Limousine after limousine pulls up and spits out flavor-of-the-week new stars, veteran actors, aging athletes and political icons.

All come to this historic temple that began as a simple paean to movie stardom, but now anchors a major entertainment complex featuring department stores, seven theaters, a ballroom for sumptuous parties, and the Kodak Theater, home of next spring's Academy Awards.

Rude paparazzi stand elbow to elbow to get photos of stars arriving for the world premiere of "Ali," Michael Mann's portrait of the seminal years in the life of three-time heavyweight boxing champion Muhammad Ali. They shout out the first names of those whose faces will sell. They wait anxiously for the bigger stars whose arrivals come last, imploring non-celebs to keep moving:

"There's free food inside."

Jon Voight, Mario Van Peebles, Mykelti Williamson, Ron Silver, Kevin James, Nicolette Sheridan, Dule Hill and others make their way past, their bodies incredibly tiny, their hair impeccably coiffed. Eddie Murphy strides along, wearing his angry man sneer, black sunglasses and, on his arm, his impossibly beautiful wife. He looks like he weighs 100 pounds.

Giancarlo Esposito, who plays Cassius Clay Sr., graciously stops to pose for photos with fans.

This is the maelstrom of bright lights that was Muhammad Ali's home for nearly 20 years as a boxer. This was the hoopla that surrounded every match, every entrance into arenas where he basked in cheers, endured the disco-ball effect of hundreds of flashbulbs and put up with the pluck-pluck-pluck of fingers that just wanted to touch him.

Here, on this night, 20 years after his last heavyweight match, Ali is the star the crowds wait for. Minor celebrities and young actors on the brink become doe-eyed celebrity hounds themselves when they hear he is about to arrive.

Neither Jada Pinkett Smith nor her husband, Will, who owns "Ali," are the main event.

Nothing really happens until the Greatest gets here. He is late, but no one cares because there would be no movie without him.

Thirty years ago he would have marched in, strong, proud, lithe, surrounded by the men who didn't make him but helped him make himself, among them Angelo Dundee and Drew (Bundini) Brown.

But tonight he makes his way slowly, head bowed, surrounded by an entourage that includes his wife, Lonnie, some of his children and his ever-present best friend Howard Bingham.

Twenty years since his last fight, five years since lighting the Olympic torch and re-igniting the torch that fans have borne for him for decades, Ali is back on top.

He came through once as the young Louisville Lip, whose bombast and poetry are now the stuff of sports fairy tales, the man who didn't invent trash-talking, but took it to new heights.

He was sleek, so gorgeous he told you so, and so commanding in the ring that watching even re-enactments of his fights by a buffed rapper-comic-actor, gives boxing fans chills.

In Ali's first life, he was an Olympic gold medalist, world heavyweight boxing champion and a Muslim. He also was a conscientious objector to the Vietnam War, which cost him years of boxing and nearly sent him to jail. His refusal to fight in the war made him at once adored and reviled.

Now, during the second coming of Muhammad Ali, he is making a greater comeback than any to win championships. He is becoming a hero for a new generation of young people who are racing to the history books and to their parents for a better understanding of a man whose story is larger than life.

"Let me tell you something. My father — boxing is his sport," said Henry Simmons, who co-stars on "NYPD Blue" and attended the premiere. "I've been watching Joe Louis, Sugar Ray Robinson, Muhammad Ali since I was about 3 or 4 years old and MA is my favorite athlete of all sports.

"I read about three or four biographies, and I did not know that his relationship with Bundini was so strong and I didn't know about Cosell as well," he said, citing the relationship that the boxer had with the sportscaster Howard Cosell. "People of color have so many stories tell. Movies like this always help."

Ali now is a humanitarian peace-keeper, a United Nations ambassador who travels nearly 200 days a year to countries around the world. His focuses are saving children and helping developing nations.

Despite having Parkinson's disease, he has personally delivered food to countries from Indonesia to Morocco to Liberia. Amnesty International gave him a lifetime achievement award. He was chairman of the committee that selected and announced the annual International Hannah Neil World of Children Award Web site last Friday. The award salutes those who have made significant contributions to the health, well-being, social environment, intellectual understanding or education of children. This year's winner, Sharadkumar Dicksheet, travels to India each year to perform surgeries on needy children who suffer from congenital deformities.

He was honored in Columbus with a $100,000 prize and meeting Ali. Ali is enjoying almost as much fame and celebrity as he did the first time around. He is Coca-Cola's newest spokesperson (infinitely more interesting than Pepsi's Britney Spears). And he will visit President George W. Bush at the White House next month for a special screening of "Ali." It's quite a circle from the 1960s when the American government called him a coward and his boxing license was taken away for refusing to go to war.

In the opening scene of "Ali," a 22-year-old Cassius Clay punches a speed bag while the audience sees flashbacks from his life — running in steel-toed boots around Chickasaw Park and along downtown streets in Louisville, Ky.; being haunted by newspaper stories and photos about the murder of Emmett Till, a 14-year-old Chicago boy tortured and lynched for looking at a white woman while visiting relatives in Mississippi; watching his father, Cassius Clay Sr., paint pictures of Jesus, a savior of Middle Eastern descent, with white skin and blue eyes.

Many years have passed since a 12-year-old boy used boxing to escape racism and race to greatness.

So how can the biggest person in the world become bigger? Let Will Smith play you in a movie that will teach another generation of young Americans about what you did.

"Ali" is the story of the 10 years between his knocking out heavyweight champion Sonny Liston in 1964 to become the Greatest at 22 to losing his boxing career to his regaining the ring and gaining millions of fans around the world.

Director Mann dealt with only 10 years. As Ali's best friend Bingham said at Wednesday's post-premiere party, "It would take a movie a week to tell the real story of Ali."

His sentiments were echoed by other stars who said they learned so much and the film made them want to know more.

"It is extremely important that a film like 'Ali' was made so that people really understand the sacrifices that a black man made, especially during the '60s when, to me, it seems like they wanted to send him off to the Army to kill him — and he knew that," actress Vivica Fox said at the premiere.

"But he stood his ground. The young generation needs to know that and not just know him for the accolades of winning the championship." Fox said. "Anytime we can have our brothers portrayed on the screen by positive actors who will sacrifice and submit themselves to the character the way Will Smith did, well, we need more of them.

"You know what was moving to me? It was that he was in Africa and he saw the things the African kids had drawn about him. You just learn so much. The only thing they've shown (in years past) is Africans running behind him like they were crazy. But they loved him. They felt a connection to him."

The scene gives clues into the psyche of the world's most famous man. People draw different lessons for their own lives from how Ali lived his and the bigger he continues to get, the more people search for the meaning of life in his actions, his history, his legacy.

No one has told people more that they should look only to themselves to learn how to live than Ali himself. As he says in the movie: "I'm going to be the champ I want to be."

Ali, who lives in Berrien Springs, his wife and Bingham, who is also an executive producer of the movie, are on a multi-city tour to attend screenings of "Ali." But it's not about the movie.

The screenings in Las Vegas, Chicago and Louisville, Ali's hometown, are expected to raise $2.5 million for his next greatest project, the Muhammad Ali Center, which is intended to increase peace and tolerance. The center is planned for construction on the banks of the Ohio in downtown Louisville.

Construction is due to begin in March, said founder and board member Larry Townsend, a Louisville businessman.

Five years ago, the center was a pipe dream.

Then it became a plan.

Then it became an office in the arts district of Louisville, the conflicted town that gave Ali to the world at a time when some of its residents were glad to be rid of the loud-mouthed kid who brought home Olympic gold in his first trip away from home, but who spoke too candidly about racial problems for their Southern tastes.

The center will keep the flame that burns now for a man who, even in his quietest times, makes more noise than ever.

The movie comes at a time when the world is learning what makes a hero. Ali holds fast to Islam, the religion that has brought him as much peace as it did trouble when he first converted. But he holds fast, at a time when extremists have sullied Islam, a time of men like Osama bin Laden, whose hatred of Americans has made him a hero to those who share his cause. Ali, who abhors violence, is bigger.

"This man's essence is the same as it was when he wasn't everybody's hero," says Jeffrey Wright, who portrays Bingham. "He's a living link to the great men who were killed in the '60s for taking heroic stances.

"What happens with Ali is he became this universal hero, but that was only after his skills were diminished — his verbal skills were diminished, his physical skills were diminished. But when he was my hero and he was somebody else's anti-hero, he had the same essence.

"I'm glad that the story can be told, a version that gives a fuller account of the journey so that young people can fully understand that he wasn't just a boxer. And when they have these debates about who was the greatest fighter, there'll be no confusion over whether Mike Tyson or Ali was the greatest fighter.

"We'll try to keep Ali's fights inside and outside the ring in the forefront of young minds."

December 14, 2001

Store owner provides kids with more than treats

Every neighborhood has that place, that one magical place where dreams come true. That place you can't wait to run to after school or on Saturdays.

For me, that place was Miss Dale's store, which was heaven — or all that children dreamed heaven to be: a long, narrow counter full of Bazooka Joe, jars of dill pickles and bins of five-for-a-penny sugar cookies.

In Detroit, for thousands of kids, for 76 years, it has been Leddy's Wholesale Candy & Tobacco. Inside the bright yellow building with fire-red doors, boxes of Mike and Ikes and Snickers are stacked politely on the floor. Shelves are stocked with barrels of Laffy Taffy and Now and Laters.

But Leddy's, which opened in 1924 on Grand River Avenue, offers more.

Through two world wars and depressions and celebrations, race riots and demographic flips, Leddy's has been constant. When Detroit's white residents began abandoning the city, the store stayed put.

And for the past half-century, the teens who live near the store have had more than candy. They've had jobs.

The store owner, whom everyone calls simply "Leddy," has hired more than a hundred neighborhood teens, nearly all African-American, to work part time, teaching them responsibility and providing not only spending change, but also college tuition.

"I always try to hire kids from the neighborhood, mostly from Redford, Cooley and Henry Ford" high schools, Leddy says.

Tyrone Raines heard about Leddy from a friend who used to work at the store. Last March, he walked in and asked for a job. He was hired on the spot and now works afternoons and Saturdays.

The 18-year-old Cooley High senior, who wants to be a photographer, artist or wrestler when he gets older, says the money comes in handy. "I'm saving it for school, getting clothes, movies, skating parties . . ."

But he says Leddy is preparing him for everything.

"He's a real nice person. He teaches us stuff, like new words. He said, 'You don't know what this word is!? Go get the dictionary or you don't get paid.' So you go get the dictionary.

"He gave me this dollar one time with writing on it. It said: 'Save this and you'll never be broke.' I've still got that dollar!"

Omar Harrison, 19, a Detroit native who attends Marygrove College, was at the counter the day I visited. He's been with Leddy for almost six years, but he says he's known about the store and the man "forever, all of my life."

"He's a good person. He does things out of the kindness of his heart," Omar says.

Omar doesn't like candy, which makes him a great employee in a candy store. But as a kid, he says, "I used to come in here all the time."

He attends classes at night and works at the store during the day. Four other students come in after school and on Saturdays.

"I've probably had well over a hundred kids work here," Leddy says. "I have one young man ...I coached him in baseball, Little League baseball. He worked for me, but then he went to college in Grand Rapids."

Leddy sometimes visits that kid, John Foley, in Grand Rapids.

"He's got three children," he says. "I've been to all their baptisms, all of their weddings. I went up there this year for his 60th birthday party. He'll call up and say I'm going to come down Sunday for a home game, for a Tigers game, and we'd go the ballgame."

Leddy is lean (and strong for 72 or any age), wears jeans and boots and has a ready smile. He sells by the bag or box and always carries women's purchases to their cars.

His customers include schools, churches, hospitals and neighborhood kids who have grown up and bring their children back.

"I've watched a lot of wholesalers go out of business," he says.

His secret? "Low overhead," he says with a laugh. "I own the building."

Leddy and his wife, Mary, raised seven children of their own: Daniel, an Air Force staff sergeant stationed in London, but is now on temporary duty in Saudi Arabia; Elizabeth, who works in advertising in Chicago; Mary, who lives in Milford; Michael, who lives in Rochester; Robert, who lives in Detroit and works for MediaOne; James, a general contractor who lives in Livonia, and Joseph, a sales representative for California Closets, who lives in Novi.

But he has shared his wisdom with children not his own.

"I've met so many people. I know their faces. If they come in and put their name in the book," he says, "they can come in and get candy on their birthday!"

In times when penny candy costs a quarter and you barely know your boss, Leddy's is a throwback to days when the corner store was more than a place to buy. It was a place to be, a place to learn, a place run by somebody special.

The business had simple beginnings in the garage of a modest Dearborn home where Leo Leddy made candy in the early 1920s.

In 1924, when the building on Grand River became available, Leo Leddy moved his candy business there.

That same year, a western Kentucky farm family relocated from Paducah to Detroit. Their son, who would become the new owner of Leddy's, was born at Grace Hospital. He attended Detroit schools and enlisted in the Navy and worked during the Korean War as an engineer aboard first the USS Okaloosa, and then the USS Arnebb, which transported Marine amphibian cargo boats used for landings. Both ships were based in Norfolk, Va., but cruised the Atlantic and Mediterranean, protecting troops.

He served for four years before returning to Detroit and finding his love, then his life.

One night, several of his friends invited him to meet some girls for a VFW dance.

"Everybody paired up, and Mary and I were the last two there," he recalled, a chuckle sneaking out in the telling. "We went to the dance and hit it off."

They married on July 18, 1953, and he worked at a tool and die plant. But he was soon out of work.

"The plant closed, and I had to find a job. My father-in-law said, 'Come work for me.' I said, 'I'm from the east side. I don't know anything about this part of town.' He said, 'I'll draw you a map.'"

His father-in-law was Leo Leddy, who owned the candy store at 15928

Grand River Ave. The son-in-law accepted and went to work Dec. 15, 1953.

"I came part time, and the way it ended up, I made it a life career."

The young couple lived in an apartment above the store for a year before buying a three-bedroom bungalow, in Melvindale.

Leddy's has closed only for sickness and funerals in 47 years. During the 1967 riots that tore the city apart, Leddy was at work.

"I was open during the riots, every day," he says. Nothing ever happened to his store, and there is no Plexiglas partition between him and his customers, no barrier to keep you from shaking his hand.

"It was a gift of God. I have a strong faith," says the lifelong Catholic who attends St. Mary's of Redford, which retains the name that the neighborhood used to have before Detroit swallowed it up and chased Redford farther west.

"He's a white business owner, but he never left that community, and the community trusts him," says Cheryl Neely, whose family moved to the neighborhood 27 years ago. "Stores opened and closed around him. And he stayed."

He never considered closing up shop and moving out of Detroit.

"Everybody would be disappointed," he says. "I know that if I'm late in the morning, and Omar is here waiting for me, the customer pulls up and says, 'Oh, he's not open?' And Omar says, 'Don't worry, he'll be here.'

"I was only sick one time. I had the flu, and I missed Friday, Saturday and Sunday. I was back to work on Monday. Another time, I'd gone in for a physical and had a low blood count ... I missed a day to get medicine."

The year after the riots, Leddy bought a house two blocks from his store, right at home in the mostly black neighborhood.

He and his father-in-law ran the store together until Leo Leddy died in 1975. His widow gave the building to her son-in-law, and he continued to run it with Mary's help.

"I haven't had a vacation in 25 years," he says. "It's been tough sometimes, not always easy. The last 10 years have been the best."

His one heartache was losing his wife to breast cancer in 1983. Since then, he has run the store with his team of neighborhood youth.

And those kids always remember him.

"I get Father's Day cards from these kids, birthday cards. I've been invited to christenings. They call me up and say, 'I'm getting married!' and I go to their weddings."

Running his father-in-law's store and turning a neighborhood of youth into a family of workers is a sweet legacy. But the sweetest irony: He doesn't remember all his kids' names, and many of them don't know his.

"I've been called Leddy so many years, I became Leddy. My father-in-law's name was Leo Leddy.

"My real name is James Nall."

October 25, 2000

Former clerks take judge's ideals across America

Judge Damon Keith remembers the Yale University law student he interviewed 10 years ago for a job as his clerk. He questioned her, listened to her, then offered her the job on the spot.

And she burst into tears.

When he asked why, she said, " 'The law school, judge! They're just beating me down. I've lost my confidence. To become your law clerk — I'm crying out of happiness.' "

The revered jurist, who sits on the U.S. 6th Circuit Court of Appeals, never forgot Yasmin Cader, now a New York attorney. But he hasn't forgotten any of his clerks.

Keith, who turned 80 last Independence Day, has hired 72 clerks in his 35 years on the bench, creating a league of passionate civil rights attorneys, scholars and jurists who live his example.

But Keith did more. During times when minority and female law students struggled for acceptance and jobs, Keith gave 61 minorities (black, Asian, Hispanic, American Indian and Arab students) as well as 28 women, a foothold.

His landmark decisions will be his legacy, but his greater contribution might be how he helped diversify America's legal ranks with attorneys and educators who are teaching his principles.

"Judge Keith's office has been a training ground for a generation of lawyers committed to social change and public service, whether through politics, the judiciary, the practice of law or academia," says Spencer Overton, a professor at the George Washington University Law School. "Judge has hired more African-American law clerks than any other federal judge in the history of this country."

Keith says his contribution was just common sense.

"I saw so many great and outstanding law clerks who were finishing these law schools and had no place to go," Keith says. "I had to tell some of my African-American colleagues on the bench who said, 'I can't find any qualified black (clerks)' ... I said, 'Well, let's assume you had to be the first in your class or editor of your law review. Would you be sitting there as a federal judge? Give others a chance.' "

His former clerks are family who call "dad" for advice. They include a governor-elect, prominent jurists, one of the nation's most recognized law professors and a California firebrand called "The Flamethrower." They all credit their success to a judge who gave them confidence and taught them justice.

THE GOVERNOR

Jennifer Granholm, who Tuesday became the first woman elected governor of Michigan, clerked for Keith from 1987 to 1988 after graduating Harvard Law.

She says she seeks the judge's counsel before making important decisions, including her decision to run for governor.

"Before I take any job, I always talk to the judge," she said. "He's like a father to me in Michigan. He's strong about several things. One is ethics. The second is standing up and being courageous and doing the right thing. The third is the little people, the average citizen out there.

"He can walk among kings but never lose the common touch. He makes everybody special."

Granholm recalls how she and other clerks used to follow the judge from "speaking engagement to speaking engagement, and he always made sure that the first people he introduced were his staff.

"He is always utterly selfless in his recognition of other people," she says.

"That was always the wonderful model for me about how you should treat people."

When Granholm became state attorney general, protocol dictated that the chief judge of the state Supreme Court swear her in.

"I said 'I've got to have the judge come to Lansing and swear me in,' " she recalls. "Even though the powers that be didn't like that, they let him. I told the judge it would be such a great honor for him to swear me in as governor on Jan 1, too."

Keith has said yes.

THE PROFESSORS

Lani Guinier was a Keith clerk from 1974 to 1976, and she, too, was hired during her interview.

The celebrated attorney, scholar and Harvard Law School professor, the first black woman to be appointed to a tenured position there, in 1998, said Keith's action gave her and other budding attorneys something they really needed: confidence.

"It was a gesture of confidence that was incredibly affirming . . ."

Guinier says the judge taught her about being a good person as much as being an effective attorney.

"Judge Keith immediately became not only my employer and my supervisor; he also became my mentor,' " says Guinier, who was a Yale Law School student when she worked for the judge. "Judge Keith knew just about everyone. He mentored me not only in the law, sharing his great respect for the rule of law, but he also guided me in an equally important tradition: He taught me to speak to everyone, to listen to their stories and to smile in recognition at their greetings."

James Coleman, a professor at Duke University School of Law, called his Keith clerkship in 1974-75 "one of the most significant experiences in my professional life."

"I think that it unquestionably set the direction that my career took after that," says Coleman, a celebrated trial lawyer who gained national attention when he defended serial killer Ted Bundy during his sentencing hearings.

"I had a chance to work for a judge who was principled and courageous and those two things don't always come together, unfortunately. The judge would make tough decisions even when I think the less courageous thing and defensible thing would have been to take a pass and let someone else deal with it. He didn't do that."

Coleman said Keith's example was the one he lives by: to always act in the public interest. Coleman was in private practice in New York before he helped set up the Legal Services Corp. in Washington to provide legal help for the poor. He also is a former chief counsel for the House Ethics Committee.

"Sometimes duty requires you to do things that may go against the popular view," he says. "But that's when our rights are most at risk, when everybody agrees on what the outcome must be. That's when someone with a cool head must come in and raise questions . . . That's what I saw when I was working with him."

Coleman, 55, a professor at Duke for the last six years, is also senior associate dean for academic affairs. That means not only is he teaching the Keith principles to his students. He also is imparting them to other professors.

Spencer Overton, the George Washington University professor, says that Keith has thrice cemented his place in history — as a passionate activist attorney, as a courageous jurist and as a teacher whose ideals will last for centuries.

"Now that Justice Thurgood Marshall and Judge Leon Higginbotham have passed away, Judge Keith is the leader of an important school of jurisprudence committed to inclusion, participation and equality," Overton says. "My scholarship on voting rights and campaign finance . . . grow directly out of my experience as Judge Keith's clerk."

Overton says the qualities he learned from the judge are numerous and include "patience, humility, commitment to excellence and concern for others." And, he says, the clerks help each other.

"I've learned through my relationships with others he's mentored, like (Judge) Eric Clay, Lani Guinier, and Jennifer Granholm," he says. "Those of us on Judge Keith's staff were extremely focused and diligent, not because we feared Judge Keith's wrath, but because we feared disappointing a man we admired."

Keith's presence is felt in Overton's classroom now.

"During the first day of each class I teach, I convey to students the importance of civility in the classroom and the courtroom by telling them about Judge Keith," he says. "I tell them that in the 1950s and '60s some white judges intentionally humiliated Judge Keith and other black lawyers in front of their clients, and that as a result of that experience, Judge Keith always gives respect to lawyers, clients and all others."

THE JURISTS

Judge Eric L. Clay, who serves with Keith on the U.S. Court of Appeals, was once his clerk.

"I was a young law student finishing up at Yale Law School and Judge Keith was famous even at that time in legal circles, having handed down the domestic surveillance case involving the White Panthers and the Hamtramck housing case ... ," he recalled, citing the judge's rulings that the government could not engage in warrantless wiretap surveillance of the White Panthers and that Hamtramck had to provide low-income housing after black neighborhoods were leveled to build a Chrysler plant.

"The judge is very committed to people who have been loyal to him or are friends of his," Clay says. "I don't know of any value that is of greater, more paramount importance to him. I try to incorporate the importance of that in my own life as much as I can."

Clay, who was an attorney with Lewis & Munday in Detroit until 1997, says the judge taught him something that helps him on the bench to this day.

"When you have an extremely complicated or difficult legal matter, where the legal precedent and the case law may not be clear and you're attempting to decide what to do, what you should do, first and foremost, is ask yourself 'What is fair?' "

Clay expressed pride at being among the numbers who worked for Keith.

"I think his clerks have been so successful because the judge selects law clerks and young proteges based upon what appear to him to be their talent and their potential for accomplishment; it doesn't matter who their parents were, whether they came from well-to-do backgrounds. It's just a matter of him evaluating their character, their intellect, their prospect for making contributions to the profession and to society."

As a Harvard law student in 1989, Judge Wilhelmina Wright left Massachusetts and came to Detroit solely to pursue a job as a Keith clerk.

"I came because of who he was and the work that he had done both as a trial lawyer and the decisions he had made as a trial judge on the Court of Appeals," says Wright, who was appointed to the Minnesota Court of Appeals in September. A former district judge and assistant U.S. attorney, she, too, was hired on the spot.

She said what she learned most from the judge was to remember the people behind the appellate arguments.

"My co-clerks and I often engaged in intellectual discussion about cases and did so with great confidence," she recalls, "but the judge also wanted to make sure that we never lost sight of the fact that behind all of these legal principles and legal arguments were people."

THE FLAMETHROWER

Two years ago, California Law Business Journal, a respected legal magazine, named Constance L. Rice one of the state's Top 100 Most Influential California Attorneys, alongside such other notables as Gov. Gray Davis and former U.S. Secretary of State Warren Christopher.

But 18 years ago, she was Damon Keith's law clerk. And even then he knew that she would be a firebrand of an attorney.

A graduate of Harvard and New York University School of Law, she clerked for the judge from 1984 to 1986, went into private practice and worked at various venues including UCLA and the NAACP Legal Defense and Educational Fund.

She is now a partner at English, Munger & Rice in Los Angeles and co-director of the Advancement Project, an L.A.-based resource agency that helps solve public policy problems involving race, ethnicity and culture.

What Rice learned from the judge, she says, is simple: "Keep your radar for justice always on. Don't turn it off."

Rice, 46, says Keith helped his clerks be themselves and proud of it.

"The thing about Judge Keith is he knows exactly who he is and there isn't an insecure molecule in his body," she says. "So he's not afraid of talent, he's not afraid of intelligence. He saw the clerkship as a partnership and I saw my job as making his chambers run like a clock and making sure the opinions that came out of his office were the best."

His commitment to law students, particularly minorities and women, has led to a league of activists to which she's proud to belong.

"He's like the father of our legal careers, a second father. We're a whole family of activist lawyers. He created a family of law clerks who pick up his perspective of using the law to advance democracy and advance inclusion and opportunity."

Judge Keith, the first of his parents' children to attend college, has never forgotten where he came from. It shows every time he meets someone.

"His outstanding quality is his common touch, his touch with the common man," Rice says. "Bill Clinton learned that from Judge Keith. There is a gentleness and humbleness to him that shouldn't be mistaken for weakness."

Judge Keith, in a way that is both powerful and humbling, keeps democracy alive in the courtroom, creating a road map to justice. But he went a step further. He decided to provide living guides on that road to ensure that no one seeking fairness can get lost. There can be no more monumental decision from the bench than that.

November 10, 2002

CHAPTER EIGHT

LIFE IN COLOR

A month that can free the imagination

Imagine being on a ship, cruising through ocean waters. Except you're in the ship's hold, shackled to the floor and to other people.

Imagine eating maybe once a day and having to relieve yourself where you sit.

Imagine sleeping spoonlike next to someone you barely know, night after night after night, while the metal cuts into your ankles. Imagine lying next to someone who has been dead for hours.

Imagine finally being free, only to learn that freedom is something other people have in a strange land where you are dragged onto stages and sold like cattle.

Imagine being boarded onto wagons and taken to houses unlike any you've seen and fields of plants you don't recognize. Imagine working in those fields sunup to sundown every day. Imagine all this happening in a language you don't understand. The only dialect you're taught is the whisper and snap of the whip.

Imagine not being allowed to read or learn or leave. Imagine knowing that this will happen to your children and your grandchildren and your great-grandchildren.

Then imagine a great war changing the economic outlook of a young nation and politically setting you free, without the means to begin a new life. Imagine packing the few rags you have and walking away from the only home you've known, a hell that kept you ignorant, stole your self-esteem, your willingness to take risks, your ability to be aggressive.

Imagine being poor because you don't know what else to be until you teach yourself something new. Imagine working hard your whole life because every hour of overtime takes your children another hour away from bondage.

Now imagine that you're white — and endured all that.

And you watch your children, the great-grandchildren of slaves, attend schools inferior to those attended by black people. Imagine your joy when your children excel anyway and build cities and invent necessities such as traffic lights and clocks. Imagine them competing for spaces at universities founded by black people's grandfathers, schools you must fight to make reflect America.

Imagine living every day knowing that only 136 years have passed since nearly 300 years of bondage ended — and that it didn't end for everyone then.

Remember now, you're white. And you endure black people resenting every effort to help you. They fight you in court to ensure you get nothing more than they have, that they've had all along.

Imagine how unfair that is.

Then fight anyway. Demand anyway. Remind America that the cost of a young country treating people like animals for centuries is that it takes centuries to correct, years for those people to stand. Some of you recover more quickly, adapt to freedom and being black, which means being successful. Black people cannot tell the difference between themselves and you except when you try to hail a cab.

Imagine having to explain to them over and over that if they've only known privilege, they can't imagine what it takes to overcome centuries of neglect.

Imagine rising from the bottom of a well you were pushed into, where you raised families, sang songs and never knew escape — until someone pulled you out.

Today is the last day of the one month each year designed to honor the contributions of your people, White History Month. It reminds of achievements, but also that you, too, are America.

Does it make a difference?

Imagine that.

February 28, 2001

Find King's message in your own life

It is telling about America and our times that our most important national debates still involve ideals that the Rev. Martin Luther King Jr. championed most of his life: nonviolence and equal opportunity for minorities.

The fact that the fight continues is a testament to the fire King lit under a nation of former victims, many of whom still suffer. The fact that there is still opposition to righting past wrongs is a testament to lasting prejudice and that America may never come to grips with its most sordid past: the enslavement of millions.

But what people might have missed most in the past week's King commemorations is that the minister was only a man. He devoted his life to what he believed. But he was still an army of one.

That is his most important message, and it is why people like Brenda Rosenberg and organizations like the American Arab Anti-Discrimination Committee are important.

Rosenberg is Jewish and so devoted to peace that she has turned it into a full-time job, giving speeches and working with peace groups to break down barriers between people of different cultures and faith and encourage dialogue among blacks and whites, Jews and Muslims, Pakistanis and Indians.

In November, she became the first Jewish woman to speak at Dearborn's Islamic House of Wisdom.

"I want to create a deeper understanding of the Abrahamic faith, especially our many shared values and to improve the common well-being of all people," she says.

She also teaches "angel lessons" to children so they can learn to be "messengers of love and peace." She taught such a class on New Year's Day at the mosque. First, she helped the children envision peace.

"Then I asked, 'Now what do we need to do to create peace?' " she said. "The children's responses were so beautiful. One said, 'We have to learn to hold hands.' And a 4-year-old said, 'We need to believe in miracles.' "

That is the answer, says Rosenberg, who was just chosen by Alternatives for Girls as Role Model of the Year.

"We have the power. We have the strength. We have everything within us. We are the miracle the world needs."

Similarly, the ADC, as it does every year, is hosting its Martin Luther King Jr. Scholarship reception Thursday to award scholarships to high school seniors.

The students were required to write essays explaining what Dr. King means to them as Arab or Chaldean Americans.

What is vital about those essays is that, instead of forcing the students to accept a generic, global portrait of King, the students had to evaluate the civil rights leader for themselves.

Long before someone asked "What would Jesus drive?" — Americans have asked in every crisis, "What would King do?"

Maybe, like Rosenberg and the ADC, those of us who care should take from this year's King season a sense of what his vision means to us in our own lives.

King's widow, Coretta Scott King, told the Associated Press this week that her husband "wanted to elevate the whole of humankind and have individuals understand that they can make a difference."

That means each of us needs to be a Brenda Rosenberg or work with an ADC.

Every one of us must find our own message in Dr. King's words, and help "elevate the whole of humankind." We must realize the power of one.

January 22, 2003

MLK used by U-M foes of fairness

It is amazing to me how often opponents of the University of Michigan's policies to create a diverse campus cite the Rev. Martin Luther King's dream as their motivation.

They obviously hardly knew the man.

If they had heard his entire "I Have A Dream" speech, they would have heard what he actually said about the debt owed to black people in America.

Those suing U-M for admission under the guise that "lesser qualified" black students took their seats still believe that white people must be first through the door.

The civil rights struggle was about allowing black people to get through those same doors, sometimes first. The lawsuits threaten the fruits of the battle.

`The litigants' seats never belonged to them. That notion, in itself, is racist. And if there's no racial motivation for the suits, why haven't the litigants questioned the special considerations given to applicants of all colors who benefit from U-M's affirmative action policy? Extra points are given to applicants who suffer from economic disadvantage or children and grandchildren of alumni or applicants from underrepresented counties in Michigan.

When America's colleges did not admit black students, where were affirmative action opponents? When activists were fighting for black children to be admitted to superior schools, none of the signs waved by screaming parents barring the doors said "Equal Opportunity!"

The reason that many white Americans do not want to discuss slavery, remember slavery or to hear discussions about the lasting impact of slavery is because inherent in that discussion is what to do to make up for it. America has never had that discussion. It has just spent years hoping that black people, once treated as animals and later as 3/5 of a person, would eventually just catch up.

And now, some Americans believe that black people have caught up and are living Dr. King's dream. Those people live in a world they view through glasses that are both rose-colored and missing the lens that shows the half of black America that has not survived slavery, that has not achieved the dream for which Dr. King so eloquently pined. He didn't ask for a color-blind society. He asked for one where color did not lead to discrimination, and he reminded America that black folks had not yet had the opportunities they were owed.

The question for those suing U-M is: Why is it wrong for the university to treat black students the way white students have been treated for years? The color of a student's skin has always made a difference. Only now it is making a difference for minorities.

America will never be truly equal until it lives up to what Dr. King demanded. For those who missed the speech, go to your history books and see what he actually said that August day — that America had given its citizens "a bad check which has come back marked 'insufficient funds.' "

U-M and other institutions are still trying to cash the checks that America wrote. Affirmative policies to provide opportunities for minorities don't make up for slavery. But they do help level a playing field long unlevel.

Proponents of affirmative action policies understand the U.S. Constitution and its tenets of fairness. They just want opponents of policies that offer affirmation to black people to treat the Constitution with the same respect that they did in the centuries that it was For Whites Only.

January 15, 2003

Keeping score on the way to the goal

Sometimes, a dear reader will call and ask me why black people keep score.

"Why," he or she will say, "does it matter whether you're the first or the second to do something?"

This is why it matters.

People, particularly white people, need to not see all black people in Tony Townsend, the monster who confessed to shooting and killing Officer Scott Stewart Sunday, then later apologized, not because he'd killed someone, but only because he'd killed a cop.

People need to see that not all black people do drugs, hold loud parties, throw trash on every Detroit street and shoot people in the head.

People need to see that black people are as diverse in the ways we live and goals we set as we are connected in our shared abhorrence for people like Tony Townsend.

People need to know that for every Tony Townsend there is a Dennis Archer who, on Tuesday, became the first black president-elect of the American Bar Association, whose members are most of the nation's lawyers.

People need to know that for every Tony Townsend, there is an Ollie Turner-Green, who didn't need the spotlight to rise from racism and poverty. She spent 30 years at Zenith Corp. and even more at Lemay Church of Christ, where she arranged music for the Golden Girls. And she raised a son who would become publisher of the Michigan Front Page, Samuel Logan Jr., another person who deserves being counted.

People need to know that for every Tony Townsend, there is another man, and another and another, thousands of them, who live in poverty, on the periphery of mayhem and don't step outside the line, don't carry guns, don't shoot people then say, "Oops, I didn't know it was a cop," as if it would have been all right to have shot someone else.

People need to know that for every mother with a crack pipe in her hand who sends her son out to sell drugs to put food on the table and a crack pipe in her hand, there are many more who sacrifice everything to send their sons to good schools and who help them with their homework and who teach them values that will keep them away from all-night parties where they might be in a position to shoot a cop.

It is hard to watch day after day, to see people look at someone who shares only your color and not your values or goals or dreams, and know that people see no difference in that person and you.

It is even harder to know that other black people see monsters like Tony Townsend and think he represents them, that because he is the same color, they must be like him, should expect that same anger to show up some day, so they let down their guard, let down their standards — and then when the moment comes, they go the wrong way because, after all, it's what is expected, isn't it?

Young black men need to know that there is nothing cool about killing someone, or killing two someones as Townsend did. They need to know that they get no props from crime that could be as valuable as the props they can get for succeeding in school, in life, in relationships.

Tony Townsend doesn't represent me or the black people I know any more than John Gotti represented every Italian-American or Kenneth Lay represents every businessman.

You see, dear readers, that is why black people count the victories and point out the differences. That is why we care that people of every color don't see all of us in any one of us.

August 18, 2002

Happy birthday, Rosa Parks!

You can feel it when you stand on hallowed ground. It moves up through you like heat, makes you think, helps you remember.

Standing on the bus where the American civil rights movement got its biggest push is like standing in a cemetery paying homage to those at the front of the freedom marches, those who withstood the fire hoses and dog bites in the name of freedom.

Standing on the Montgomery City Lines bus that Rosa Parks rode into history, I can smell the bone-tiredness of those forced to stand in the back because front seats were for whites only.

I can see you, Mrs. Parks, getting off your job Thursday evening, Dec. 1, 1955, leaving work as an assistant tailor at Montgomery Fair department store. I can see you climb aboard the bus at Court Square and take a vacant seat. You take this bus all the time. It has 36 seats, 22 for negroes, 14 for whites.

But this time, you recognize the driver. It's the same man who put you off the bus 12 years ago, told you to get off his bus in 1943 because you didn't come on through the rear door.

You sit in the fifth row, the first colored row. But when the bus approaches the Empire Theater and white passengers get on, the driver calls back, "Let me have those front seats."

You do something to change the course of the civil rights movement. You don't get up.

Others head to the crowded back, the back that represents the rears of restaurants where my grandmother refused to accept food, the balconies of theaters where we couldn't be seen, second-best.

But you let a man climb past you from the window seat and you slide into that seat and into the encyclopedia. And the bus becomes hallowed ground, another place where one person decides to say, "No more."

You are arrested and fined, but your arrest sparks the Montgomery Bus Boycott, which begins four days later and lasts for 381 days, until the U.S. Supreme Court declares segregated buses unconstitutional.

When you were born in Tuskegee, Ala., 89 years ago today, you didn't know the place history was holding for you. The new America was not won by celebrities or presidents. It was won by everyday people, ministers and cab drivers, people like you, who said, "No more."

February 4, 2002

Just saying you're sorry isn't good enough

The angry man called again.

His name is different every time, or sometimes he doesn't leave a name at all. This time he called to tell me to stop writing about slavery. He said his ancestors died fighting in the U.S. Civil War so slaves could be free.

He called because I wrote on Wednesday that the United States walked out of the United Nations World Conference Against Racism, not because of Yasser Arafat, but to avoid discussions of slavery and reparations. He called me a whiner for not getting over what happened to millions of black people hundreds of years ago. He said if I didn't like the United States, I could go back to Africa.

I've never been to Africa. But that's not the point.

The point is the angry man feels he owns America and that only he decides what is right for it. He doesn't believe what I do: that the United States government should convene hearings to discuss the travesty, impact and lingering ill effects of abducting millions of Africans, killing millions more through three centuries.

From the 1500s to the mid-1800s, Europeans captured and shipped 10 million black slaves from Africa to North, Central and South America. Nearly two million died on the way, their bones littering the bed of the Atlantic. Only one-fourth of white Southern families owned slaves, but slaves made up nearly a third of the southern U.S. population. They worked like animals in the fields or as servants in the homes. They had the right neither to learn to read nor to marry nor to own property. Owners gained loyalty by granting privileges or threatening to sell family members.

It's easy to say slavery was abolished 136 years ago in America. It's harder to talk about what happened next. We lament the educational, mental and physical health of a population of people who were treated like animals for 300 years. But we never consider that taking off the shackles and saying "You're free!" didn't fix the damage.

And that's why, 136 years later, the debate continues.

The only sane thing to do is to actually talk about slavery: what happened, what it did to generations of Americans and whether anything can be done to repair the damage.

That's what reparations means.

It means more than talking about ways to improve black students' scores on tests without talking about why generations of black children need help.

It means more than talking about how discrimination still exists in housing, banking and schooling, making it harder for some black people to succeed.

It means doing something, legally — I'm not sure what — to fix it.

The angry man and I see our country differently. He believes that America is perfect, like a diamond and shouldn't be touched.

I see America as a natural pearl, polished to amazing luster by the friction of daily existence, and the continual resolution of challenges. Its sheen becomes stronger only when it's hit by waves of understanding that come from existing in different situations with different people.

The angry man likes it when I write, Anna Quindlen-like, about cultural trends or education or life events that I see through my daughter's eyes. But he doesn't like to be reminded that I'm black. Then it's harder to connect with me and laugh with me. It makes him uncomfortable.

What slavery did to America affects all Americans. So maybe the only way to find peace is for people to understand that saying slavery was a shame isn't enough.

September 7, 2001

Historian shares the simple truths of discrimination

"The body of Benjamin Franklin, Printer (like the cover of an old book, its contents torn out and stripped of its lettering and gilding), lies here, food for worms; but the work shall not be lost, for it will (as he believed) appear once more in a new and more elegant edition, revised and corrected by the Author."

Centuries after a 22-year-old Benjamin Franklin wrote his own epitaph, an eloquent commentary that wouldn't be needed for 62 more years, his words resonate.

Such is the way of testimonies, whether made in churches, such as the fiery oratories that marked the civil rights movement, or in court.

In the University of Michigan admissions policy court case — whose resolution may determine whether a university can make itself reflect society — such testimony occurred.

The words of Dr. John Hope Franklin, the world's greatest historian, resound weeks after he told a rapt courtroom the story of a black boy growing up in an America changing from segregated to integrated, from disjointed to united. He recalled his education: graduating magna cum laude from Fisk University in 1935 and earning a master's and PhD from Harvard. But he also recalled taking his first foreign language classes at Fisk because, unlike the white high schools, his black school in Tulsa, Okla., didn't offer them.

He told simple truths of racism, which endure.

For instance, he recalled visiting the North Carolina State Archives for his Harvard dissertation on free Negroes and the director telling him: "When we built this building, we didn't anticipate that anyone of your color would work here. And so we don't have any place for you to work."

After a three-day wait, Franklin returned and was shown to a separate room. He was given a key to fetch his own materials because white pages could not be asked to get them. But two weeks later, the director took the key back because white students had complained about Franklin having more access than they did. From then on, white staff fetched his materials.

"It was at that point that I realized the inconsistency and the remarkable ingenuity ... of racial discrimination and those who practiced it," he said.

That ingenuity of racism was displayed again at three libraries within three blocks of each other in Raleigh. In one, blacks could not sit in the stacks. In another, blacks could not take materials from the shelves, but could sit in the stacks and read materials retrieved by white staff. There were no restrictions in the Supreme Court library, he said.

"That gave me to understand that the practice of racial segregation was sort of improvisational," he said. "That is, they made it up as they went along."

The discrimination was not limited to educational institutions. He also recalled two barbecue joints outside the city. At one, blacks could be served in the car, but not inside the restaurant. At the other, blacks could be served inside, but the waitresses couldn't bring food to their cars.

"You need a road map or you need an encyclopedia and a number of other aids to help you navigate your way through these racial mines ," he said.

After the racial slights in and out of school, reality became clear.

"I decided that that was a kind of sickness, a kind of searching for something that would give them a sense of security and superiority and advantage."

Thus the man who has 128 honorary degrees, worked with Thurgood Marshall on the Brown vs. the Board of Education case before the U.S. Supreme Court and wrote the authoritative history of blacks in America, "From Slavery to Freedom," visited Detroit to explain that passing time may not be the only cure to racism.

He did offer hope.

"Yes, I could sit all day and talk about changes for the better that have taken place," he said. "And if they hadn't taken place, one would wonder whether this was a country worth fighting for or living in."

But even as an elder, he said, he still sees the sickness.

"I was in Oklahoma City about three years ago. I was waiting for the man who owned the largest bookstore there because he was having an autograph party for me that afternoon. We were having lunch first. I was just in the hotel. A man walked up to me and said, 'Here's my keys. Go and get my car and bring it around to the front.' I'm standing there with my white hair and my broken-down self and I said 'I don't know where your car is and I'm a guest in the hotel just like you.'

"Apparently the person at the desk must have said something to him because in the midst of the afternoon ... while I'm autographing books and the line is from here to the door, this man walks in ... and comes all the way to the front of the line and interrupts me and says, 'I want to apologize for what I did. I didn't know who you were.' I said, 'Well, who am I? I'm a human being.' Seems that's all he needed to do was treat me like a human being."

The legal question facing university officials is this: Should the improvisations of racism that have resulted in biased standardized tests and segregated classes be the only measure of a student's ability to excel? If John Hope Franklin had not had parents who refused to attend segregated affairs, who had not raised a family on a foundation of education, who had not overcome the improvisations of racism, would the world's foremost historian be an 86-year-old black man who had attended inferior schools in Oklahoma?

Franklin's words must carry weight in deciding whether a nation and its institutions have the authority to right past wrongs.

His words are the kind that, like Benjamin Franklin's and Dr. Martin Luther King Jr.'s, will teach long after this case is finished and the dust has settled.

March 4, 2001

Holes are supposed to be repaired

Every day, Mr. Jones gets into his car and heads to work. And every day, he runs into a huge pothole right in front of his driveway.

He has tried filling in the hole himself, but it is larger than his meager tools can repair. He has tried to get loans for a house in a better neighborhood, but the banks decline. So he drives into the pothole every day, complaining to everyone that it's ruining his life.

His growing frustration leaves him depressed. So he overeats, vents and has too many drinks every now and again.

At work, he runs into Mr. Smith, a coworker who lives across town in a spacious colonial on a pristine, tree-lined drive. Mr. Smith has never seen a pothole up close. He has heard that it can do damage, but he figures people should just avoid them.

He doesn't understand what can be so upsetting or why Mr. Jones tends to blame the pothole for everything that goes wrong in his life. He warns him that he's making himself sick by worrying so much about the pothole. And he lets him in on a little secret: All his coworkers are tired of hearing about the doggone pothole.

Mr. Jones vainly tries to explain how the pothole does more than damage the car. When the car doesn't work, he says, he can't get to work, and his children are late for school. When he's late, it affects future promotions he might get. When his children are late, it affects their schoolwork.

That pothole does a lot of damage and has lasting effects, he says.

His coworkers believe that Mr. Jones is a whiner who uses a minor complaint to blame for his tardiness and bitterness. After all, they tell him, there are few potholes left around the city, and most people just drive around them.

Mr. Jones says he cannot escape the pothole. It is right in front of his home, all the time.

They ask why the city doesn't fix the pothole. City officials, Mr. Jones says, have told him that it is HIS attitude about the pothole that needs fixing. They are not convinced that the pothole is doing any real damage.

They tell him not to make such a big deal out of nothing. There are bigger problems in the world, like succeeding at work, vacationing in Maui, choosing a president. Potholes are a thing of the past, he believes, and this last one will eventually get repaired.

Mr. Jones drives home from work, feeling worse than ever. Why can't he convince them that the pothole affects his performance at work and how much he earns for vacations and for whom he votes? That pothole can make his daughter miss ballet and his son miss debate.

He knows he must find a way to stop talking about it because as long as the pothole doesn't affect his coworkers, they are not interested in fixing it. And Mr. Jones has begun to notice them avoiding him at work. "There's Mr. Jones, and if you don't watch out, he'll talk your ear off about this pothole that he says is making his life miserable. We wish he'd get over it."

The pothole is racism.

It is as real for the people who face it every day as sunshine is for those who don't. It's hard for those who cannot even see it to understand its lingering damage.

But that doesn't make the damage — or the problem — less real.

And I want the pothole fixed before my daughter learns to drive.

January 12, 2001

We mustn't let any little girls get lost

It was bound to happen.

The case of Elizabeth Smart, a bright, beautiful girl in Salt Lake City has received the same coverage as our attack on terrorists.

The case of Alexis Patterson, a bright, beautiful girl in Milwaukee, has received scant national attention, save questions about why it hasn't gotten as much coverage as the Smart case.

And now the media is questioning itself for its disparate coverage.

For those few Americans who still feel that race doesn't matter, the missing girls represent yet more evidence that it does. Race and class and a sense of connection all matter.

But I'm less interested in what pundits feel than how the different coverage makes little black girls feel, little girls like my daughter, little black girls like the one in me.

It was hard to hear about either case. As a mother, the thought of someone snatching anyone's child causes my heart to skip.

I feel for the mothers of two daughters who aren't in their own beds, safe and warm. I pray for a miracle and the unexpected positive coverage that probably won't come.

But I also feel for the mothers of black daughters everywhere whose kids see once again that, for whatever reason, it seems to make a difference if you're black.

Journalists make judgments, whether they admit to them or not. Elizabeth's father is a wealthy white businessman. Alexis' stepfather is an ex-con.

Elizabeth was snatched from her bed in a mansion. Alexis never made it to school after her stepdad walked her halfway. She is 3-feet-8-inches tall and 42 pounds with brown eyes and light brown skin. She was last seen wearing jeans and a purple shirt and carrying her pink Barbie book bag.

The Milwaukee Journal Sentinel, which examined the coverage of the two cases, found about 67 stories on Nexis about Patterson, but more than

400 about Smart, whose disappearance also was featured on "America's Most Wanted," CNN and MSNBC.

Now there may be a suspect in the Smart case. But the Locate Alexis Patterson group must contend with racists who call the family home and who put a flyer on the Black Holocaust Museum in Milwaukee asking why white people should care about a missing black girl.

I spend sleepless nights wondering how to prepare my child for so much to come. I send her to good schools. I provide extra experiences to help determine where her aptitudes, and her future, lie.

We travel within and outside of the United States so she can see more of the world than I did at her age. And I've told her she can be president one day, even if my heart knows it might take another hundred years.

But what I cannot prepare her for is the wall, the one all black children hit one day whether they've been raised in mansions or tenements.

One day, my daughter will meet a person who treats her badly because she is black. That person will try to make her feel inferior, less important, try to make her believe that a 7-year-old black girl being nabbed on the way to school doesn't really strike fear in the hearts of parents like a white girl being nabbed from her bed.

My fear is that she'll believe that Alexis isn't as important as Elizabeth. I worry that she'll forget that both, after all, are little girls.

My greatest fear is that she won't be strong enough to overcome the hate, to aspire for the presidency anyway.

For those who think race doesn't matter in America, the little girl in me says it does.

June 26, 2002

AIDS is still a devastating public enemy

It's hard to remember what else we cared about before Sept. 11.

The terrorists who attacked our largest city also attacked our national agenda. Everything got moved down. It eclipsed not only government operations, but also personal concerns about our health, our bills, our travel itineraries, our plans to buy new cars.

Everything seemed so important. Government forays into the Social Security Fund. The plight of Medicare and Medicaid. National problems with illiteracy. Faith-based initiatives.

AIDS.

Now that we're working our way back to normal, we must focus in two directions at once: the growing global crisis and other issues at home.

Few are more important than the growing numbers of people — particularly African Americans and heterosexual women — who are contracting the virus that causes AIDS.

The latest figures for the silent killer haven't changed: AIDS remains the leading cause of death among African Americans aged 25 to 44, according to recent studies by the National Center for HIV, STD and TB Prevention, one of the Atlanta-based Centers for Disease Control.

About 40,000 new HIV infections occur every year, 54 percent among African Americans, who represent only 13 percent of the U.S. populace.

A third of new infections occur during heterosexual sex. One in every 160 black women and one in every 3,000 white women is infected every year.

Thirty percent of gay and bisexual African-American men aged 23 to 29 were HIV positive, according to a recent CDC study, compared to 7 percent of white gay and bisexual men, with whom the epidemic began 20 years ago.

As the world prepares for possible war, and the families of those who lost loved ones in the Sept. 11 terrorist attack await official declarations that hope is gone, why should we care about anything else?

Because America, with God's help, will survive the tragedy and the challenging days ahead.

And when life resumes, not as we used to know it, but the way we choose to live it post-tragedy, we still have other work to do.

That's why 11 AIDS walks across Michigan this weekend have not been canceled. That's why organizers of the Detroit Walk are urging residents of the nation's second blackest city to turn out big.

Why? Maybe you missed it a few graphs up. Black people account for more than half of new HIV infections.

This weekend's walk won't be just about exercise or fund-raising. It will be about education for all people. Detroit's walk, which begins at noon Saturday at Belle Isle, will help us celebrate and teach us not to be victims.

Registration for the 5K walk begins at 10 a.m. But organizers are encouraging families to come out all day by offering live entertainment on two stages and interactive playscapes for children.

Those who attend also can see 30 quilt blocks from the AIDS Memorial Quilt, which honors those who have died and the effort to halt the spread of the disease.

Mayor Dennis Archer and former Detroit Police Chief Benny Napoleon are honorary chairs. Sheryl Lee Ralph of "Moesha" fame will be shown on a big screen discussing the issue.

If you're a Detroit area family, please come to Belle Isle, for the sake of our kids and our future. We will have a future, hopefully one without terrorists, and one without AIDS.

September 28, 2001

This disease calls for fire and brimstone

The Rev. Kenneth J. Flowers was in Atlanta when the Centers for Disease Control released a new report on AIDS showing its disproportionate impact on America's black population.

Those numbers led him to stand in the Greater New Mt. Moriah Baptist Church pulpit two Sundays ago and preach about AIDS. It was a good Baptist sermon — fiery, strong, demanding, rising in volume and passion until he was done.

And then there was silence.

"There was a pall over the congregation," he said. "I think they were shocked that I was preaching about it. In a black Baptist church, folks get pumped up and shout 'Amen!' But there was a quietness. I don't know whether it was because the statistics were so sobering and they were in a state of shock, or whether there was resistance to it: 'Why is he preaching about that? That doesn't affect us.' "

It not only affects us, but it is doing so in crisis proportions.

AIDS is the leading cause of death among African-Americans aged 25 to 44. Let me say that again: AIDS is the leading cause of death for black people aged 25 to 44.

Not cancer. Not strokes.

Not diabetes. Not homicides.

AIDS.

We are waiting for numbers to go away that are only getting worse: There are about as many new AIDS infections every day as people living in Highland Park — 16,000.

Black people, 13 percent of the U.S. populace, account for half of new infections. A third of new infections occur during heterosexual sex.

One in every 160 black women in America is infected, compared with 1 in every 3,000 white women.

One in seven gay black men, aged 23 to 29, is infected with the AIDS virus every year, six times the rate of white gay men, with whom the epidemic began 20 years ago.

And AIDS is the biggest sermon not being preached.

In the small town where I grew up, folks turned to ministers for everything, from counseling to legal advice. Ministers preach against police brutality, drug use, racism. Yet the largest black health crisis in American history is getting short shrift.

One reason black ministers "have not gotten on board is because the black church still views AIDS as a gay disease," Flowers said.

He called AIDS "the modern-day leprosy," citing the skin disease whose sufferers were shunned as unclean. What he didn't say is that many of the shunners are ministers.

"AIDS is not a gay disease. It's a people disease that's killing folk," he said. "Until we wake up and see what's happening, we're going to find an entire group of people wiped out."

A father of three and his church's pastor for six years, Flowers recently celebrated his 40th birthday. He spoke of a seminary friend who didn't because he died of AIDS in 1999.

"I did the funeral at my church. He said he wanted me to talk about AIDS. He joked that if I didn't talk about it he was going to raise up out of the casket and talk about it himself."

Flowers did preach on AIDS at the funeral, and he's preaching now about our resistance to a world crisis. It is AIDS. It isn't pretty. It isn't comfortable. And it is no longer a gay disease.

It is a black disease.

July 15, 2001

Journalist worked to add color to America's newsrooms

Sometimes we journalists miss the point. Sure, we want to win Pulitzers and other awards. We want the recognition and salaries that accompany stardom.

But in an industry still struggling to make its newsrooms diverse, we must remember those who don't seek glory, but who fight to make newsrooms reflect America. They help women and minorities get hired so every journalist has a chance to earn the kudos.

My friend, Charles Jackson, was one of those people.

His efforts to make American newsrooms diverse are as great an achievement as his work at the Washington Post and the Oakland Tribune, two of the papers he worked for during a 35-year-career.

He died March 7 at 55.

In film, Charles might have been the long-suffering high school music teacher in "Mr. Holland's Opus," so busy teaching students he doesn't recognize his legacy.

Newsrooms across America are filled with Charles' "children" — Young Turks he helped mentor, thus creating a symphony of bright journalists whose music will last long after many of us are gone.

He was born Willis Charles Jackson on Aug. 3, 1945. He attended an all-black high school in Ft. Worth, Texas, then studied journalism in Kansas at the predominantly white Wichita State University. In 1966, in his first job at the Wichita Eagle-Beacon, he was the only African American in the city room.

He spent his life trying to make sure no other minority journalist felt that alone in a newsroom. He helped people find jobs, and when he could, he hired minorities himself.

In 1969, he became only the second African-American reporter to work at the Ft. Worth Star-Telegram. He told the story of that first interview so many times it has become legend. He walked in off the street to apply, and the personnel director told him: "I'm sorry, we don't have any porter jobs available." Charles didn't blink as he told the man: "No! You misunderstood. I said RE-porter!"

Listing all the places he worked, all the honors he won and all the titles he earned would be accurate, but wouldn't reflect his greatest achievement — touching people who might have quit without his encouragement.

He spent his summers teaching high school students in journalism workshops. He spent his spare time counseling veterans as they charted rough waters in an industry that is still mostly white.

You don't have to be black to cover black people. And Asians, Arabs and Hispanics have stories, too. Those were Charles' lessons. He simply wanted minority journalists in the room to help tell the story.

He spent his life holding that door open. He helped keep the door open so long, it almost stays that way.

Charles died last week and declared to his wife that if she planned some huge funeral, he'd come back and haunt her — and he would. Instead, she's planning a huge party to celebrate his life and to remind us that some others of us had better step forward and put our feet in that door. He told his wife to tell people: "I'm down to my last reporter's tablet."

News coverage that leaves some people out isn't accurate. Coverage by and about people of all cultures is what Charles wanted.

And that would be accurate.

March 18, 2001

ABOUT THE AUTHOR

Rochelle Riley has been an editor or reporter at the Courier-Journal in Louisville, Kentucky, The Dallas Morning News, The Washington Post, the Fort Worth Star-Telegram and the Greensboro (N.C.) Daily News. Her column is published three times a week in the Detroit Free Press on topics ranging from politics to parenting, culture to convenience, family to furniture — the emotional kind. The Knight-Ridder News Service syndicates her columns nationwide. You can read them online at www.freep.com.

Named Michigan's Best Columnist in 2002, Rochelle is a tireless advocate for children, winning awards — as well as the respect of teachers, parents and students — for her commentary on education and children's issues. She also offers incisive, sometimes spiritual commentary on local and national news. In 2002, Rochelle helped the Free Press launch Metro Detroit Reads, an adult literacy campaign to expand opportunities for adults to learn to read.

Born and raised in Tarboro, N.C., just hours away from the incredibly beautiful Outer Banks, Rochelle has true Southern roots and an occasional accent. She received her bachelor of arts degree in journalism from the University of North Carolina at Chapel Hill. She enjoys the culinary arts, but only after the artwork is done. She finds it impossible to become a vegetarian because it would mean giving up barbecue. And she spends most of her time away from work barefoot and writing. She also is the author of "From the Heart," a collection of Courier-Journal columns, and she is completing her first novel.